WITHDRAWN
from the
MANITOWOC PUBLIC LIBRARY

D0078364

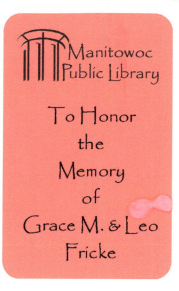

Manitowoc
Public Library

To Honor
the
Memory
of
Grace M. & Leo
Fricke

MANITOWOC PUBLIC LIBRARY

JUN 1 2 2003

MANITOWOC WI 54220

946.03 ANDERSON
Anderson, James Maxwell,
Daily life during the
Spanish Inquisition /
Manitowoc Public Library
3312005728514

MARILYN PUBLIC LIBRARY

JUN 1 2 2003

DAILY LIFE DURING

The Spanish Inquisition

The Greenwood Press "Daily Life Through History" Series

The Age of Sail
Dorothy Denneen Volo and
  James M. Volo

The Ancient
Egyptians
Bob Brier and Hoyt Hobbs

The Ancient Greeks
Robert Garland

Ancient Mesopotamia
Karen Rhea Nemet-Nejat

The Ancient Romans
David Matz

The Aztecs: People of the Sun and
  Earth
David Carrasco with Scott Sessions

Chaucer's England
Jeffrey L. Singman and Will McLean

Civil War America
Dorothy Denneen Volo and
  James M. Volo

Colonial New England
Claudia Durst Johnson

Early Modern Japan
Louis G. Perez

18th-Century England
Kirstin Olsen

Elizabethan England
Jeffrey L. Singman

The Holocaust
Eve Nussbaum Soumerai and
  Carol D. Schulz

The Inca Empire
Michael A. Malpass

Maya Civilization
Robert J. Sharer

Medieval Europe
Jeffrey L. Singman

The Nineteenth Century American
  Frontier
Mary Ellen Jones

Renaissance Italy
Elizabeth S. Cohen and
  Thomas V. Cohen

Traditional China: The Tang Dynasty
Charles Benn

The United States, 1920–1939:
  Decades of Promise and Pain
David E. Kyvig

The United States, 1940–1959: Shifting
  Worlds
Eugenia Kaledin

The United States, 1960–1990:
  Decades of Discord
Myron A. Marty

Victorian England
Sally Mitchell

DAILY LIFE DURING

The Spanish Inquisition

JAMES M. ANDERSON

The Greenwood Press "Daily Life Through History" Series

GREENWOOD PRESS
Westport, Connecticut • London

946.03 ANDERSON
Anderson, James Maxwell,
Daily life during the
Spanish Inquisition /
Manitowoc Public Library
33128005728514

Library of Congress Cataloging-in-Publication Data

Anderson, James Maxwell, 1933–
    Daily life during the Spanish Inquisition / James M. Anderson.
        p.   cm.—(The Greenwood Press "Daily life through history" series, ISSN 1080–
    4749)
    Includes bibliographical references and index.
    ISBN 0–313–31667–8 (alk. paper)
    1. Inquisition—Spain. 2. Spain—Church history. 3. Spain—Social
conditions. I. Title. II. Series.
    BX1735.A72   2002
    946'.03—dc21   2001040597

British Library Cataloguing in Publication Data is available.

Copyright © 2002 by James M. Anderson

All rights reserved. No portion of this book may be
reproduced, by any process or technique, without
the express written consent of the publisher.

Library of Congress Catalog Card Number: 2001040597
ISBN: 0–313–31667–8
ISSN: 1080–4749

First published in 2002

Greenwood Press, 88 Post Road West, Westport, CT 06881
An imprint of Greenwood Publishing Group, Inc.
www.greenwood.com

Printed in the United States of America

The paper used in this book complies with the
Permanent Paper Standard issued by the National
Information Standards Organization (Z39.48–1984).

10 9 8 7 6 5 4 3 2 1

Cover photograph: Bernard Picart, *Procession of the Auto de Fe in the Plaza Mayor in Madrid
1723* (Madrid: Biblioteca Nacional). Used by permission of the Biblioteca Nacional.

For Sherry
companion, colleague, and friend of fifty years

Contents

Acknowledgments

The author expresses his gratitude for assistance to Dr. Barbara Rader, Executive Editor, and Betty Pessagno, Senior Production Editor, Greenwood Publishing Group. Also to Dr. Siwan Anderson, Dr. Joel Prager, Dr. Stanley Goldstein, Howard Greaves, Dr. Henry Kamen, Sr. and Sra. Fernando Lopez, Dr. Marilyn Mohan, and Dr. Rodney Roche.

Thanks also go to Maria Concepción Ocampos Fuentes at the Prado Museum and Javier Docampo at the Biblioteca Nacional in Madrid as well as Margarita Becedas González at the University of Salamanca, Spain; Ziva Haller of the Israel Museum; the Library of Congress; Christina Schwill of the Bayerische Staatsgemäldesammlungen in Munich, Germany; Martin Durrant of the Victoria and Albert Museum; the National Gallery; J. Symons and Sonya Brown of the Wellcome Library in London; and Mark Bills of the Russell-Cotes Museum in Bournemouth, England.

The map was produced by Paul Killinger, Ford Graphics, Ringwood, England. The line drawings are by Myrna Johns.

Chronology of the Spanish Inquisition

1469   Isabella marries Fernando II of Aragón.

1474   Isabella I becomes queen of Castilla.

1478   Pope Sixtus IV authorizes Spanish Inquisition.

1479   Fernando II becomes king of Aragón (and Fernando V of Castilla);
        Isabella and Fernando begin joint rule.

1480   Inquisition begins operations in Sevilla.

1481   First public auto de fe held in Sevilla.

1482   War begins with Granada; number of inquisitors enlarged.

1483   Pope Sixtus IV appoints Torquemada first Inquisitor General of Cas-
        tilla and of Aragón; Jews expelled from Sevilla, Córdoba, and Cádiz.

1484   Inquisition has thirty people burned alive in Ciudad Real.

1485   Rabbis in Toledo ordered to inform on Crypto-Jews.

1486   First auto de fe performed in Toledo; Jews expelled from Zaragoza;
        order rescinded.

1488   Founding of the *Suprema* and unification of the inquisitional tribu-
        nals of Aragón and Castilla; Torquemada made Grand Inquisitor for
        all Spain.

1490   Jewish books burned in Toledo.

1491   Rumors circulate of a kidnapped child of La Guardia murdered by Jews.

1492   Conquest of Granada; Columbus sails westward; Jews expelled from Spain.

1493   Cathedral at Toledo completed.

1498   Death of Torquemada.

1499   Promises to Moriscos broken; first of royal decrees against Gypsies; general hospital founded at Santiago de Compostela.

1501   Catholic Kings decree that offspring of those condemned by the Inquisition could not hold important positions; Arabic books burned in Granada.

1502   All Muslims in Castilla ordered by the crown to convert to Christianity or suffer exile.

1504   Death of Isabella; first of several foundling hospitals established in Toledo.

1506   Death of Felipe I.

1508   University of Alcalá de Henares founded.

1516   Death of Fernando; regency of Cardinal Cisneros begins.

1517   Carlos I arrives in Spain from Flanders; Protestant revolt initiated in Germany by Luther.

1518   Carlos I enhances the judicial power of the Inquisition.

1519   Carlos I becomes Carlos V of the Holy Roman Empire.

1520   Revolt of the *comuneros*; uprisings in Valencia.

1521   Defeat of the *comuneros*; Aztec empire falls to Hernán Cortés; chocolate introduced into Spain; war with France begins; Inquisition bans Lutheran books.

1522   Death of Nebrija, author of first Spanish grammar.

1525   Royal decree orders all Muslims in Valencia and Aragón to convert to Christianity or suffer exile.

1526   Forty-year agreement between Moriscos, king, and Inquisition.

1527   Construction begins on royal palace at Granada.

1528   Leper houses put under state supervision.

1533   Cortes of Aragón complains of Inquisition seizure of Morisco property; Inca empire falls to Francisco Pizarro.

1535	Expedition to Tunis.
1540	Founding of the Jesuits.
1541	Military reverse at Algiers.
1542–1544	Hostilities with France.
1545	Opening of the Council of Trent.
1547	Birth of Miguel Cervantes.
1548	Punishment in the galleys ends.
1552	Books deemed heretical burned publicly.
1556	Abdication of Carlos I and ascension to the throne of Felipe II.
1559	Pope authorizes inquisitorial jurisdiction over bishops; archbishop of Toledo arrested; first papal Index of forbidden books.
1560	Jesuit schools appear in Spain.
1561	Madrid established as the capital.
1562	Birth of Lope de Vega.
1563	Construction of El Escorial begins; prohibition on the use of firearms.
1565	Synod in Granada condemns Moriscos.
1567	Laws clamp down on Moriscos; beginning of struggle for independence of the Netherlands; Burgos Cathedral completed.
1568	Death of Don Carlos, son of Felipe II; revolt of the Moriscos.
1569	Morisco uprising in Andalucía.
1570	Morisco revolt winds down; Moriscos dispersed.
1571	Battle of Lepanto.
1572	Regulation of prostitutes; Fray Luís de León arrested by the Inquisition.
1575	Felipe II cancels foreign debt; Gypsies indiscriminately sent to galleys.
1576	Public bathhouses banned; mutiny and sack of Antwerp by the Spanish army.
1580	Felipe II succeeds to the Portuguese throne; Francisco Gómez de Quevedo born.
1583	The popular dance *saraband* banned as being too risqué.
1584	Valencia outlaws the carrying of flintlocks.

1585	War with England begins; severe famine.

1585   War with England begins; severe famine.

1587   Sir Francis Drake destroys the Spanish fleet at Cádiz; general hospital established.

1588   British destroy the "invincible" Armada; clashes in Aragón between Old Christians and Moriscos; census of Morisco inhabitants in the country ordered by the government.

1590   Royal decree forbids women to use the veil.

1597   Outbreak of plague in the north of Spain.

1598   Death of Felipe II and ascension of Felipe III.

1599   Plague reaches epidemic proportions; birth of Velázquez.

1600   Calderón de la Barca born; theaters reopened after period of closure by royal decree.

1601   Court moves to Valladolid; Madrid municipal law prohibits employment of slaves.

1602   End of the plague begun in 1596.

1604   Peace with England arranged.

1606   Court returns to Madrid; mutiny of Spanish troops in the Low Countries.

1607   Cessation of hostilities between Spain and the United Provinces.

1609   Expulsion of Moriscos from Spain begins; twelve-year truce with the Dutch; starvation in Galicia due to poor harvests.

1610   Royal edicts to control police corruption.

1611   First of the Sumptuary Laws decreed by Felipe III.

1614   End of process of expulsion of the Moriscos; torture abolished.

1616   Death of Cervantes.

1618   Beginning of the Thirty Years' War.

1619   King visits Portugal; Gypsies expelled from Castilla.

1620   French cut the Spanish Road from Milan to Flanders.

1621   Death of Felipe III; Felipe IV mounts the throne; Cortes denounces church wealth.

1623   Further Sumptuary Laws decreed by Felipe IV.

1624   Gypsies expelled from Valencia.

1625   Jesuit Imperial College established in Madrid; death of Lerma, a powerful statesman under Felipe III.

1627	Suspension of payments to foreign bankers by Felipe IV.
1630	Spain and England sign peace treaty.
1631	Revolts in Vizcaya.
1635	Death of Lope de Vega.
1637	Royal decree sends personal slaves to the galleys.
1638	Victory over French at Fuenterrabía.
1640	Independence uprisings in Portugal and Cataluña.
1642	French occupy Roussillon.
1643	Battle of Rocroi in France.
1644	Felipe IV swears to respect the Catalán *fueros*.
1645	Death of Olivares; death of Quevedo.
1647	Worst harvest in Andalucía in a century; severe outbreak of the plague lasting five years.
1648	End of Thirty Years' War; popular uprising in Granada; price of bread triples in Andalucía; food riots follow.
1650	Bad harvests; outbreak of plague; uprising in Andalucía and La Mancha.
1651	Plague strikes Barcelona and surrounding area.
1652	Pacification of Cataluña; royal treasury bankrupt; uprising in Sevilla and Córdoba.
1655	English settle Jamaica; war between Spain and England.
1659	Peace of the Pyrenees; end of Spanish power in Europe; first of the new-style autos de fe held in Valladolid.
1660	English sailors (Protestants) burned at the stake in Sevilla.
1665	Death of Felipe IV; Carlos II assumes throne.
1668	End of war with Portugal.
1676	Major flood and famine, followed by drought, plague, and typhus, begin, lasting six years.
1680	Large auto de fe held in Madrid with king present.
1683	Drought in Andalucía devastates the harvest.
1687	Locusts devastate Cataluña and famine precipitates rebellion.
1700	Death of Carlos II; Felipe V proclaimed king.
1701	War of the Spanish Succession begins.

1704	British capture Gibraltar.
1707	Anglo-Portuguese army invades Spain but defeated at Almansa; Aragón and Valencia lose their autonomy.
1713	Treaty of Utrecht recognizes Felipe V as king of Spain; Spain cedes Gibraltar to Great Britain.
1714	End of the War of the Spanish Succession, resulting in loss of autonomy in Cataluña.
1721	Spain joins the alliance of England and France.
1724	Felipe V abdicates; son Louis I dies; Felipe V returns.
1727–1729	War with England and France.
1738	Vatican declares war on Freemasonry.
1746	Death of Felipe V; Fernando VI assumes throne; birth of Goya.
1748	Serving in the galleys as punishment ended.
1751	Freemasons condemned to death.
1756	The Seven Years' War begins.
1759	Death of Felipe V; Carlos III becomes king.
1762	Spain joins war against England.
1763	End of Seven Years' War.
1766	Palace guard fire on a protesting crowd; long capes (under which ill-gotten goods could be concealed) forbidden by royal order.
1767	Jesuits expelled from Spain.
1779	Spain joins France in War of American Independence against England.
1781	Last victim of the Inquisition burned alive.
1783	Treaty of Versailles; Spain recovers Florida.
1785	By royal decree, women allowed to earn a doctorate degree.
1787	Burials forbidden in the cities.
1788	Carlos IV becomes king.
1789	French Revolution.
1793	War against revolutionary France begins.
1795	War with revolutionary France ends.
1796	Spain joins France in war against England.
1797	Defeat of Franco-Spanish fleet at Cape St. Vicente.

1799   Sale of the assets of the Inquisition; law proscribing wearing any other color than black for women.

1800   Louisiana ceded back to France.

1805   Alliance with Napoleon; defeat of the Franco-Spanish fleet off Trafalgar.

1807   Popular uprising at Aranjuez.

1808   Napoleon forces abdication of Carlos IV and his son Fernando VII and seats Joseph Bonaparte on Spanish throne; Spanish War of Independence begins.

1809   Large cemetery built outside the city of Madrid.

1810   France occupies most of Spain.

1812   Liberal Constitution drafted by Cortes of Cádiz.

1813   End of the War of Independence.

1814   Fernando VII restored to the throne; torture abolished.

1815   Edict published denouncing non-Catholic views.

1820   Military uprising of Spanish troops.

1822   Congress of Vienna and war with France.

1823   French recalled to Spain to aid Fernando VII.

1826   Last death sentence by the Inquisition for heresy.

1833   Death of Fernando VII; ascension of Isabella II.

1834   Inquisition abolished.

Introduction

The three and a half centuries of Spanish history encompassing the introduction of the Spanish Inquisition in 1478 to its demise in 1834 denote the period of transition from Medieval to Modern Spain. The sixteenth and seventeenth centuries are generally called the Early Modern period.

What was it like to live in Spain during these times, in a preindustrial, agricultural, class-stratified society? A country relatively isolated from the rest of Europe and in the process of consolidating politically diverse regions under one authority in Madrid. A budding nation in the throes of eliminating racial and cultural differences by any means, while at the same time embarking on world empire, only to see its territorial gains slip away. A powerful church disposed to bring about religious unity at the expense of all else. A time when the Spanish Inquisition spread its grasping tentacles throughout the country, its inquiries and operations instilling alarm and fear among large segments of the population.

While courtly functions, political and social institutions, laws, education, manners, fashions, technology, and other facets of society underwent changes that affected the daily lives of the citizens to varying degrees, persistent religious, anti-Semitic, and xenophobic themes remained a strong and continuous factor in their lives.

The overall framework and organization of society changed only slowly, and throughout most of the period some aspects of it remained fairly constant. The peasant class made little headway to improve its standard of living, the upper classes remained in firm control of the wealth of the country, and the monarchy and its institutions continued to function as the ultimate arbiter of justice and the source of foreign policy. The powerful, all-embracing Roman Catholic Church maintained a firm grip on the religious conduct of the populace and punished nonconformists through the Holy Office of the Inquisition—one of those institutions in the history of human endeavor that cast a long shadow over humanitarian ideals. A law unto itself, the Inquisition came to define the limits of its own power. This was a time gratifying for some, dark and ominous for others.

The reader will note the political and social parallels between the period covered in this book and recent events: The religious intolerance of Early Modern Spain has an echo in the antagonisms of Catholics and Protestants in Northern Ireland and Muslims and Hindus in India. The ethnic hatreds of the time have an analog in Kosovo between Albanians and Serbs, and the idea of purity of blood in sixteenth-century Spain finds its counterpart in so-called ethnic cleansing in the Balkans and the Aryan doctrines of the Nazis; the latter, like the Inquisition, also resorted to censorship and burning of books. The notion of guilt by association, a characteristic of the McCarthy hearings in the U.S. Congress in the 1950s, was a vivid reflection of the same principle manifest in the Spanish Inquisition.

A good deal of information about the period investigated here has emphasized and sometimes sensationalized the cruelty and injustice of the Spanish Inquisition. In their point of view, however, many inquisitors felt they were fair and were genuinely concerned about the spiritual welfare of the people. In their efforts to save souls from what they believed was eternal damnation, the body was irrelevant; only the soul mattered. In this belief they had the support of the majority of the population.

The following pages strive for a balanced account of the everyday activities of all classes, and minority groups, concerning their religious attitudes, morality, struggle for survival, and encounters with the Inquisition. Each chapter examines a different aspect of daily life in order to develop a composite picture of the times. A wide range of sources, some contemporary with the period, some general, and others specific in nature, have been consulted. Names of persons are kept in their Spanish form.

1

Early Modern Spain

At the end of the Middle Ages, much of the Iberian peninsula was a barren, isolated expanse on the fringes of Europe, half its land unproductive, the rest sustaining a meager living for the inhabitants. There were no easy routes over the monotonous, burning plains and lofty mountains, no political center, no single ruler.

On 15 October 1469, eighteen-year-old Isabella, a princess of Castilla, and her cousin, seventeen-year-old Prince Fernando of Aragón, met for the first time in Valladolid. Three days later they married. In 1474, on the death of her brother, Enrique IV, Isabella I was crowned queen of Castilla, inheriting a turbulent kingdom in which nobles warred with each other for estates and power and lorded over their serfs with tyrannical and arbitrary authority.

Upon the death of his father in 1479, Fernando acquired the throne of Aragón as Fernando II (but became Fernando V of Castilla). Later known as the Catholic Kings, the pair became joint rulers of the two major Christian kingdoms—Castilla and Aragón—that comprised Spain, each monarch exercising sovereign power in her or his own realm.

During this time, the two kingdoms differed from each other by the legacy of their history, by divergent customs, and by political institutions, laws, privileges, and administration. Both sustained populations of Christians, Muslims, and Jews, along with a diversity of dialects and languages.

While Castilla's interests had for centuries been oriented southward toward reconquest of the peninsula from the Muslims (climaxing in the

W. H. Mote (1850). *Isabella I, Queen of Spain*. (Library of Congress).

fall of Granada in 1492), the energies of the people of Aragón were projected eastward throughout the Mediterranean in the domination of the Balearic Island, Sardinia, Sicily, and Naples. By the fifteenth century, the crown of Aragón was the dominant power in southern Europe. French interest in Italy and Turkish naval strength in the eastern Mediterranean were the primary inhibiting factors to total supremacy. However, as Aragonese overseas expansion lost its impetus, that of Castilla was just beginning.

KINGDOM OF CASTILLA

Although subject to the authority of the crown of Castilla, the Basque region, peopled by a unique race of mysterious provenance, had a special position allowing for considerable autonomy. The economy was based on iron ore, and both the raw material and locally forged agricultural tools and weapons made up exports. With an abundance of sturdy forests that fed the forges, wood was also used in another major activity—shipbuilding.

Further west, Asturias consisted of a tangle of lofty snow-clad peaks and sparsely populated valleys, ancient Celtic lands of dark superstition

Sixteenth-century Spain.

and legend, where bears and wolves still roamed the hillsides. Clustered in small woodland clearings, the hamlets were often cut off by snow, and the lean inhabitants survived the winter on dried vegetables and the milk and meat from their emaciated sheep. The few passing strangers were watched with deep suspicion from the dark, cold doorways of the stone cottages.

Where the mountains gave way to hill country lived the Galicians, in groups of four or five houses scattered among the valleys and along the inlets of the sea, whose livelihood, farming and fishing, was precarious at best. With the alleged tomb of Saint James, Santiago de Compostela (a site of pilgrimage attracting many worshippers) and Orense on the Miño River were the largest towns.

To the south lay León and Old Castilla, broad empty spaces where an entire day of travel could pass without sight of a village, a house, or even another individual in the immense open landscape of the central *meseta* (plateau). This vast, fertile, windswept, undulating plateau, where the treeless skyline was only occasionally interrupted by distant hills, stretched to the Guadarrama mountains a little north of Madrid. Wheat was the principal crop that sustained life, along with sheep, goats, and cattle.

South of the mountain chain lay New Castilla and, to the west, Extremadura—continuations of the same monotonous plain interspersed here and there by low knolls shimmering in the summer heat but offering no obstacle to the icy north wind in winter. Both regions continued as flat, desolate, sun-scorched landscapes of scrub, wild thyme, heather, and occasionally a poor adobe village.

Separated from New Castilla and Extremadura by the low-lying Sierra Morena mountains, Andalucía, with its long Moorish traditions, formed the southernmost region. The verdant valley of the Guadalquivir River and the warm climate of the coastal lands allowed the cultivation of oranges, olives, and sugarcane. In the eastern portion of the region loomed the Sierra Nevada mountains of Granada, the last independent Moorish stronghold on the peninsula.

East and northeast of Andalucía was situated the old kingdom of Murcia, lying in a direct path of hot Saharan winds off the desert across the sea. Founded by the Moors in the ninth century, it was an intermittently independent or a Christian vassal kingdom until it was absorbed by Castilla in 1243. The region was one of the driest, with impoverished villages and stark gray landscapes; the soil was nevertheless fertile and responded luxuriously to irrigation from Moorish canals and water wheels.

MAJOR TOWNS OF CASTILLA

Until the latter half of the sixteenth century the ambulatory monarchy of Castilla took up residence from time to time in different towns: Burgos, Valladolid, Medina del Campo, Segovia, and Toledo were all sometime royal capitals. These developed into agricultural and commercial centers and continued to flourish even after the court settled down in Madrid. Crumbling medieval walls were still used to control traffic in and out of the cities. Carts, coaches, and pack mules were often relegated to several main gates and were inspected for contraband goods of those drivers trying to evade the excise taxes on merchandise brought into the town.

First to be seen when approaching Burgos was the great cathedral completed in 1567. The city was a major stopover on the pilgrims' route to Santiago de Compostela and the main staging center in the north for the export trade in wool shipped through the northern ports to France and Flanders.

Valladolid, the last residence of Christopher Columbus and where Felipe II was born in 1527, was a major grain depot and market for the surrounding area; and nearby Medina del Campo, where Isabella passed

Typical Castillian town beginning to expand beyond its walls.

the last days of her life, became famous as a commercial town and for its fairs. Merchants came from all over the country to participate. In the first half of the sixteenth century it was the supply center for Spanish cloth destined for the New World.

The ancient Roman city of Segovia on the road south became the site of a textile industry sustaining 600 looms and reached its greatest prosperity about 1580. Queen Isabella was crowned in its castle.

Once the capital of the Visigothic kingdom of Spain and later under the Muslims a center of trade, Toledo, on a bluff above the river Tajo, often served as the royal capital from the time it was retaken from the Moors. In the center of the city stood the massive Gothic cathedral with forty chapels completed in 1493. Nearby were several synagogues to serve the large population of Jews who lived there. With the resettlement of the court to Madrid, Toledo declined in prosperity. However, it never lost its expertise in the manufacture of finely tempered (damascene) swords.

Benefiting from the presence of the royal family and its entourage, Madrid grew enormously. From about 20,000 inhabitants in 1561 when Felipe II installed the court permanently in the town, the population soon doubled. The old ramparts were demolished to make way for urban sprawl. For the inhabitants of Madrid participating in its rapid growth, the intense street life, and the presence of the court with its army of officials, the town was the center of the universe.

In the south, Sevilla also grew rapidly. As a bustling river port on the Guadalquivir with access to the Atlantic Ocean, the city attracted people from all parts of Europe, owing to its burgeoning West Indian trade. With its phenomenal growth, Sevilla eclipsed all other southern towns such as Córdoba, Málaga, Cádiz, and Granada.

KINGDOM OF ARAGÓN

The land of Aragón consisted of a confederation of separate realms that included the kingdoms of Aragón and Valencia and the principality of Cataluña. Aragón itself extended from the Pyrenees, over the lands of the middle Ebro River to the mountainous terrain that separated it from Castilla. Much of it was a sparsely settled, desiccated region, hot in summer, cold in winter, treeless and arid with outcroppings of dry stony hills and flat scrub-covered plains. In some places irrigation from wells or streams created small oases in the thirsty landscape.

The prosperous kingdom of Valencia, taken from the Moors in 1238, remained autonomous until 1319 when it affiliated with Aragón under one crown. Nevertheless, the idea of kingdom remained in general usage. This garden paradise with its elaborate system of irrigation channels and water wheels implemented by the Moors, and blessed by abundant sunshine, produced a continual series of crops and products: grapes, oranges, lemons, limes, almonds, oil, hemp, sugarcane, date palms, rice in the marshy areas, and mulberries for the silk industry.

The principality of Cataluña was once ruled by Frankish kings, but the local counts gained independence in the ninth and tenth centuries when they were recognized as sovereign princes. United with Aragón in 1137 through royal marriage, the region differed substantially in language and culture from the rest of the peninsula. The land was fertile with a gentle climate and produced wine, fruit, and oil. The industrious people, whose culture was closely related not to Castilla or Aragón but to Provence, felt more akin to southern France than to Spain.

MAJOR TOWNS OF ARAGÓN

Of the three major cities of the realm, Barcelona, capital of Cataluña, was the hub of Aragón's trade, the mercantile center of its Mediterranean empire. It was a middle-sized city of about 40,000 to 50,000 people and supported a variety of crafts and small-scale industries. Its prosperity diminished steadily as commercial interests shifted to Sevilla and the West Indian trade.

The city of Valencia, once ruled by the Cid at the end of the eleventh century when it was captured from the Muslims, reverted to Moorish rule but, later conquered by Aragón, became a flourishing town, usurping some of the Mediterranean commerce once controlled by Barcelona. The city declined in the early seventeenth century, remaining a maze of mostly unpaved streets and dilapidated buildings.

Conquered from the Moors in the twelfth century, Zaragoza became the capital of the kingdom of Aragón and the agricultural center for the surrounding region. The Moorish citadel served as the royal residence.

A bustling city on the banks of the Ebro River with its flourishing trade market, Zaragoza began to decline in the late fifteenth century when it ceased to be the permanent home of the kings of Aragón.

POPULATION AND LANGUAGES

Early in the seventeenth century two major cities stood out—the imperial capital of Madrid and the commercial river port of Sevilla—whose populations each reached about 150,000. The opening of America to Spanish commerce after the voyages of Columbus proved very profitable for Sevilla as trade developed between the two continents. Regional capitals of lesser importance such as Barcelona, Valencia, Granada, Toledo, and Valladolid had populations of about 50,000. Below these in number of inhabitants and importance were the market towns such as Medina del Campo, with about 15,000 inhabitants.

Aragón was only about a quarter the size of Castilla, with 17.2 percent of the peninsular land mass compared to 65.2 for Castilla, and contained a little over a million inhabitants, compared to Castilla's 8 million or so. The latter had about 73 percent of the population of the peninsula, Aragón about 12 percent. While the Jewish people of Spain constituted the single largest Jewish community in the world, they formed about 2 percent of the population, or around 100,000 inhabitants, during the Middle Ages. When Isabella came to the throne of Castilla in 1474, there were about 80,000 practicing Jews living in the realm, as many had already converted to Christianity.

In some regions of the country the quarter of a million or so Muslims were in the majority. The most dense concentration was in the kingdom of Granada, where they formed 54 percent of the population. In the Alpujarras mountains south of the capital, they constituted nearly 100 percent of the occupants. A third of the population of Valencia in the sixteenth century was Muslim, about one fifth of Aragón. In Cataluña they were few. They were even less in northern Castilla, with about 20,000 in 1502.[1]

About a quarter of all inhabitants spoke languages other than Castillian—a direct descendant from Hispano-Latin spoken on the Iberian peninsula centuries before. Aragonese, with only dialectal differences, was close enough to Castillian to be mutually comprehensible. Similarly, Andaluz was at the time becoming a dialect of Castillian as independent linguistic changes occurred in both Castilla and Andalucía. Catalán, on the other hand, spoken by the majority of people in Cataluña, Valencia, and Mallorca, was a separate language also developed from Latin but closer to Provençal spoken in southern France (from which it evolved) than to Castillian. Galician was akin to Portuguese and not readily understood by Castillian speakers. Spoken in the western Pyrenees, Navarra, and west as far as Bilbao, the ancient Basque language was not related to any of the others and entirely incomprehensible to all but Basque speakers. Another major language, employed especially in the south, but with no relationship to the others, Arabic, spoken by the Muslim population and remotely related to Hebrew, was easier for Jewish scholars to learn than it was for speakers of the Hispano-Latin languages. Jews and their brethren converted to Christianity spoke the local languages and often acted as intermediaries and translators between Christian and Muslim cultures.

TRAVEL: ROADS, TRANSPORTATION, AND INNS

In Early Modern times, the vast and underpopulated country was connected by little more than mule paths, muddy grooves in the winter rain, and dusty and shadeless in the dry summer heat. Roads had seen little improvement in a thousand years, and this did not change until the eighteenth century when some development was introduced. There were, however, travelers and, from the sixteenth century, guidebooks that helped the populace move from one location to another: businessmen to fairs and markets, ambassadors going to the court, the royal courier service, import-export merchants, military planners, pilgrims in search of shrines, and a few tourists.

The upkeep of roads and bridges was the task of the municipalities that on rare occasions were aided financially by the crown. In both cases the minimum amount of money was spent on maintenance—even less in hard economic times. The wooden bridges rotted away quickly and roads washed out in bad storms. Not many places could afford extensive repairs. Only the few remaining Roman bridges and roads could be counted on to survive under all conditions. Some parts of the country had no roads at all connecting towns. In western Andalucía there was one between Sevilla, Córdoba, and Granada but nothing between Huelva and Cádiz, or Córdoba and Jaén, until the eighteenth century. Navigable stretches of rivers in Spain were few and far between, offering little help to the traveler or in the transportation of goods.

The count of Gondomar, ambassador to England between 1613 and 1618, accustomed to traveling between Madrid and the northern coastal ports, stated that the journey was worse than any other in Europe. There were few inns, no food, and few good horses—only mules were generally available. Horses were in such short supply that smuggling one out of the country was considered a grave offense.

The winter roads from the port of La Coruña in Galicia were sometimes impassable for weeks due to snows and flood; so a letter from London to Madrid might take two months to arrive.[2]

As late as 1796 Robert Southey reported that it took him eighteen days from the northern Bay of Biscay to reach Madrid. He walked most of the way (presumably beside the coach) to keep warm, while the mule-drawn vehicle broke down several times and overturned once.[3]

The journey from Barcelona to Madrid of some 370 miles generally took about two weeks. As late as 1807 it still required ten days in heavy carriages drawn by six mules to make the journey from Sevilla to Madrid. At this time a party of four passengers would be gathered together by the coachman who fixed the day and hour of departure, arranged both the length of the stages and the time to arise each morning, and took care that each among them attended Mass along the route.[4]

The young Bostonian George Ticknor, who arrived in Spain in 1818, reports: "Traveling from 4 o'clock in the morning until 7 at night would not bring us forward more than 22 miles."[5]

Few ordinary people traveled far from their towns and villages unless they were on commercial business. For most journeys undertaken by foot the traveler could cover about two or three miles in an hour and maybe twenty in a day. On horseback, a rider could make about thirty-five miles a day.

The nobility generally traveled on horseback; the peasant walked or rode a donkey. Traders, where possible, used two or four-wheel wagons pulled by two or four mules. A wagon with a load of 1,200 pounds and two sturdy mules could manage about twenty-five miles a day. Carts and drivers could also be hired for most occasions. In addition, pack animals were used to carry loads and were the only source of transporting goods over mountain ranges or rough terrain where wheeled wagons could not proceed.

When great numbers of often heavily loaded wagons traveled across the land, such as an army on the move or an aristocrat changing residence, progress was slow. William Beckford, the English millionaire who left Lisbon for Madrid in 1788 with his entourage of servants, footmen, cooks, musicians, his piano, private bed, carpets, and collected works of art, was able to travel about ten miles a day. His diary, 10 December, reports crossing the Tajo River (the border with Spain) and continuing "through heavy sands for five tedious hours without perceiving a habitation or meeting any animals . . . except herds of swine in which I believe consist the principal riches of this part of the Spanish dominions."[6]

The mule train was the normal means of moving goods across the peninsula, but the dangers of the road dictated a certain style of journey. The *arrieros* (muleteers) congregated in convoys and traveled in well-armed caravans on appointed days. Their entire fortune might have been on the back of a few mules, and their guns were always near at hand, but numbers ensured their safe passage among bands of thieves. Individuals going their way contributed to the strength of the party. The muleteer lived frugally: Saddlebags of coarse cloth held his provisions, and a leather bottle hanging from the saddle contained water or wine. A mule cloth spread upon the ground served as his bed, and his pack saddle his pillow.

The demeanor of the muleteers was frank but courteous.[7] They never passed another person on the road without a nod or a solemn salutation such as "Vaya usted con Dios" (Go with God). The mules were brightly adorned with tufts and tassels, and their approach was heralded by the tinkling of the bells around their necks. Sometimes the men sat sideways on a mule for hours, singing ballads about former Spanish heroes, their battles and loves, Moors and highwaymen. Bandits and smugglers were often considered heroes among the peasant people of Spain who envied their adventurous lives. Sometimes the song was improvised on the spot, commemorating an incident on the trail.[8]

Along the road were reminders of bygone days: a half-ruined walled town situated high on a barren hill; a broken-down watchtower on a rocky crag; relics of heroic times when the Christians and the Moors were locked in mortal combat, fighting on charging steeds with sturdy lances and flashing scimitars. An ominous cross protruding from a pile of stones might mark the grave of a recent traveler ambushed by a highwayman.

For many travelers, Spain was the worst of the European countries to visit. A group of Cistercian monks journeying through the country in 1532 complained that they were lodged like pigs in filth and dirt and that horses were better treated than people.

An account by a contemporary of the travels of Santa Teresa, the famous Spanish mystic, tells of her staying in an inn located near Córdoba in 1575 at a time when she was racked with a fever: "The only room available had previously been inhabited by pigs and the ceiling was so low that we could hardly stand upright." With vermin everywhere, she was forced to lay on an uncomfortable bed, listening to loud shouting and cursing of other people lodged at the inn; finally, she decided to leave and continue on her journey "in the blazing midday sun; that night, rather than risk enduring a second inn like the first," she and her group camped in the fields.[9]

Conditions did not change much over the next 100 years. The French countess Madame d'Aulnoy visited the country in 1679 and commented on the inns: "You enter into the stable, and from thence to your chamber; this stable is ordinarily full of mules and muleteers, who make use of their mules' saddles for pillows in the night and in the day-time they serve 'em for tables." To reach the rooms, she had to climb a staircase more like a ladder. Once there: "You are showed a chamber whose walls are white enough, hung with a thousand little scurvy pictures of saints."

Besides complaining about the beds and blankets and absence of forks in the inn, other things annoyed her:

They have only a cup in the house; and if the mule-drivers get first hold of it . . . you must stay patiently till they have done with it or drink out of an earthen pitcher. It is impossible to warm one at the kitchen-fire without being choked, for they have no chimneys, and 'tis the same in all the houses on the road; there is a hole in the top of the ceiling and the smoke goes out thence.[10]

Entering Spain from France or Portugal or traveling from one kingdom to another involved passing through customs and paying duty on goods. At the beginning of the nineteenth century, Fray Servando Teresa de Mier complained that the guards at the custom house searched everything in an unseemly manner and left the contents of one's luggage strewn about the ground if their palm was not greased. Unregistered money, when found, was confiscated. All along the roads and at bridges there were tolls that had to be paid for their upkeep.

Mier found the difference in language, laws, and value of money in each region a vexing problem and the inns abominable.

To top it all they ask whatever price they like for a damnable meal, a hard, dirty, filthy bed in a garret, where one is assailed by the smoke from the kitchen, and then they demand payment for the noise a person has made even if he has been as quiet as a dead man . . . and there is nothing one can do but pay, because if the inn is an isolated one, it is the innkeeper himself who administers justice.[11]

Mier goes on to say that taking a coach (here he means cart) is of little value since it proceeds at the pace of the coachman, who usually walks beside it and stops frequently to let the mules graze. The jolting in such carts is unbearable, and the risk is always present that they will overturn and the load kill the passengers.

While traveling through Aragón, he noted holes in the earth outside the village where rainwater collected; the green-crusted holes constituted the water supply for the village.

Ticknor also found the inns troublesome:

I have not been in a single inn where the lower storey was not a stable and the upper one as full of fleas as if it were under an Egyptian curse. . . . Not once have I taken off my clothes except to change them.[12]

MEALS ON THE ROAD

Inns were forbidden to keep a stock of food, so guests had to either bring their own or buy it locally. This measure prevented the innkeeper from defrauding the public and the royal treasury of taxes, called *millones*, due on the sale of food. Only certain individuals such as the butcher or grocer, who purchased the tax concessions in each town or village, could sell provisions.

Madame d'Aulnoy found the meal to be a problem. What one brought to the inn would be cooked on the open fire, where the smoke made the meat so black it turned her stomach to look at it. She compared the kitchen to hell, and in it were men and women black as devils, clad like beggars and smelling none too good. She went on:

There are always some of 'em impudently grating on a sorry guitar, and singing like a cat a-roasting. The women . . . have glass necklaces which hang twisted about their necks like ropes of onions.. . . .They are as great thieves . . . urgent to serve you only to have an opportunity to steal something from you.[13]

By the end of the eighteenth century, however, this was beginning to change. Leucadio Doblado reported that upon stopping at an inn in 1801 "travellers were not here obliged to starve if they had not brought their own provisions."[14]

The prices (fixed by royal decree) were chalked up on a board that the landlord had to display. Bed, wine, a candle, and service charges would all be listed. The food supplied by the guests was served up in the dining room. Here, everyone ate at a long, wooden communal table that had a large knife fastened to it by a chain. The knife was shared by everyone, which included guests, muleteers, owners, and servants. All would be poured a cup of wine. Wine was kept in goat skins (only in Cataluña and Valencia did they use wine barrels at this time) and tended to take on the flavor of the rest of the kitchen odors along with smells of hide and pitch.[15] To drink from the skin, one had to hold it high and pour the wine into the throat without touching the lips to the opening.

A traveler on the road during the fruit season might wish to purchase and consume oranges, figs, grapes, cherries, pears, and apples and other succulent items and not dine at the inn at all.

BANDITS

Inns were not the worst problems of the traveler. Bandits and high-waymen were always a clear and present threat to the unwary wayfarer. Sometimes the bandit only asked for alms by placing his hat or pistol belt in the middle of the road while he hid behind a rock, rifle in hand. Those who failed to stop and leave something might be shot at. On other occasions, gangs ambushed the unprotected and took everything right down to their clothes.

The extreme heat of the summer day in parts of the country forced travel at night, making robbery even more likely and requiring an armed retinue. Some highwaymen who refrained from plundering churches or who always left the robbed and dejected traveler with enough money to complete his journey were romanticized into virtual Robin Hoods.

Whatever the case, the bandits roamed the byways of the country sometimes with bands of outlaws numbering several dozen. Highway robbery was always an important consideration for the traveler, but this was only one of the hazards. One could be easily robbed at an inn, sometimes by the innkeeper himself. In remote areas there was no recourse to justice.

Travel remained a risky venture right up to the nineteenth century. In 1829, the writer Washington Irving left Sevilla for Granada, where he was to remain several months writing his *Tales of the Alhambra*. He and his Russian companion went by mule with an armed guide and carried extra money to be given, if necessary, to highwaymen in exchange for their lives. Being familiar with the scant larders of the inns, they rode with saddlebags full of cold provisions and a wineskin of what Irving called "portly dimensions."[16]

CURRENCY AND COST OF LIVING

One type of monetary system was used in Aragón and another in Castilla. That of Aragón employed the libra, made up of 20 sueldos; 1 sueldo was equivalent to 12 dineros.

In Castilla reckoning was done in maravedís along the following lines; 1 ducat (a gold coin) equaled 375 maravedís. The real, made of silver, was equivalent to 34 maravedís. After 1534 a new gold coin was issued, the escudo, which slowly replaced the ducat, but the latter continued as a unit of accounts. 1 escudo = 10 reales = 340 maravedís.

Salaries and prices differed from place to place, but on average, a daily wage for a laborer in Castilla around 1550 was about 50 maravedís; sailors earned about the same, soldiers a little more, and skilled carpenters and masons over twice that amount. Servants in a well-off household with food and lodging included might make about 16 reales a month. Salaries went up in the following century but often not as fast as inflation. In contrast, the income of a wealthy grandee family about the same time was in the vicinity of 60,000 to 100,000 ducats annually.[17]

In 1657 the marquis of Helicia gave a party for Marie-Anne of Austria with plays, concerts, and a banquet for a thousand people. It cost him 16,000 ducats.[18]

Purchasing power in maravedís on average was about as follows:

1	kilogram (2.2 pounds) pork or veal	30
1	chicken	20
1	partridge	25
1	dozen eggs	24
1	kilogram fish (varied with the type)	20

100	sardines	15
10	loaves of bread[19]	25
1	liter of milk	5
1	liter cooking oil	15
1	liter red wine	10
1	liter white wine	6
1	liter spirits	45
1	lettuce	1.5
1	melon	3
1	kilogram apples	2.5
1	kilogram grapes	3
1	kilogram sugar	85
1	kilogram pear preserves	85
1	kilogram marzipan	69[20]

Bread, sardines, fruit, and vegetables were inexpensive. A single person could eat reasonably well on 50 maravedís a day, but meat and most fish were affordable only to the wealthy. A laborer with a family to house, clothe, and feed was hard-pressed to maintain a healthy diet for his household.

When out of work, with no pay forthcoming, as was often the case with the day laborer or a seaman between sailings, it was a strain to make ends meet. Certain items such as sugar, preserved fruit, and marzipan would entail nearly two days' work to buy 1 kilo and were destined only for the tables of the affluent.

If a person fell ill and required medical treatment, a doctor's visit could cost 136 maravedís—a nurse, as much or more; a purge, 340 maravedís. So-called curative powders made of various ingredients such as emeralds and coral were 714 maravedís. A Mass said at home would cost 34. It was not long before a sick man or woman was destitute, the cost of the medicine and care being about as high-priced as the treatment was ineffective.

Fine clothes were not cheap. Some examples (prices in maravedís):

stockings	272
shoes	153
shirt	510
waistcoat	1,800
cap	1,100
cloak	4,500

loose coat   4,500
sword   1,900[21]

For a laborer or a sailor to aspire to dress like a gentleman of even the lesser nobility was beyond hope. Purchasing only a fine cloak or coat would consume around three or four months' wages.

NOTES

1. For these figures see Kamen, *The Spanish Inquisition*, 23.
2. Hillgarth, 44.
3. Southey, 1:104.
4. Doblado, 328.
5. Mitchell, 47.
6. Boyd, 285.
7. Irving, 17.
8. Ibid.
9. See Hillgarth, 40–44, for these examples and others of early travelers.
10. Aulnoy, in Ross and Power, 70.
11. Mier, 112.
12. Mitchell, 47.
13. Aulnoy, in Ross and Power, 69–70.
14. Doblado, 162.
15. Defourneaux, 15–16.
16. Irving, 16.
17. For figures based on thirteen noble families, see Elliott, *Imperial Spain*, 313. For wages of seamen of the Atlantic fleets in the 1588–1655 period, see Goodman, *Spanish Naval Power*, 187, and Pérez-Mallaína, 115.
18. Defourneaux, 58.
19. The 10 loaves of bread in the inventory of Pérez-Mallaína were presumably small, not the usual 2-pound loaf. Bread prices differed from place to place and fluctuated wildly in times of shortages. See Casey, 129.
20. For these items and others, see Pérez-Mallaína, 116.
21. For more detailed prices and salaries, see Pérez-Mallaína, 115–116. Figures here have been averaged and rounded off.

2

Political Setting

Throughout the Middle Ages grievances of a peasantry downtrodden by a repressive aristocracy and by overbearing clergy always had undercurrents that threatened to break out into serious violence. The Catholic Kings, Isabella and Fernando, consolidated their royal authority by bringing to heel disobedient nobles, dismantling troublesome castles, and establishing governing bodies loyal to them. With no fixed royal abode, they traveled around their realms, dispensing laws and justice where necessary, which enhanced their authority and endeared them to the common people.

During the ten-year war against the kingdom of Granada beginning in 1482, Christian forces whittled away at the last Muslim state on the Iberian peninsula. The war terminated when the city of Granada itself fell on 2 January 1492. This was followed on 31 March by a royal edict giving all Jews four months to convert to Christianity or leave the country. On 17 April, less than three weeks later, the Catholic monarchs signed the agreement that would send Christopher Columbus on his westward voyage in search of the Indies. The death of Isabella in 1504 ushered in a new dynasty to rule Castilla—the Habsburgs.

In 1493, the Habsburg Maximilian I became emperor of the Holy Roman Empire, a loose confederation of German states, and through diplomacy and marriage policies established Habsburg domination throughout much of central Europe. In 1496 his son, Philippe, duke of Burgundy, married Juana, a daughter of Fernando and Isabella. Because Juana and Philippe were absent in Flanders, Fernando continued to rule

Titian. *Carlos I of Spain (Carlos V of the Holy Roman Empire)*. (Madrid: Prado).

Castilla (as regent) and Aragón until 1506 when the couple arrived to claim the throne of Castilla. Philippe, now Felipe I, the founder of the Habsburg dynasty in Spain, died shortly thereafter, whereupon Juana went insane. Fernando continued to rule until his death in 1516. The son of Felipe and Juana, Carlos, then became ruler of all the Spanish domains.

CARLOS I (CARLOS V OF THE HOLY ROMAN EMPIRE)

Born in 1500 and educated in Ghent (now in Belgium), Carlos I inherited the Burgundian realm, which included the Netherlands (now Belgium and Holland), Castilla and Aragón, and Spanish territories in Italy and in the newly discovered Americas.

He arrived in Spain in 1517 to consolidate his new inheritance with an entourage of Flemings (residents of Flanders, today mostly in Belgium) who displayed haughty disdain for the Spanish and occupied the best government positions. When his grandfather, Maximilian I, died in 1519, Carlos inherited the Habsburg lands in central Europe (today Austria, Germany, the Czech Republic, Slovakia, and territories in north-western Hungary) and was elected Holy Roman Emperor as Carlos V. He was now by far the most powerful sovereign in Christendom.

After extracting a good deal of money from the reluctant Cortes (parliaments) of Castilla and of Aragón, Carlos departed in May 1520 for the Netherlands. The unhappy Spaniards wanted their own king and not simply a part of an emperor whose worldly ambitions would be financed to a large extent by them. The final insult was that a foreign regent, Adrian of Utrecht, was left behind in Valladolid to govern.

Seething with anger, the townsmen of Castilla revolted. The uprising of the *comuneros* (communities) led by the city of Toledo, which expelled its *corregidor* (crown-appointed governor), became a revolution that soon spread to most of the cities of Castilla. A revolutionary junta was established that drove the royal officials residing in Valladolid from the city, including the regent Adrian.

The junta sought to impose conditions on the power of the king, but it soon succumbed to infighting. Forces loyal to Carlos, mobilized by the aristocracy, took advantage of the dissension and captured the town of Tordesillas near Valladolid, the headquarters of the junta. The *comuneros* were no match for the army arrayed against them, and on 24 April 1521, they were defeated at the battle of Villalar near Valladolid. Their leaders were executed. The following October Toledo fell, and the revolution was over. The revolt of the communities underscored the unrest rampant in the country and the difficulties of the monarchy and aristocracy to subdue the common people permanently.

Carlos I had other pressing problems besides maintaining political control in Spain. After 1517, the year Martin Luther rebelled against the Catholic Church, the number of Lutheran followers grew rapidly, and conflicts ensued between Protestants and Catholics over religious issues in the Holy Roman Empire. Carlos tried to stem the tide of religious revolt. At the same time, he was involved in struggles with the Ottoman Turks, who were threatening Europe from their base in the Balkans; with the pirates of the Barbary coast; with wars with the French Valois dynasty, which challenged his authority in Flanders, Italy, and elsewhere; with his need to control Spain, especially the rebellious Catalans who never wanted him as king; and with keeping the defiant Dutch in the fold of the empire. Other matters, too, were pressing: By the 1550s Spain exerted its influence over portions of the South American continent, Central America, Mexico, Florida and Cuba and disputed the East Indies with Portugal that claimed the islands.

TOWN PRIVILEGES (*FUEROS*)

Early Modern municipalities were not unlike small city–states, an outgrowth of earlier times when concessions and liberties were granted to them by the monarchs or nobility to attract settlers to the frontier areas under their control where Muslims and Christians confronted each other. The inhabitants were authorized to surround their towns with defensive ramparts, to carry out their own internal administration, to maintain a militia, and in whole or in part to elect their own magistrates. To the community was often given the right to tax itself to pay for local improvements, with only a light tribute destined for the monarch. Sometimes freedom from persecution of the town officials was guaranteed by the crown against charges brought by royal agents.

Thus, personal liberty and fiscal and administrative autonomy were the primary features inscribed in the municipal charters, or *fueros*, which differed somewhat from town to town, depending on the historical circumstances. In 1025 Barcelona obtained a charter of privileges from Count Ramón Berenguer, and Zaragoza was given extensive privileges in 1125 by Alfonso the Battler. Toledo, Córdoba, Sevilla, and other towns all received their *fueros* from the reigning monarch as they were reconquered from the Muslims.

Some communities were designated cities and had jurisdiction over larger territories or several parishes that might include neighboring villages and hamlets. Towns, on the other hand, were usually limited to the areas encompassed by their walls and immediate surroundings. Those magistrates charged with communal affairs formed the *ayuntamiento*, or municipal council. There were also many other officials such as the *alcaldes*, responsible for civil and criminal justice; the *regidores*, who administered the affairs of the city, and the *alguacil mayor* (principal peace officer), who commanded the militia. Other officials controlled the building crafts and communal property. Cities sent representatives or deputies (*procuradores*) chosen by the municipal council to the Cortes, the body that looked after the interests of all the subjects of the kingdom but that was summoned to meet only at the will of the king. As guardian of the local *fueros*, the Cortes could refuse to obey orders from the crown if the demands jeopardized the interests of the region.

While the Cortes advised the monarch on numerous matters including royal marriages and foreign alliances, its real power lay in controlling financial matters. The king could not levy new taxes or raise old ones without its consent.

As *procuradores* left their towns for meetings of the Cortes, they took with them detailed instructions. They were entrusted with the mandate to present complaints to the king from their constituents, and while in Castilla they had no power to legislate, their suggestions were sometimes made into law by royal edicts. Some remote areas of the two kingdoms of Castilla and Aragón were underrepresented or not represented at all, such as Galicia and Extremadura with no important cities.

In Castilla the Cortes consisted of the three estates: the nobility, the church, and the commoners. Since it only had real authority over taxes and the first two groups paid none, nobles and clergy often absented themselves from the meetings. In time they were not summoned, and the king went directly to the cities and towns for his requirements. Unable to withstand the pressure exerted by the sovereign, the towns gave him what he wanted, and the Cortes gradually became a useless body. In the reign of Carlos II, the last Habsburg king, it was never called to session, and the money required for the crown treasury was solicited directly from the town councils.

The Cortes of Aragón, Valencia, and Cataluña were not so compliant, and various kings were often frustrated by their refusal to grant them money, to levy troops for wars, or to house soldiers on their territory without considerable concessions. In these realms the Cortes shared legislative power with the king and approved or denied royal edicts. Here the nobility did not shun the sessions and scrupulously watched over their own interests. The Cortes was often more interested in submitting their complaints than listening to the king's pleas for money. Always finding obstacles to put in the way of the king's demands, they were also seldom called.

COUNCILS AND *CORREGIDORES*

The administration of each region was overseen by the Council of Castilla. This royal body was designed by Isabella and Fernando in 1480 to be the central governing body of the kingdom. It was the supreme court of justice and supervised the workings of local governments. Under Carlos I, it had about twelve members, all university-trained lawyers, since the king preferred them to the grandees (the high landowning nobility). Early in the sixteenth century, other councils were formed to deal with Aragón, finance, the Indies, war, and foreign policy. The Council of the Supreme Inquisition, known as the *Suprema*, was founded in 1488. There were others of lesser importance, such as the Council of Military Orders, but none had much authority except the *Suprema* and the Council of Castilla. The latter appointed *corregidores*, or civil governors, who served as representatives of the crown at the local level throughout the kingdoms. Their seats were in the larger cities where they presided over the town council and maintained vigilance over the area under their jurisdiction. By the end of the sixteenth century there were sixty-eight *corregidores*; this number increased to eighty-six over the next century.

FELIPE II AND THE SPANISH EMPIRE

When Carlos I (V) abdicated in 1556 he bequeathed Spain (Castilla and Aragón), the Netherlands, the Italian domains, and the overseas empire

Sanchez Coello. *Felipe II*. (Madrid: Prado).

to his son Felipe II. On the emperor's death in 1558, the Austrian branch ruled by Carlos's brother Ferdinand I retained the Holy Roman imperial title.

Toledo, the current capital, gave way to Madrid in 1561 when Felipe II moved the court to this small town on the Manzanares River seventy-one miles northeast. Madrid became the permanent political and administrative center of the country. About 10,000 government officials and members of their families accompanied the king to the new location, rapidly changing the face of Madrid from a humble town to a noisy, cluttered, unsanitary city of narrow streets left over from earlier times combined with more spacious new avenues.

The Spanish empire reached it zenith under Felipe II, but as Spain became an imperial power, strong defensive measures became necessary to hold the empire together, and an effort was made to convert the country into an international military power. Mighty Mediterranean and Atlantic fleets were constructed, and both the armed forces and the technology were upgraded. For all of this, foreign resources were needed, and with financial backing from European bankers, Spain developed an impressive military capacity drawing on the expertise, weaponry, and human resources of Italian and German states.

The expenses were an enormous drain on Castillian revenues, which had a negative effect on development as money poured into military undertakings and not into industrial enterprises or increases in agricultural production. In spite of the flow of gold and silver from the Americas into Castilla, it was never enough to keep the government out of debt.

THE MUSLIM THREAT AND THE ECONOMIC COST

Along the Barbary coast of North Africa, extending from Libya to the Atlantic Ocean, the name derived from the Berber tribes who were the principal inhabitants of the region, pirates preyed on European shipping. Beginning in the sixteenth century this coast was occupied by several independent Muslim states under the sovereignty of the Ottoman Empire. Encroachment of the Ottoman Turks westward in the Mediterranean led many to believe that sooner or later another Islamic invasion of Spain would occur.

In the space of a decade and a half after 1560, Felipe II had 300 galleys constructed for the Mediterranean fleet at a cost of 3.5 million ducats. In 1571 Don Juan of Austria was selected to lead a formidable Spanish, Venetian, and Papal fleet of over 200 ships to destroy the Turkish Armada in the Gulf of Lepanto (now the Gulf of Corinth) and halt Muslim expansion in the Mediterranean. Felipe II paid half the costs of the expedition, which was entirely successful and devastated the Turkish fleet.

The costs of victory at Lepanto and maintaining a large fleet in the Mediterranean against the Turks and Barbary pirates, troops stationed in Italy, an army in the rebellious Netherlands, and a navy of galleons in the Atlantic to protect the treasure fleets from America ravaged by English and French corsairs were staggering. In spite of spiraling expenses, Felipe II ordered the construction of a colossal palace at El Escorial, which helped ensure that the crown remained heavily in debt while Spanish industry stagnated. Interest on money borrowed from foreign bankers was already astronomical and growing. Several times the king confiscated the entire gold bullion imports from the New World, but it was not enough. In 1575 he arbitrarily canceled his foreign debts and had to renegotiate loans from Italian creditors. He hammered the Cortes into approving a large tax raise—a burden that fell on the merchants, artisans, and peasants that many could not pay. People lost their property, farms, and jobs, and the streets became overrun with beggars. Returning soldiers, often maimed from the wars with no means of support, became vagabonds wandering from city to city looking for work. The country was rife with derelicts of all sorts with no money and no hope. While perhaps not totally oblivious to the plight of the people, the king thought it better to spend great sums on wars in defense of the

Titian. *The Empress Isabel of Portugal* (wife of Carlos I and mother of Felipe II). (Madrid: Prado).

Catholic faith in distant lands than to worry about the state of affairs at home.

PORTUGAL AND ENGLAND

With the end of the Portuguese House of Avis in 1580, Felipe II (with a strong claim to the throne through his Portuguese mother) overcame rival claimants through force and persuasion to become king of Portugal. This union, incorporating the Portuguese overseas possessions, created the largest and most far-flung empire that had ever existed.

Still troubles accumulated. Felipe had a zealous devotion to Roman Catholicism and to the preservation of absolute rule. This combination proved disastrous in the Low Countries where his persecution of Protestants and his attempts to rule the Netherlands as a province of Spain led to war with England. Under Queen Elizabeth I, England had become a Protestant power whose foreign policy included unofficial support for the Dutch rebels and for the English privateers who raided Spanish colonies and treasure fleets in the Americas. From the Spanish point of view, Elizabeth I ruled a nation of despised heretics.

When Catholic Mary, Queen of Scots was put to death by order of

Elizabeth on 8 February 1587, her death provided Felipe with an added stimulus to deal a lethal blow to England. To put an end to English belligerency and force the country back into the Catholic mode, he took unprecedented measures. In 1588, a huge fleet costing 10 million ducats was sent against England, but the great Spanish Armada met disaster from English cannon and North Sea storms, and most of the surviving ships were wrecked in gales on the way home. Meanwhile, the domestic situation continued to deteriorate. American treasure alone could not support Spain's wars; taxation remained oppressive, and the state defaulted on loans. In addition, as Felipe strengthened the Inquisition, intellectual life became narrower and less open to new currents of thought.

Felipe II died in 1598 and left a bankrupt country, rapidly declining domestically and internationally.

FELIPE III AND FELIPE IV

Unlike his father, Felipe III was not interested in the day-to-day running of government and entrusted this task to others, restoring to authority the Councils of State and of War and others that had been neglected by his father. The Castillian aristocracy regained its former political power, and the king allowed his favorite minister, whom he titled the duke of Lerma and on whom he bestowed a fortune, to control the government. The duke's friends and relatives were also well taken care of and promoted to high posts. The duke accompanied the king everywhere, controlling access to him, sold favors for his own profit, dominated court patronage, and married his children into the wealthiest of the grandee families from which they gained noble titles. The duke of Lerma set the pattern that was to be followed throughout the seventeenth century in which a favorite of the king (known as a *valido*) drawn from the aristocracy controlled the government.

There were some matters neither the king nor his *valido* could do anything about. In 1597 an outbreak of the plague in the north of the country gravitated southward and reached epidemic proportions in 1599 and 1600, killing about 15 percent of the population. To compound the disaster, harvests were poor and in places failed completely in the last years of the century, while abroad, the illustrious Spanish army met with the first of a series of reversals. The campaigns against the Dutch were halted, and cutbacks were made in other foreign ventures. Peace with England was arranged in 1604, followed a few years later by a truce with the Dutch in 1609.

In that same year the government rounded up and expelled from the country the vast majority of Moriscos who had not melted into the fabric of Spanish society. With their expulsion, the economies in some areas, as around Valencia where they were in great numbers, were devastated.

The king nevertheless continued to spend long periods absent from the court, ignoring these problems.

The overly pious Felipe IV succeeded to the throne at age sixteen after his father's untimely death in 1621. Like his father, he had little aptitude for his lofty calling but instead patronized the arts and became a respectable scholar. Felipe IV allowed Gaspar de Guzman, count-duke of Olivares, to run the government. Olivares sought to restore and even expand Spanish power abroad: He resumed the Dutch conflict and involved Spain in the Thirty Years' War, a series of European conflicts lasting from 1618 to 1648 engaging most of the countries of western Europe, and fought mainly in Germany. This involvement led to war with France after 1635, but in spite of some successes, Spain's military effort could no longer be sustained at home. Olivares's attempts to increase taxation and conscription led to revolt in 1640, first in Cataluña and then in Portugal. Spain was further weakened by the rapid exhaustion of the American silver mines after 1640. Politically and economically the country entered a long period of decline. On 19 May 1643, the severe defeat of the once invincible Spanish infantry, the army of Flanders, by the French at the battle of Rocroi in northern France symbolized the decline of military power that had long sustained the imperial ambitions of the country.

With the home front in chaos and failing abroad, Olivares was ousted, but the wars and revolutions his policies had helped engender haunted Spain for another three decades. Cataluña was recovered in 1652, but Roussillon and Cerdagne, then Spanish territory, were returned to France in 1659. Dutch independence had to be recognized in 1648, but the war with Portugal dragged on. When the king died in 1665 the country was in grave economic crisis.

CARLOS II

The new ruler, Carlos II, a product of Habsburg inbreeding, acquired the throne in 1665 but could not govern effectively because of physical and mental infirmities. Factional strife characterized the country at home; lost wars typified it abroad. The period was the low point in the country's fortunes as the grandees ran the country for their own benefit and silver shipments from America often never arrived, having been waylaid by buccaneers from their Caribbean bases.

The war with Portugal finally ended in 1668, but over two decades of campaigns left parts of Castilla in dire straits. Portugal regained its independence, but Extremadura on the Portuguese border lost between a third and one half of its population and remained up until the present day a depressed area.

The king, who had married a niece of Louis XIV of France, was apparently impotent, and no heir was foreseen. The unanswered question of the Spanish succession became the dominant theme in European diplomatic intrigues. When the king died on 1 November 1700, his will for a successor read in favor of the French Bourbon Philippe, duke of Anjou and grandson of Louis XIV of France, to succeed him (as Felipe V). Philippe's accession would make possible an enormous increase in the power of France and threatened to overthrow the balance of power in Europe. Many statesmen viewed the Bourbon acquisition of Spain's still vast territories with alarm and thus favored the Habsburg claim to the throne as represented by Charles, son of the Holy Roman emperor Leopold I. As the storm clouds gathered, England, the Netherlands, Austria, Prussia, and several smaller countries formed a coalition against Louis XIV of France and against Spain.

FELIPE V, WAR OF SUCCESSION, LOSS OF PRIVILEGE

The young Bourbon king arrived in Madrid in February 1701 as Felipe V and shocked the dignitaries by declining to attend the auto de fe, a major ceremony of the Inquisition in which the condemned were sentenced and which the inquisitors held as a traditional welcome to a new king. In spite of his refusal to attend the act of the Inquisition, the king, nevertheless, did not try to prevent it functioning as normal. He had many other things to worry about, especially his throne. The Spanish War of Succession, fought from 1701 to 1714, in which the Austrian House of Habsburg and the French House of Bourbon contested the Spanish throne, changed the political face of the country.

After a series of engagements fought in Italy, in the Netherlands, and in the German states, the war came to Spain. In 1704 the English captured Gibraltar and an Anglo-Portuguese army invaded the country in 1707. After much devastation it was routed by a Franco-Spanish force at the battle of Almansa southeast of Toledo, and Felipe V's supporters retained control of most of the country.

In 1707 Felipe V decreed the abolishment of the *fueros* of Aragón and Valencia on the basis of their rebellion and disloyalty, as some of the nobles had supported the Habsburg side. The war came to a close with a series of treaties at Utrecht in the Netherlands between 1713 and 1715, with the Spanish Bourbon still on the throne and by pledges from Louis XIV and Felipe V that their two kingdoms, Spain and France, would not be united.

In 1714, Cataluña's constitution and ancient privileges were abolished when the French invaded and sacked the city of Barcelona for supporting the wrong side. The political bodies of the principality were remodeled in 1716, the laws of Castilla were implemented, and the Castillian language (instead of Catalán) was imposed in the law courts. The country was occupied by the military. The traditional crown of Aragón now no longer existed, and Spain became a politically unified nation with the seat of authority in Madrid. The only exception was the Basque country that had remained loyal to the Bourbons and retained its ancient privileges of self-government.

Felipe V died in 1746, and his son Fernando VI succeeded him on the throne. Fernando kept Spain free from foreign entanglements, giving the country a decade of peace. He also promoted internal welfare by encouraging industry, and the economy generally improved under his rule. When he died, childless, in 1759, his brother Carlos III inherited the crown.

CARLOS III AND CARLOS IV

In 1762 Spain entered the Seven Years' War, a series of conflicts fought from 1756 to 1763 for the control of Germany and for supremacy in colonial North America and India. It involved most of the major powers of Europe, and Spain acted as an ally of the French against Britain. As a result, Spain lost Florida to the British, but the Louisiana Territory was given to Spain by France as compensation. The two nations allied again in 1779 to support the American Revolution against Britain, and by the Treaty of Versailles in 1783, Spain recovered Florida. The Spanish presence now extended over much of the North American continent. Under Carlos III, an enlightened ruler responsible for many foreign and domestic achievements, Spain regained some of its former greatness.

Carlos IV came to the throne in 1788, but the extraordinary upheavals that the French Revolution engendered throughout Europe after 1789 had especially adverse effects on Spain. Fear that revolutionary ideology might spread there caused repressive policies to be revived. In 1793, after French king Louis XVI was beheaded, Spain joined other European powers, including Britain, in declaring war against the revolutionary government of France but soon had to admit defeat as French armies ravaged its northern provinces.

In 1796, as rebellious fervor diminished in France, Manuel de Godoy, the chief minister, who had gained the favor of Carlos IV and Queen María Luisa, reversed course and formed an alliance with France against Britain. British naval supremacy could not be overcome, however, and Spain was frequently cut off on the high seas from its American colonies with disastrous economic consequences. Worse still, France began to act more like a master than an ally once Napoleon gained effective control in 1799. In 1800 Louisiana was ceded back to France, and in 1805, Spain, now a French puppet state, saw its fleet destroyed in the battle of Trafalgar by the British under Admiral Horatio Nelson. Godoy became unpopular and in March 1808 was overthrown, and Carlos IV was forced to abdicate in favor of his son, Fernando VII.

A Napoleonic army then invaded Spain, and father and son were summoned by Napoleon to Bayonne across the French border. Both were forced to abdicate and to hand over the crown of Spain to the French emperor; they were then detained in France. On 2 May 1808 the population of Madrid rose up in bloody rebellion against the French occupation. Napoleon then summoned his brother Joseph from Naples and placed him on the throne of Spain. A pro-French faction of Spaniards acknowledged this decision, but most of the population resisted.

WAR OF INDEPENDENCE, RESTORATION OF FERNANDO VII, LIBERAL CONSTITUTION OF 1812

By January 1810 the French had defeated the major Spanish resistance and occupied most of the country, but the Spanish people refused to recognize Joseph as king. Guerrilla bands effectively harassed French forces, preventing them from completely taking over the country, while the British, who had landed a force in Portugal, kept the French army off balance. The war against Napoleon was a heroic period for Spain and contributed to the emperor's eventual defeat. Six years of warfare greatly harmed the economy of Spain, however, and its American colonies began to win their independence. By 1826 only Cuba and Puerto Rico remained under Spanish rule.

While Fernando VII had been residing at Valençay in France as an idle and pampered prisoner of the French government, the Spanish Cortes met in Cádiz outside of French-controlled territory to draft a constitution (the first in Europe and the second one in the world after the United States). This national assembly proclaimed a constitution that placed sovereignty in the hands of the people, not the king, who received only limited veto power over legislation. It established parliamentary government and universal male suffrage and eliminated the special privileges of the nobles and clergy. Catholicism remained the official religion of the country, and heresy remained a crime, but the Inquisition was abolished.

When the defeat of Napoleon allowed Fernando VII to return to Madrid on 4 May 1814, he was greeted with rejoicing. The return of the king signaled a peaceful and, it was hoped, prosperous new beginning. But Fernando had another agenda. Unwilling to except limitations on his rule by the Cortes, he decreed all the body's acts null and void and reinstated the Inquisition. He declared that anyone who upheld the constitution would be guilty of treason. Those voicing objection to absolute monarchy were imprisoned, tortured, and some murdered.

While it seemed that nothing had changed, under the surface of society transformations of the very kind the king, the church, and the Inquisition feared were emerging. Liberal attitudes introduced by French and English officers during the War of Independence, aided by the appearance of Freemasonry, lent support to the views of the Cortes. Revolution hovered on the fringes of the despotic regime gaining momentum. Then, in 1820, Rafael de Riego, commander of a military battalion, incited his men to revolt. The insurrection spread throughout the country as leaders emerged, and men and women demonstrated their desire for constitutional government. With few options open, Fernando VII took the oath to the Constitution of 1812, thereby restoring it to political prominence. Celebrations again resounded throughout the country; the prisons were opened and political prisoners freed.

The new constitutional government proved inept, however, and disorder verging on chaos continued unchecked in much of the country. In April 1823 it called in a French army under the command of the duke of Angoulême to restore order. This time the French were welcomed by the populace. The king, supported by French troops, rescinded all the government's acts, and the prisons again filled with political dissidents. Fernando VII died in 1833, and his three-year-old daughter, Isabella II, ascended the throne, while her mother, María Cristina, served as queen regent until Isabella came of age in 1843. It would be another forty years before a republic was established.

3

Social Setting

A NEW WORLD

Centuries of peninsular reconquest from the Moors had finished, and a new epoch of overseas conquest began. During the fifty years after Columbus's epic voyage, Castillian explorers and adventurers departed their homeland looking for a better life in the New World. The powerful Aztec nation in Mexico fell to Hernán Cortés in 1521, and by 1533 the Inca empire of South America succumbed to Francisco Pizarro and Diego de Almagro. The men who were beginning to subjugate the American continents were private adventurers, many of whom came from poor Castillian towns. The new continent offered an opportunity for adventure, wealth, and status, an effective appeal that led many people to emigrate. It has been estimated that about 150,000 Spaniards braved the ocean crossing for America before 1550 and maybe about a quarter of a million during the sixteenth century as a whole.[1] After 1600 more and more people fled the poor regions of Galicia and Asturias along with Basques to seek prosperity in the New World.

Soldiers, sailors, unemployed workers, farmers, artisans, ecclesiastics, merchants, servants, pages, writers, and poor nobility all sought passage to America. Many younger sons of farmers and of the lesser nobility, whose chances of inheriting land or money were poor or nil, hoped for better possibilities abroad.

On occasion, the crown provided transportation for colonists, especially if they were bound for the West Indies such as the islands of Cuba,

Hispañola, Jamaica, and Puerto Rico. Here population was needed to ensure Spanish dominance against pirates bent on establishing bases and raiding the Spanish fleets returning with gold and silver to Sevilla; or against encroachments of rival powers such as the English who, for example, finding few Spaniards in residence, occupied Jamaica in 1656.

In spite of opportunities abroad, the great majority of people were in no position either financially or psychologically to seek a long, uncomfortable passage on an oceangoing vessel sailing away to a doubtful future. Most remained at home, marveling at the stories they heard of men who ventured into the unknown in search of gold or glory or to spread the gospel.

ARISTOCRACY

The kingdoms of Castilla and Aragón were chiefly agricultural societies, and the vast majority of the people were peasants who worked the land. The upper class, the nobility, monopolized land, education, and public offices but was itself a diverse institution of privilege ranging from the extremely wealthy grandees at the highest level down to the poor hidalgo, with the lowest aristocratic standing. The impoverished hidalgo might scrape a living in a rural village from a petty estate or cultivation of a patch of ground. But poor or not, he invariably felt himself far above the demeaning, vile class of taxpayers, namely, the artisans, bourgeoisie, and the peasants.

Some hidalgos went off to conquer new lands in the Americas, but most remained at home where they kept locked away their precious testaments to their noble rank that insured their privileges. Some came to the large cities in search of an occupation suitable to their station and found employment as squires or chaperons of high-class ladies; others just wandered the streets. Contempt for manual labor, considered degrading by the upper classes, often kept them idle and hungry. Disdain of manual work was not confined to the aristocratic class, however, but was widespread throughout society, as many people aspired to noble rank and adopted a noble attitude even if they did not have the credentials. In northern Castilla much of the population claimed hidalgo status, legitimately or not.[2]

UPWARD MOBILITY

Hidalgos with money who usually resided in the cities preferred to be called *caballeros* and were there considered middle-rank aristocracy. They lived in town houses and drew income from their estates, supplemented by investments. From the rank of *caballero*, they attempted to enter the ranks of the *titulados*, or titled nobility, and rise to the status of viscount,

count, marquis, or even duke. For this significant leap in status, which had to be granted by the king, money, land, vassals, a life of ostentatious spending, and enough cash to make loans to the royal treasury were generally required. Those in possession of great wealth might move up to the level of grandee, the highest rank short of the royal family. They were addressed as cousin by the king and allowed to keep their hats on in his presence.[3] In 1520, when they were legally defined by Carlos I, only twenty-five families held this lofty position, many of whom were lords of hundreds of villages from which they received taxes, rents, and other revenue. By 1600 there were forty-one families of this elevated rank.

MIDDLE CLASSES

Below the nobility were the guild masters, merchants, manufacturers, shipowners, modest property owners, and proprietors of mills. Having money and imitating the aristocracy with fine clothes and houses was not enough for many of them, however. Such people squandered their wealth in pursuit of noble rank to the detriment of expanding their businesses or initiating new enterprises. The use of profits to buy estates, to supply a dowry for a daughter, or to acquire securities deprived industry of investment.

To achieve noble status involved proving that the family lineage was free from Jewish ancestry. This entailed expensive litigation, as the claim could be contested by enemies. The struggle and expense involved to obtain some kind of noble status were worth the effort for many families for several reasons, the most important, apart from the honor of the title, being exemption from direct taxation and access to the best jobs in public office. Other rights included the privilege of bearing arms; immunity from debtors' prison; release from jail for petty crimes, from torture if accused, or from the galleys if convicted; and in the event of a capital crime, avoiding the dishonor of the gallows—decapitation being considered the aristocratic punishment. Noble status also exempted the family from the billeting of troops in their private houses.

Aristocratic rulers of the towns often tried to thwart this upward pretension by keeping commoners from important positions—for example, by passing laws that only noblemen could serve as aldermen or in other official capacities with the self-justifying argument that nobles were above the petty self-interest of trade and presumably more impartial. But wealthy merchants founded entailed estates (by which the inheritance of property was restricted to the owner's lineal descendants) that continued to grow until the family's voice had to be heard and its demands met. Another way to advance socially was to buy a title from the king, who always needed more income. Thus a man could become a hidalgo with the same privileges as those who were so by birth. Many claims of noble lineage were made and rejected, often on the basis that granting noble status deprived the crown of tax money.

LOWER CLASSES AND TAXES

Many of the lower classes could find jobs only at certain times of the year such as the period of planting and harvesting on the farms around the towns. The remainder of the time they had little to do. Numerous people, mostly young, standing around idle in the marketplace or cathedral squares was a common sight.

There was little prospect for improvement of the living conditions for the vast majority of peasants in the fields and for laborers in the towns. That they might slide lower on the scale of social values into the world of beggars, thieves, and vagabonds was a definite possibility aggravated by a fiscal policy that weighed most heavily on the poor. The *alcabala*, a Castillian sales tax levied at about 10 percent for most of the period, and the *millones*, a special tax on consumer items such as meat, wine, and oil, hit hardest those who could least afford it.

High taxes led to a vicious circle. As residents fled from the tax collector, the tax quota for the district fell on those who remained, increasing the amount due to diminishing contributors until they, too, were driven away. More than a few Castillian villages fell vacant and derelict as the inhabitants migrated to the big cities or went abroad. The cities also had little to offer by way of employment for the unskilled, but there was a glimmer of hope. With charitable institutions such as monasterial soup kitchens and benevolent alms-givers, there was less chance of starving to death. Sometimes the disquiet beneath the surface in peasant society boiled over into violence. Bad harvests, high prices, and high taxes often provided the catalyst to ignite popular revolt. In 1648, for example, collusion between grain merchants and government officials in Granada to push up grain prices led to a popular uprising in which the city was held for some weeks by the insurgents before they were pacified. In 1652 rebels from the poor districts of Córdoba and Sevilla took control of the cities, set up barricades, and demanded cheaper bread prices. Such outbursts were crushed by city authorities and local aristocracy.

The peasant was a victim of a seignorial society that placed greater value on honor and status, the pursuit of luxury, and conspicuous spending than on productive manufacturing and agricultural enterprises that might have raised his standard of living. The close alliance of crown and aristocracy kept the malnourished peasant in his hovel.

LIMPIEZA DE SANGRE, OR PURITY OF BLOOD

Old Christians (those people whose families had always been Christian and hence supposedly of pure blood with no taint of Jewish or Muslim ancestry) enacted laws to restrict opportunities for minorities, especially Conversos and Moriscos (Jews and Muslims converted to Christianity, also called New Christians).

As the number of Conversos increased with the Catholic Kings forcing Jews into conversion or exile, so suspicion of them grew and the more entrenched became the notion of purity of blood, a constant theme that affected all levels of society. The stigma of a family's non-Christian origins and hence impure blood remained throughout future generations.

Many municipalities enacted laws restricting the activities of New Christians, and military orders, pious brotherhoods, and even guilds of merchants and craftsmen demanded credentials of pedigree. Purity of blood became an obsession, and sincerity or demonstrations of religious fervor could never offset the blemish of converted ancestry.

The Catholic Kings issued decrees in 1501 forbidding the offspring of those condemned by the Inquisition, which were mostly Conversos, to hold any important posts or to become physicians, surgeons, or notaries. Later came the practice of exhibiting in cathedrals and churches placards bearing the names of those punished in order to distinguish their descendants of impure blood. The Inquisition maintained records of family bloodlines, and before a person could marry or seek office, registers were checked back as far as possible to see if any Jewish or Moorish names appeared in the family tree.

Since it was often impossible to prove ancestry for most people not of illustrious families with a public record and history, a flourishing trade in genealogies developed—some true, some false—to assist a person's eligibility for office. They could also be used to discredit him by showing tainted blood due to some past marriage or affiliation.

The Cortes that met in 1593 was concerned with the proliferation of investigations into ancestry. University colleges, the courts, monasteries, and cathedral chapters all piled up extensive archives on family backgrounds, claims to nobility, and *limpieza de sangre*.

FOREIGNERS

In 1650 there were about 150,000 foreigners living in Spain. They came thinking it a land of riches with all the gold from Peru and silver from Bolivia. Needless to say, a lot of them were disappointed, and Spaniards cursed them, complaining that they took the bread from Spanish mouths.[4]

Prominent and quick to expand in the maritime business were the French. The less-than-friendly feelings toward them and their enterprises were compounded by an old resentment when people of humble origins had begun to arrive in some numbers in the fifteenth century from France in order to benefit from the higher wages paid in Spain. Workers came from southwestern France to Aragón during the plowing and harvesting seasons to find employment. Others took jobs as coachmen, foot-men, grooms, tavern keepers, and servants as well as artisans, bakers, and laborers. Some came to sell merchandise in the cities, and some found jobs working in masonry or the carpentry trade. If employment was not readily available, they took advantage of Spanish charity and strained the resources of local generosity at the gates of the monasteries and hospitals. Vagrancy increased with the influx of these workers, and soup kitchens sometimes were swamped with foreign nationals.

The major complaint was that they brought nothing into Spain and returned home in the same clothes that they came with—only this time their pockets were filled with gold coins. Working harder and for less, they took the jobs from locals and built up considerable resentment in the minds of the xenophobic Spaniards. Frenchmen that remained in the country often took Spanish wives, enabling them after ten years of mar-riage and residency to apply for Spanish citizenship.

Complaints were also directed against the Genovese and the Portu-guese, both active players in the Spanish maritime trade in Sevilla and later in Cádiz. Many of them also married in Spain and became natu-ralized subjects, but for most Spaniards this was only a devious way to further their commercial prospects. The stubborn Castillian disinclination for menial jobs favored the foreigners.

BEARING OF ARMS

The development of the public well-being was beginning to take a more concrete form in the Early Modern period as the state assumed a bigger role as the guardian of the peace. It was no longer enough to secure a pardon from a family through payment for an act of aggression. Before, the victim of a crime decided if he or she would prosecute; now, the state began to make such decisions based on the common good. One outcome of this more general authority was further limitations placed on the carrying and use of arms. Some restrictions were already in place in many localities such as the carrying of weapons inside city walls dur-ing hours of darkness. The local constable was charged with ringing the church bell every evening to inform the peasants returning from the fields and travelers that the time of curfew had arrived: ten o'clock in summer and nine in the winter. During the curfew, the constable had the right to detain and, if necessary, disarm anyone who looked suspi-cious—for example, someone not carrying a lantern.

Some people were permitted arms under all circumstances such as muleteers and travelers who needed to protect themselves on the roads, but these had to be unloaded at the entrance to towns. Tax collectors, knights of the orders, and public officials as well as agents of the Inquisition were permitted to carry arms day or night. The idea of bearing arms, however, was slowly becoming a privilege, not a right.

The development of improved guns, the flintlock, made new legislation more urgent. A pistol having a flint in the hammer for striking a spark to ignite the charge became the prevailing type of handgun from the end of the seventeenth century to the middle of the nineteenth. The pistol could be concealed under the cloak, and no longer required the slow match and cumbersome firing mechanisms of earlier types. In 1563 the government decided that the use of a firearm constituted aggravated assault and carried a penalty of the loss of the aggressor's property. Authorities in troubled Valencia outlawed flintlocks altogether in 1584, but the law was unpopular, and many claimed that the traveler could not now protect himself and that the crime rate had risen since the ban went into effect. In time, as the laws were enforced, the risk of carrying a gun was judged greater than that of needing it.

Knives and swords did not seem to offer the same threat to the public as did the gun, however. Madame d'Aulnoy wrote that Spaniards did not abandon their swords either for Confession or for Communion, saying they were needed to defend the religion. When they put it on in the morning, they kissed it and made the sign of the cross with it.[5]

JUSTICE

Roguish literature of the times often made allusions to corrupt officials. The police of the Santa Hermandad (Holy Brotherhood), responsible for law and order in the countryside, had a despicable reputation for corruption. Royal edicts of 1610 and 1613 illustrate the lack of confidence the government had in its own judicial officials and police by ordering that these officers were not to frequent taverns and that tavern owners, innkeepers, and wine merchants were not to advance them any money.

The fact that some criminals met an untimely end on the gallows suggests that not all officials were scoundrels, however. Punishment intended to set an example was severe for those who were sentenced. The condemned prisoner, wearing a blue hat and a white tunic (the uniform was supposed to give the wearer some heavenly indulgences), made the journey from the prison to the scaffold riding a donkey or mule, his hands tied to a crucifix, a halter fastened around his neck. He was flanked by two monks saying prayers and exhorting the condemned man to die bravely. In front of this little group, the town crier marched along loudly heralding the crimes of the prisoner, and on horseback behind the condemned came the constable who had captured him and the judge who had sentenced him. The procession halted at each shrine or church along the way while prayers were recited, then moved on toward the rendezvous with death. The execution was generally by hanging unless the malefactor was a nobleman, in which case he had the right to be decapitated.

Sometimes there was a general call-up of citizens to chase outlaws—a kind of posse system. At other times soldiers were employed to hunt down criminals, paid for by the royal treasury or by the municipalities. Robberies and banditry were such problems that some towns adopted draconian methods to deal with them: Friends or relatives who sheltered criminals were themselves subject to the galleys, and in 1603, in the region of Alicante, it was proposed that if a wanted man was found in his home town, his family, parents, and siblings would be sent from their homes into exile.

A refuge for criminals was sometimes found on the estates of the upper nobility over which the king had little jurisdiction. Most high-ranking aristocracy resented royal authority and wanted to maintain their independence from the crown. But the immunity from the law that the nobles had long enjoyed began to slip away. During the sixteenth century the government gradually brought the grandees to its point of view by threatening to confiscate their land unless they were more active against bandits; eventually the feudal lords agreed to turn over to the law thieves or highwaymen found on their properties.[6]

Sanctuary for criminals was a discordant issue between government and clergy. Anyone, cleric or layman, could claim immunity from the law by entering the sacred space of a church.[7] Here in its inner recesses the law had no authority. Sometimes, as a result, the church was turned into a meeting place of brigands where they planned their exploits, but such matters differed from town to town. In Valencia, for example, only the main church could be used as a sanctuary, but even then, someone who had murdered with intent or was engaged in brigandage on the roads was excluded. The conflict between church and state was part of a broader struggle between the conservatives who wished to maintain the old order, the status quo, fearing arbitrary government rule, and the new proponents of strong government who felt the safety of the nation, backed up by wide-ranging laws, was the best way forward.

Discretionary methods were employed by civil courts where individual magistrates had wide powers. In one case in Toledo in 1613, not only was a man detained without trial for manslaughter, but the family of his victim was also held in order to prevent retaliation. In the filthy Toledo jail suspects languished for as long as seven years awaiting trial, and in 1614 an arbitrary decree of the government sent all suspects who were awaiting appeal of their sentences to the galleys where oarsmen were in short supply.

Aragón had among its special privileges limitations or prohibition on torture and habeas corpus, but these safeguards were often denounced by the authorities as making their work more difficult. Such conflicts and debates were, in a general way, searching for the limits of government. For the greater good of public order, the state gained more and more adherents to its point of view in the wake of widespread criminal activity. In 1626, the Valencian Cortes tried to limit the sacrosanct right of dueling, for example, and allowed those thugs who attacked people to be prosecuted by the state, that is, by the magistrates of the crown, without waiting for a complaint from the victim as had previously been the case. Social attitudes were clearly changing toward more judicial absolutism, and the old nobility who had always marched to a different drummer gradually bowed to new legal constraints.

To enforce state authority, a fairly steady stream of men went to the scaffold, after which in some places the bodies remained strung up in the market square. Bandits received special treatment and were dragged through the streets before being hanged, drawn, and quartered. Various confraternities were dedicated to the assistance of fallen humanity: the Valencian brotherhood of Our Lady of the Forsaken, every 24 February, Saint Mathias' Day, gathered up the bones of those executed during the year and whose bodies had been left dangling from the gallows in the center of town or, in more enlightened communities, a mile or so outside the gates. The remains were solemnly interred in the common ground of the General Hospital. Other cities also had their confraternities to retrieve the corpses of the executed and bury them, even picking up the pieces of those who had been drawn and quartered. Penal reform began only slowly in the eighteenth century. Sentences to the galleys, where a man might spend a lifetime at the oar, ended in 1748; torture was abolished in 1814.

SUPERSTITION

While most of the population professed to be Christian, people in the main were ignorant of the gospels. The Latin Vulgate Bible was written in a language they did not know even if they could read, and the incantations of the Mass in Latin were meaningless to the uneducated. More understandable were the saints to whom most people attributed miraculous qualities and who were invoked for guidance, protection, and cures. Equally genuine for many people, especially country peasants, were witches, werewolves, vampires, hobgoblins, black magic, and the power of amulets to protect the wearer. Certain rituals were practiced by men and women of all ages and classes. Some claimed the power to cure illnesses; others to predict the future through readings of the palms, the cabala (Jewish mysticism), and by means of astrology. Some, especially women, engaged in magical practices through rites, incantations, and invocations using cards or tossing beans to see how they landed. The sorceress might also throw salt into a fire in order to read the flames and make her predictions. Such devices were often designed to bring about the seduction and conquest of a suitor.

In Galicia, peasants believed the spirits of the dead rode upon the misty sea haze bearing lighted candles. This assembly of souls cast a fearful uncertainty over the population, as it could be encountered on any lonely moor on a dark night, thousands of lights flickering above as the ghostly horde made its way across the sky. Many peasants swore they had seen it.[8]

More general throughout the country among the lower classes was the concept of the evil eye. It was thought that some people carried venom in their eyes, and staring fixedly with evil intent at someone, they were able to do that person harm. Men or women suspected of this power were denounced to the authorities or to the Inquisition. Superstition was a powerful component in the lives of the peasants, but equally potent, regulating the lives of both upper and lower classes, was the concept of honor.

CODE OF HONOR

Personal honor stemmed from the centuries of the Reconquest of the country from the Moors. The proud knight often possessed little more than his horse and sword, but he had a high sense of his own self-worth sustained by his courage, trusted name, and reputation. A man's honor was a sensitive issue that, by extension, applied to all members of the household. For example, a woman's virtue had to be maintained inviolate; but if blemished, the affront had to be avenged.

Dishonor could arise from malicious slurs on the virtue of a wife or daughter. To protect their reputation, all male members of a wronged family—father, sons, and uncles—would seek revenge as their duty. Dishonor might arise from the infidelity of a wife or from the promiscuity of a daughter, in which case a husband might kill an unfaithful wife and her lover; a brother, his sister if she brought shame to the name of the family. Courts took a lenient view of crimes of passion involving honor, but acts of vengeance often brought on prolonged and bloody feuds between families.

On another level the glorious Reconquest, the carving out of a great empire in the Americas, the defeat of the Turks at Lepanto and of the French in Italy, the acquisition of a European empire from Sicily to the Netherlands—all were a source of God's grace and of great pride. It was an honor to be Spanish. No one knew it better than the swaggering and arrogant soldier who might be hungry and in rags but who was unbeatable.

A challenge to a duel could not be ignored. To face death bravely and to die unruffled was the pinnacle of honor. Even the convict who died on the scaffold commanded great esteem when he showed disdain for his fate.

The French countess Madame d'Aulnoy found that the major defect of the Spaniard was his unchristian passion for revenge and the means by which he accomplished it. According to her, when a Spaniard received an affront, he assassinated the offender.

For example, if one gave another a box o' the ear, or strikes him on the face with his hat, his handkerchief, or his glove, or has wronged him in calling him a *drunkard*, or lets drop any words that reflect on the virtue of his wife, these things I say must be no otherwise revenged than by assassination.[9]

Carried to extreme degrees the concept of honor brought on a reaction in which antihonor became fashionable among society's outcasts, as seen in various novels of the time where the cynical protagonist rejects and mocks such noble values by rejecting public opinion and exalting actions such as cowardice and deceit.

THE FRINGE SOCIETY

In times of crop failures and famine, numerous people from the countryside sought refuge in the cities and swelled the ranks of already destitute city dwellers. The glamour of Madrid with its opulent court aristocracy and Sevilla with its affluent bourgeois merchants attracted impoverished people from all over.

The lowest person in the hierarchy of the dispossessed was the beggar. This occupation, for those who could not work, **Beggars** was recognized as a right under the law, but the beggar was obliged to obtain a license furnished by the local priest that allowed soliciting alms in the immediate locality. Among the legal beggars was a privileged subgroup of the blind who held a monopoly on the recitation of prayers intended to protect individuals and the community from all manner of evil. In some cities the blind formed brotherhoods whose statutes, recognized by the municipal authorities, guaranteed their privileges. In Madrid the statutes assured members of the right to sell gazettes, that is, gossip sheets, and almanacs. In Zaragoza, a blind man who had fallen ill did not lose his benefactors, as other members of the brotherhood would take over his duties and say the required prayers in the houses of those who customarily used his services. The money supported the sick man until he could resume his duties.

However, the cities abounded with bogus blind and crippled people who crowded around the church doors and the public market and squares, assailing the populace with groans and entreaties. During the reign of Felipe III, a discourse was written on the protection of the gen-

uine poor and the lessening of pretenders in which the figure of those
living on charity was given at 150,000, the majority of them frauds. Reported also were the stratagems used by the pretenders to deceive the
public, such as covering the body with false scars, feigning to have only
one arm, or faking a death scene while companions passed the hat for
money to bury the poor fellow.[10]

Pícaros, Peddlers, and Vagabonds A degree above the beggars, the pícaros passed much of their time scrounging and engaging in petty theft while working just enough to avoid the charge of vagabondage. They might be employed in the kitchens of
a tavern or run errands as delivery boys or help shoppers as street por-
ters. In such jobs they were able to steal scraps of food or small pieces
of merchandise and share it among others of the same genre. On about
the same social level were the peddlers whose wares included such items
as knives, rosaries, combs, needles, drinks, tidbits of food, and other
sundry goods that were sold along the thoroughfares of the city.

In a class of his own was the vagabond. Attracted to a carefree life,
rising when he wished, waiting on no one nor being waited upon, un-
afraid of losing possessions since he had none, he roamed the country,
sleeping and eating in the open air under the stars or spending the cold
hungry nights of winter in a haystack; the blistering days of summer he
spent under the shade of a willow tree by the river. The exhilarating
flight, with a melon under the arm, from an irate farmer was an adventure. Like the pícaro, he lived by his wits. The comforts of a conformist
existence had no appeal to him. Even the last walk to the scaffold was
worth the freedom encountered along the way.

Thieves and Assassins At the top of the hierarchy and dominating those who lived by their ingenuity were the professional thieves and assassins. Among the thieves were various specialties by which an individual might be known. Some were highwaymen, others were housebreakers adept at climbing ropes to upper
floors, still others were skilled at rustling cattle from the farms and outlying villages, and some were experts at prying open the church alms
boxes and depriving statues of saints of their rich ornaments.

The most feared and revered were the assassins. They wore clothes
not unlike that of a soldier (as many had once been), a large brimmed
hat often plumed with feathers, a sword in their belt, and a leather doublet that might hide a coat of mail. They hired out their services to anyone wishing to have an enemy dispatched and set up the fatal encounter
either by provoking a quarrel as an excuse or by ambush in which the
victim was simply murdered in the night. Sometimes they were apprehended and sent to the scaffold, leaving this world with a nonchalant
air that enhanced their reputation for arrogance and bravery.

Authorized gambling houses were found in the cities, generally managed under license by disabled war vet- **Gambling and** erans in lieu of a pension. More prevalent, however, **Prostitution** were gambling dens where professionals lurked to extract money from gullible clients. Those who worked the tables also performed every trick known to card cheats. Sometimes they worked in gangs, one to entice the unsuspecting from the street into the den, one to fleece them at cards, and a third to disappear rapidly with the marked cards, the evidence, when the game was over.

Another widespread source of income in the world on the circumference of society was prostitution. Every town of any size in Spain had a brothel. Some cities were renowned for their number, such as Valencia and Sevilla, where an entire quarter consisted of houses where the prostitutes could engage in their work in comfort and freedom. The rows of little cottages surrounded by pleasant gardens belonged to the overseers, to the municipality, or to wealthy individuals who installed the girls in them. The success of these establishments was considerable.

Not unlike the tiered male community, the women also had a ranking order. The lowest were those working in the houses of ill repute. Their vocation had once been regulated by Felipe II in 1572 and again in 1575 when each girl was placed under the jurisdiction of an overseer, female or male, recognized by the public authority. On taking charge, this supervisor swore an oath to obey the royal edicts that forbade the admittance into the house of married women, a young virgin, or a woman burdened with debts since she would not be able to escape her occupation. Overseers were also prohibited from lending money to their charges, as this could potentially bind them indefinitely to their profession. At least once a week the women were obliged to be examined by a doctor. In the event of a contagious disease, they were sent to hospital.

The overseer was responsible for orderly conduct in the house to which entry was forbidden to any man carrying a sword or dagger. The price varied with the charms and physical qualities of the woman and with the requirements of the patron; for example, less money *on* the bed than *in* it. So they might not be mistaken for respectable women, the dress code of prostitutes was also fixed by regulations that differed from city to city. Usually they were not permitted to don high-heeled shoes or wear trailing dresses. A short red cloak was worn over the shoulders, and they were denied the comfort of kneeling on a hassock in church.

Prostitutes were banned from plying their trade during Holy Week, and during Lent they were packed off to the local church to receive a lecture on repentance with the usual theme of Mary Magdalene. The few who followed the priest's advice were then sent to a convent for fallen women.

A step above the house girls were the streetwalkers who themselves were surpassed in the hierarchy by the women who pretended to be great ladies. To heighten respectability and price, they often went about accompanied by a squire; his real status of pimp was immaterial.

Meeting Places   The shady world of the marginalized citizens of Spain had its own particular jargon that served as a means of recognition between the inhabitants. A tavern became in the local slang a *hermitage*; the torture chamber was the *confessional* where one did not *sing* (talk) even if silence led one to *wed the widow* (the gallows). There were also special well-known meeting places where dubious characters came together. In Madrid it was the Puerta del Sol and the Plaza de Herradores (Blacksmiths' Square). In Segovia it was a little square in the shadow of the great Roman aqueduct that spans the city, while in Toledo the old Arab bazaar served the purpose, as did the Strand (Arenal) in Sevilla, which ran down to the river. The Potro of Córdoba stood out among the other meeting places, and if born there, it made one almost high nobility among fellow companions. The supreme hideout and place of rendezvous, however, seems to have been Zahara, a fishing port in Andalucía. To have even been there was recognized as an accomplishment of the highest degree, or so says the literature of the time. Cervantes refers to Zahara as the place where one drinks, sings, blasphemes God, disputes, fights, and steals.[11] A place of true freedom! There were some people in Spain, however, who were not free in any sense of the word.

SLAVERY

Traditionally slaves in Spain had been Muslims, taken captive during the Reconquest. This supply continued into Early Modern times. Eighteen thousand prisoners were taken by the Spanish in the battle at Tunis during the reign of Carlos I and thousands more at the battle of Lepanto under Felipe II. Most were considered the property of the king and served in the galleys or worked in the royal mercury mines at Almadén in Andalucía under terrible conditions.[12] But captured Muslims were not the only source of slaves.

Portugal, united with Spain under one monarchy from 1580 until 1640, maintained a monopoly on the black slave trade from Guinea, Angola, and Mozambique. For the most part the black slaves were destined for America, but a small percentage found their way to Andalucía, where they were baptized and mostly functioned as domestics in private homes. The influx of slaves into Spain declined when the Portuguese lost much of the control over the trade to the English and French. Nor were there any longer prisoner-slaves from Mediterranean sources, as the large battles had ceased.

Slaves were present in Madrid among the families of the very wealthy despite a city law in 1601 that prohibited their employment. In the north and central regions of the country they were very few. Reports from the period by foreign travelers show surprise that slavery was still rampant in the south of the country. Brunel noted in 1665 that slaves made up most of the servants.[13]

The slave market in Sevilla functioned on the steps of the cathedral, and nearly all well-to-do families had one or two slaves. Dealers had their businesses also in other port cities such as Málaga and Cádiz. Sevilla about this time was estimated to have between 7 and 8 percent of its population enmeshed in bondage, of which the majority were black servants.[14]

Not uncommon was the exploitation of slaves for private gain. Allowed by their masters to live at liberty and engage in any calling, they handed over a percentage of their earnings to their owners. Guilds refused enrollment of slaves into their societies, so they were always reduced to the most menial occupations.

In 1637 Felipe IV could not find enough convicts to row his galleys and tried to draft personal slaves for this duty. The municipality of Sevilla complained about this measure, stating the need of individuals, often widows, pensioners, or others who relied upon their slaves for assistance and income. The king's wish was little enforced.

GYPSIES

The transient poor roaming the countryside for anything to beg or steal were augmented by Gypsies who appeared in western Europe in the late fifteenth century. The first in a series of decrees was issued in 1499 directing them to take up fixed residence, till the land, desist from cattle trading, dispense with their style of dress, and abandon their language for Castillian. The Cortes of Castilla made repeated demands to punish them for failure to conform, and the city of Madrid continuously expelled them from the municipality where they set up camp in any convenient open space. The kingdom of Navarra prohibited their passage on pain of a hundred lashes or a turn in the galleys. In 1525 the Cortes, meeting in Toledo, asked that the Egyptians, as they were mistakenly thought to be, not wander about the realm since they stole from the fields, destroyed the orchards, and engaged in deception. These laws had no effect. The Gypsy bands grew larger, often supplemented by other oppressed people such as runaway slaves and wanted criminals.

In 1575 many were rounded up regardless of whether they had committed a crime or not and condemned to the galleys. In 1619 Felipe III decreed their expulsion from Castilla, and in 1624 they were expelled from Valencia. Neither state nor church objected to this treatment. The church was annoyed that the Gypsies never made any overt sign of being

Christian and did not baptize their children unless forced to. The state showed little sympathy toward them since they avoided service in the king's arms and were reputedly responsible for many robberies, frauds, and murders. Their nomadic life, disdain for religious observances, and reluctance to participate in society alienated them from the Spanish people. Although a few Gypsies settled down to become law-abiding vassals of the king in such places as Sevilla and Granada, the majority continued to lead a wandering existence, moving from pasture to pasture and town to town. Government measures to curb the perceived Gypsy problem were harsh but ineffective.

NOTES

1. Elliot, *Spain and Its World*, 11; Casey, 25.
2. Kamen, *Spain in the Later Seventeenth Century*, 226.
3. Ibid., 227.
4. Defourneaux, 23.
5. Aulnoy, in Ross and Power, 372.
6. Collection of taxes, local justice, the nomination of officials, and the recruitment of soldiers were often in the hands of the aristocracy. About 60 percent of the region of Salamanca and its population was under the jurisdiction of the duke of Alba. Another 6 percent or so was under ecclesiastical control. Similarly, the enormous landholdings of the duke of Osuna in Andalucía or those of the duke of Grandía in Valencia were practically independent domains where the only orders recognized were those of the lord.
7. Sanctuary in churches did not apply to anyone sought by the Inquisition.
8. Borrow, 210.
9. Aulnoy, in Ross and Power, 289.
10. Defourneaux, 218.
11. Ibid., 226.
12. Kamen, *Spain in the Later Seventeenth Century*, 283.
13. Brunel.
14. Casey, 122.

4

The Church

The Roman Catholic faith pervaded every aspect of social life. Spaniards identified their country as the one chosen by God, the kingdom with the most solid and pure Catholic religion. The formidable and victorious armies of Castilla under the banners of the Almighty and Catholicism were clear examples of His favor. The minister, Olivares, stated in 1625, "God is Spanish and fights for our nation."[1] On the other hand, manifestations of collective piety and the office of the Holy Inquisition were in large part responsible for the foreigner's view of Spain as the universal seat of intolerance—an attitude accepted with pride by many Spaniards, for it demonstrated their steadfast adherence to the principles of Christianity.

CHURCH CONTROL OF SOCIETY

The life cycle of every individual was guided by the Holy Roman Church. At baptism the child's name was registered in the parochial archives; later Confession and Communion took on its special significance, guaranteeing strong control by the church over the lives of the congregation and by the priest over their conscience. The marriage and death of each of the faithful were also recorded in the parish registers.

To show no interest in church affairs or not to attend them was considered a public scandal and could result in punishment by the bishop such as a fine or, if repeated, a jail sentence. The important Easter ceremonies were carefully watched to detect who was missing. In some

Bishop.

places people were given a voucher to prove they attended church. The menacing presence of the Inquisition deterred any behavior that was contrary to Catholic doctrine.

The tolling of the church bells called the people to Mass and, at canonical hours, regulated daily activity in most villages—for example, interrupting work at noon, when the sun reached its highest point, and at vespers, about seven o'clock in the evening, which summoned people to pause and say a prayer for the souls of the dead.

CHURCH WEALTH, PRIVILEGES, AND CHARITY

A French ecclesiastic visiting Spain, impressed by the number of priests and monks and the wealth of the churches, reported that in comparison the French houses of worship were only stables.[2] The vast wealth of the Spanish church derived from the *diezmo*, or tithe (a tax on the peasants), from both rural and urban property holdings and investments from which it drew large sums of money and from income brought in from Masses, administering of the sacraments, the sale of indulgences, and from private donors. It was often the case that rich people left behind money and land for the church in the hope that this would help open the gates of Saint Peter when they were ready to pass through. It was not uncommon for an entire monastery to be built with money donated by a wealthy aristocrat who died with no heirs.

From the point of view of the lower classes, the *diezmo* was the most hated and the most reluctantly paid tax, consisting of a tenth part of all the agricultural gross earnings paid in cash or crops. The church considered the *diezmo* to belong to it by divine right. There were no deductions for costs of seed and equipment or for hardship. The peasant was obliged to pay and warned not to defraud that part of his harvest owed to God nor to make trouble for the tax collector.

When a peasant defaulted on the tithe, generally for lack of the means to pay it, he was excommunicated. If the debt was not paid within the year, the threat was always present that he would be denounced to the Inquisition. A farmer in Galicia who complained that the tithe was an act of human and not divine origin was ordered by the Inquisition to retract his statement before the church congregation and pay a fine of 800 ducats and then was banished from the village as a troublemaker.[3] While some monasteries appeared to the peasants who worked their lands as grasping landlords rather than spiritual leaders, the church argued that its wealth and income were necessary to its authority.

Through outright purchases and endowments from wealthy families the church acquisitions were boundless. The large number of ecclesiastics and the comfortable living conditions of the clergy, the bishops' grand palaces adorned with luxurious furnishings and the finest table, with their numerous servants, pages, squires, and even jesters, and the golden and bejeweled splendor of the churches themselves never failed to impress foreigners. Nor did the size of the monasteries that in Valladolid and Toledo seemed to some visitors to incorporate half the town.

Church-owned land in the countryside was considerable. The Cortes of Valladolid petitioned the king, Carlos I, in 1523 to halt the expansion of church properties before it owned all the land in Castilla. The king wrote to the pope about the situation, but nothing came of it. In 1563 and 1579 the same problem was raised with Felipe II, but again nothing changed.

It has been calculated that by the end of the seventeenth century the church owned about one sixth of all cultivable land (always of the best soil).[4] In towns it owned businesses that included fruit marketing and furniture making, and in some major cities such as Sevilla and Zaragoza, one third to one half of the houses belonged to it. It did not invest readily in industry but preferred safer and more tangible investments such as mortgages and annuities. The most obvious riches were the paintings, jewels, and gold and silver that adorned the churches. There were many complaints throughout the century concerning this enormous wealth: The Cortes in Madrid denounced the ecclesiastical accumulation of riches in 1621, and on several occasions Felipe IV promised to halt transference of property to the church but without success.

Overall ecclesiastical income was not evenly distributed. The well-being of the parish priest and of the regular clergy was contingent on their geographical location. The annual revenue of the Episcopal See of Toledo was around a quarter of a million ducats, and that of Sevilla was over 100,000, while for others, for example, Almería, it was a mere 4,000 ducats. In very poor districts the parish priest depended on the charity of the parishioners to keep food on the table. Religious orders tended to cluster around cities or rich agricultural areas, however, and avoided or eventually abandoned poor villages and regions.

The privileges accorded the church were impressive. Like the nobility the clerics paid no taxes except special levies from time to time for military enterprises and the *millones*, the special tax on certain food items. Its members were not subject to military duty nor to the jurisdiction of secular courts for most offenses short of murder.

The eight archbishops and forty-six bishops who made up the jurisdictions of Castilla and Aragón were selected by the king, primarily because of their noble birth and not often through achievement. Regardless of qualifications, men were generally appointed who were members of the royal family or others of the nobility who coveted the richest sees for personal gain. Some never so much as visited their parishes but drew income from them. At age ten, the son of Felipe II received a cardinal's hat and was made archbishop of Toledo or Primate of Spain, the highest ecclesiastical post in the land.

Not all was greed and gluttony, however. An important part of church income was given to help the poor and was also used to maintain a system of charitable institutions such as schools, asylums, orphanages, and *Inclusas* where abandoned babies were collected. This social assistance was often the only form of support that could be counted on. Hospitals and hospices for the poor were fairly numerous. Most convents and monasteries maintained soup kitchens and distributed food free or at a minimal cost to legions of needy people who crowded the large cities. The gates of the monasteries were opened at noon every day, and monks or lay brothers issued forth carrying a large cauldron of soup and baskets of bread to be shared with the indigents clustered at the entrance. For the unemployed, beggars, crippled soldiers, and hungry students, this was often the only meal of which they could be certain. The *sopa boba*, or convent broth, rescued many in the streets from starvation.

NUMBER AND RECRUITMENT OF CLERICS

With its privileges the clerical establishment offered a desirable occupation within reach of many people. As a result, and to escape from hunger and abuse and from the restrictions of the class system, many men and women from poor families took up the religious orders. Peasant and bourgeois families often made heavy sacrifices in order that at least one son might achieve the education necessary to qualify for a church career.

Often the educational, intellectual, and moral fiber of young clerics did not inspire confidence, and their lifestyle was frequently far from exemplary in spite of the efforts of some bishops to watch over their comportment. The line between the lay and ecclesiastical worlds was fine indeed to the point of obscurity, and the simple priest could live a life that in most ways was ordinary and secular.

Due to lenient recruitment procedures, parish priests were often of mediocre intelligence and little endowed with high spiritual values. Many entered the profession with no aptitude for it but simply to find freedom from toil. Some, no doubt, felt a genuine calling, but the sheer numbers and the poor performance of many suggested that other, less spiritual factors were involved. It was a relatively safe haven from the cares and obligations of the world, and besides the many privileges, bread and wine were guaranteed, as was a certain amount of respect.

During the sixteenth and seventeenth centuries the number of people devoting their lives to piety rose spectacularly. In 1624 the bishop of Badajoz complained that religion had become a way of earning a living and that people took to it as they would any other trade.[5] The following year the Cortes informed the king that there were 9,000 monasteries in the realm. The number of convents was probably close to this figure. It has been estimated that among monks, nuns, and lay clergy there were about 200,000 people and rising in the religious establishments in a country of about 8 million.[6] The growing number alarmed the civil authorities, who worried that too much manpower was being channeled into a vocation that offered little to the economic development of the country, that the number of ecclesiastics harmed agricultural production where men were needed and reduced population growth through celibacy.

Those young men of noble families whose place of birth in the line of inheritance left them with nothing could use the church as an honorable way out of their predicament. They could easily attain high rank and respect in the ecclesiastical hierarchy by virtue of their class, which guaranteed them good economic and social positions.

A poor son of a peasant showing promise might be instructed by the parish priest in exchange for household or church chores. A boy as young as seven might become a tonsured cleric, in which case he was sent to a church-sponsored school to learn reading and writing and the basics of the church liturgy. From the age of about ten or twelve he attended a grammar school to learn Latin and eventually might be sent to the university for advanced education. On the other hand, a boy might be sent to a monastery, although he was not obliged to remain there after he had come of age.

It was not rare among clergy to have a mistress. Concubines in the bishops' palaces and in the more humble houses of the priests were common knowledge, and sometimes the arrangement resulted in children. It was, however, among the regular clergy that the greatest contrast between lofty spiritual values and low moral standards were found: For example, much admired for piety was Teresa of Avila of the reformed Carmelites and Juan of the Cross of the reformed Augustinians. In contrast, there was great permissiveness in many monasteries. In the words of Father de Cabrera, "They [the monasteries] are full of lazy and sensual people, incorrigible vagabonds always ready to disturb religious peace and concord."[7]

Most religious orders were selective when it came to the social status or racial background of the potential novice and, as in other sectors of society, the orders, who demanded proof of *limpieza de sangre* of their new members, were on the lookout for those of low birth wishing to join simply to find a steady supply of meals. The Jesuits recruited their members from among the elite and congratulated themselves when a titled person joined. Members from the upper classes were expected to bring a donation into their monastery.

COUNCIL OF TRENT

During the late fifteenth and early sixteenth centuries the need for a council to reform the church was widely recognized. Such a council finally opened at Trent in northern Italy on 13 December 1545, which addressed the central doctrinal issues posed by the Protestants. One of the first decrees affirmed that scripture had to be understood within the tradition of the church—an implicit rejection of the Protestant principle of "scripture alone," that is, that salvation could be achieved without priests.

The council refused any concessions to the Protestants and, in the process, crystallized and codified Catholic dogma: It directly opposed Protestantism by reaffirming the existence of transubstantiation, purgatory, and the necessity for the priesthood. Clerical celibacy and monasticism were maintained, and decrees were issued in favor of relics, indulgences, and the veneration of the Virgin Mary and the saints. The sole right of the church to interpret the Bible was asserted along with many other decrees issued to deal with the problems of corruption and ignorance of clergy. The council was dominated by Italian and Spanish prelates, and its pronouncements gave a certain unity of purpose to Spanish ecclesiastics and a clear (Protestant) enemy to counter.

CULT OF THE VIRGIN AND OF THE SAINTS

Encouraged by the Council of Trent, the Spanish church took up with enthusiasm the worship of saints, whose biographies became one of the preferred genres in the reading habits of the literate populace. The deep-seated belief in saints was clear from the portrayal of them with characteristics attributed to average people. For example, when a group of clergy desired to have Santa Teresa canonized in 1622 and made the patron saint of Spain, others objected on the grounds that the traditional patron, Saint Iago (Saint James) of Compostela might be offended by the competition and withdraw his protection.[8]

Worship of the Virgin Mary was an integral part of the Spanish Catholic faith and was represented variously in the different regions. The attraction for pilgrims and their money may help account for part of this; nevertheless, the Virgin appeared in different outward manifestations such as the Virgin of Pilar in Zaragoza, the Virgin of Guadalupe in a monastery in the mountains of Estremadura, the Virgin of Montserrat in a monastery high in the rocky crags of Cataluña, and the black Virgin of Sevilla.

PROCESSIONS AND HOLY WEEK

A characteristic of religious life was the fondness for outward display. A visible expression of religious sentiment was important to keep the faithful entertained and loyal. Events such as the canonization of a saint gave way to spectacular festivities lasting sometimes for several days. The procession organized by the Franciscans in Madrid in 1627 in honor of the martyrs of their order illustrates the pomp and splendor of such occasions. From the church of Saint Francis, effigies of the martyrs, dressed in cloth of gold and silver, were carried in great splendor. After these came the high officials wearing rich vestments, followed by some 400 Franciscans and barefoot Capuchins. Bearing lighted torches, 500 tertiaries (lay members of a monastic third order) brought up the next rank with the standard carried by the duke of Medina and accompanied by most of the grandees of Spain. The procession passed by the palace so that the king and queen could observe it. At the finish line, the richly decorated church of Saint Giles, eight sermons were delivered by the most outstanding of the preachers of the court.

Religious festivities frequently gave way to a meeting of the sacred and the profane. During Holy Week beginning with Palm Sunday, solemn rites were observed commemorating the passion, death, and resurrection of Christ. Throughout this time the church bells were silent, the use of carriages was forbidden, and in an act of humility the gentry had to go around on foot, unescorted by squire or page. The churches remained open all day and night (unintentionally offering brief adventures in clandestine meetings between the sexes).

The week took on a carnival atmosphere, and the processions that occurred daily through the streets were spectacular and extravagant. A legion of public officials would lead the parade, followed by the members of the attendant confraternity holding high its banners and crosses. Each man in the phalanx carried a lighted candle. The penitents then marched by, their heads concealed in pointed hoods revealing only their eyes through slits, and laboring under heavy wooden crosses that chafed the skin on their backs and shoulders until it bled. Others passed by flagellating themselves until the blood ran freely. Some penitents, even of high rank, had to be carried home in a state of near collapse. While sincerity was probably a strong factor in the masochistic exercise of self-flagellation, in some cases other reasons may have been paramount. For instance, it was reported by travelers that some young men whipped themselves in front of their mistresses' houses for extended periods, soliciting both pity and admiration. Playwrights of the time poured scorn on amorous penitents who began lashing themselves only when they happened upon a fair young lady.

The chaplain to the French Embassy in Madrid, Muret, reported that upon entering churches in the city during Holy Week, men dressed in white with shoulders bare and bleeding flogged themselves so severely that blood spattered on the bystanders.[9]

RELIGIOUS ORDERS

Depending on their income and the amount of land they possessed, monasteries ranged from a few members to hundreds. The regular orders underwent prodigious growth during the first half of the seventeenth century. Some, such as the Carthusians and Jeronimites, had lost their impetus or they had grown lax and lazy, turning over all manual labor to hired help, but the Mendicant Orders, which renounced all possessions both personal and communal, grew alarmingly. Their popularity was based on the spirit of reform prevalent at the time among the austere and prestigious Carmelites. The order of Saint Francis was popular and possessed hundreds of monasteries. In addition to preaching and charitable work, the Franciscans were noted for their devotion to learning, as were the well-organized Dominicans.

Founded in 1534, the Jesuits' primary interests were the spread of the church by preaching and teaching and thus to strengthen Roman Catholicism against Protestant expansion. The Jesuit order, also known as the Society of Jesus, grew faster than any other, supported by the middle classes and the nobility. Conflicts and rivalries between the various orders were constant and prolonged, sometimes culminating in scandals that called for the intervention of the king or pope. Doctrinal debates, theological disputes, jurisdictional conflicts, jealousy, personal ambition— all led to ill feeling between them.

DAILY LIFE IN A MONASTERY

After morning Mass the business of the day was conducted in the chapter house. This was the time to administer discipline for any offenses charged by the monks, who were encouraged to report on one another. The abbot might sentence a guilty party to a beating or some other penance that could involve, in serious cases, a prison sentence.

Although monks were sworn to a life of poverty and could own nothing, the institutions were often rich. They were organized from the abbot, who was the chief authority, down through the second in command, the prior, to the various officers in charge of the library, kitchen, monastic church, divine services, clothing, food supplies and fuel for the fires, the infirmary, and a host of other duties. The sacristan looked after the donations and ceremonial equipment for the church; a porter took care of guests. Some of the offices changed hands regularly, giving everyone an opportunity to perform them. The routine revolved around the daily cycle of the divine office or divine duty, a series of services of prayer to be chanted or recited at determined hours of the day.

Those who enlisted in a monastery in order to keep hunger away from the door were generally not disappointed. The dietary standards were usually high for the times, and servings were ample. Wine was the standard drink. In sickness or old age the inhabitants of the monasteries were well looked after. Sanitation was about as good as could be expected, and barring some highly contagious disease, the monks could expect to have long, healthy lives. Perhaps more difficult to become accustomed to than the discipline, absence of privacy, and the monotony of events was the lack of heat. Apart from the kitchen, the rooms were generally unheated, and in winter, keeping warm was a problem.

An integral part of many monasteries were the lay brothers who were recruited from the lower classes to provide manual labor for the monks. They formed the echelon of bakers, wood cutters, and water carriers or filled in on other jobs as needed. They had only limited participation in monastic affairs, and most were illiterate. Those monasteries that lacked the use of lay brothers would hire laborers from the outside as required.

Alms giving was an essential characteristic of the establishment, and surplus food and clothing were distributed to the needy. Sometimes food and shelter were provided for travelers, especially pilgrims en route to visit a shrine. Monasteries also provided housing and care for the elderly over a long term when the person in need had given or had promised a substantial legacy.

Monks were generally literate, and monasteries played a role in intellectual life. At one time they were the sole perpetrators of education, but that role had declined by the end of the Middle Ages as secular schools became more abundant. With the advent of the printing press, the monkish endeavor of copying manuscripts also declined, but they often preserved valuable texts and provided places of study for both monks and laymen.

Bathing was not one of the favorite pastimes of monks and priests. This habit of the Muslims and of the Jews was frowned upon and could incur a suspicion of heresy if performed too often.

NUNS AND CONVENTS

While the male orders dedicated much time to study, preaching, teaching, and missionary work and as such were considered useful to society and hence supported financially, the female convents struggled along with none of these redeeming features.

Convents were often refuges for women of high position in which to live out their widowhood and at the same time asylums, or even prisons, for the young daughters of the nobility shut away by their families often without the girls' consent and against their wishes. The cause of this was generally the fact that not all the young ladies could find suitable husbands in their own class, or the family could not afford the expensive dowries for more than one or two daughters when they might have several more. Families that could not afford to marry their daughters at the level they thought fitting sent them instead to the convent. Some convents demanded a dowry from the aspirant, although it was generally much smaller than that required in marriage and thus more affordable for many families.

Generally the women were cloistered (that is, had little contact with the outside world), lacked strong financial backing, and were often deprived of material benefits that made daily life easier. Most convents were poor with a few exceptions such as the Real Monasterio de las Huelgas in Burgos and the Descalzas Reales in Madrid. Most lived a life of austerity that included hunger at times and manual labor on the land, or sewing, embroidering, or making jam or pastries to sell. Tensions and conflicts were bound to arise within the convent as places were limited, most being taken by aristocratic or upper-middle-class women so that hierarchies were established with the women from the lower classes at the bottom.

In many convents life overall was generally boring and centered around religious piety. In some, which were notorious for the easy and ostentatious life within, however, it was just the opposite: The upper-class convents of Madrid—the Comendadoras de Santiago y Calatrava, the Encarnación, or the Descalzas Reales—that attracted the most noble-women engaged in a style of life both lax and convivial. It is not surprising that many of these inmates, unwilling participants in their own incarceration, were not inclined to give up the pleasures of the world outside and as much as possible created that world within the seclusion of the convent.

According to Madame d'Aulnoy, the wealthy inhabitants of the convents, generally nuns of noble birth, might have two or three maids to look after their needs, and the rooms both private and public were richly furnished as if they belonged in the private houses of the ladies. Not only was the convent furnished as if it were a house in the city, but anyone could come calling, anytime. The noblewomen, bright, clever, and inventive, might see more men than their counterparts would see on the outside. Contemplation and penitence were not on the minds of these ladies. Hence, these convents, rich and exclusive, were frequented by numerous visitors of both sexes. Gifts were exchanged, and the nuns flirted with the male visitors while engaging in festivities, amateur plays, and the then-popular literary tournaments and poetic jousts that might include salacious premises for discussion.[10]

THE *GALÁN DE MONJAS*

An extraordinary practice was that of the *galán de monjas* (courtier of nuns), where a young man who fancied himself in love with a nun made every effort to see her, even from a distance. He might meet her in the parlor of the convent or pass notes to her through the intermediary of another sister. Many nuns enjoyed this game of having a suitor of sorts with whom they carried on a generally platonic romance that at least kept them in touch with the outside world.[11]

These excesses in so-called holy places and, as news items from the period sometimes reported, the seduction or rape of nuns (often by monks) prompted Felipe IV to draft a decree prohibiting all intercourse between the sexes in the monastic orders. It was never issued, however, as churchmen opposed it on the grounds that it was discriminatory by oppressing the clergy more than other men.

Monasteries and convents were on many occasions the subject of the satirical literature of the times, and the alleged immoral comportment of priests and nuns was the subject of many cartoons. Some people were irritated that they behaved just like anyone else and did not set an example of rigid moral conduct for society. The lack of interest by the Inquisition in prosecuting those writers who exposed the church to public ridicule only suggests that the accusations were true and that the Holy Office was not unaware of the magnitude of monastic diversions from their professed ideals.

PREACHERS IN THE COUNTRYSIDE

Prompted by the Counter Reformation in the wake of the Protestant threat to the Catholic Church, members of the clergy traveled around the country to reinforce the values of Catholicism and to arouse the populace to better compliance with their religious obligations. The regular orders fervently took up this endeavor throughout the peninsula. Friars went in pairs, stopping even in remote villages, and preached to the assembled locals. Prayers, Masses, and confessions were performed, terminating in penitential processions of the entire town or group of villages. To impress and frighten the audience, various kinds of theatrical devices were used, simulating the flames and screams of the condemned souls in hell, highlighted by grisly skulls among sulfurous fumes. The torrid speeches awakened the attention of the most dimwitted, and the scenes of hell made the women swoon. Foreign travelers who witnessed these dramatic performances were impressed by the extreme vehemence of the orators, the fixed attention of the audiences, and the sighs of the women. On some occasions the speaker would slap himself forcefully, and the audience amidst great howls and moaning would do the same to themselves.[12] The drama, the visual effects, the collective piety, and the great solemnity were events prolonged over several days that the locals were not likely to forget.

CHURCH, STATE, AND THE INQUISITION

The sacred self-governing status of the church and its exemption from civil laws was a matter that preoccupied the government. Church punishments for offenses, except in cases of heresy, were generally more lenient than those set out by the civil authorities for similar offenses. This and the fact that many men were given the tonsure to escape civil justice were contentious issues. When a magistrate condemned a member of the clergy for an offense, he was subject to harassment by church officials and priests thundering their condemnation from the pulpit, even to excommunication. "You did not hang a man, you hanged Christ," roared one Jesuit priest from his pulpit in Granada after the state had executed a priest for a grave offense in 1556.[13] Cases occurred when the entire town was denied the sacraments for the actions of its secular judges. Often the judges backed down and underwent a church-imposed penance for their defiance.

A major dispute arose between the papacy and the Inquisition over the jurisdiction of bishops. The latter could only be tried by Rome according to a rule established during the Middle Ages and extended to Spain. The papacy vacillated between exerting its authority and giving in to the Inquisition when bishops were under investigation. The most famous case involved the archbishop of Toledo, Bartolomé de Carranza y Miranda, the highest church authority in the country. The Inquisitor General Valdés accepted the opinion of Carranza's archrival Melchor Cano that the archbishop was tainted with heresy based on a book he wrote, in spite of opinions to the contrary of most theologians. The exceptional archbishop of humble origins had jealous aristocratic enemies who frowned on his rise to eminence and some who had coveted the wealthy see of Toledo for themselves. Valdés made appeals to Rome, and in January 1559 Pope Paul IV empowered the Inquisition to act against bishops for a limited time of two years. In April of that year Valdés called for the arrest of the archbishop, sanctioned by the king, Felipe II. Taken off to Valladolid and quartered in two rooms of a private residence, the prelate spent the next seven years under house arrest. The papacy wanted him sent to Rome for trial, but the king, seeing the papal claim on Carranza as interference in Spain's affairs, refused to allow him to go. Eventually an agreement was reached, and the archbishop was dispatched to Rome, where he spent the next nine years in prison. Finally, having abjured his "sins" he ended his life in a monastery in Orvieto (Italy) in 1576.

NOTES

1. Hillgarth, 126.
2. Alcalá-Zamora, 256. The view of a French Capuchin monk who visited Spain in the seventeenth century.
3. Casey, 234.
4. Alcalá-Zamora, 257.
5. Defourneaux, 107. See also Alcalá-Zamora, 261, for a little different figure, and Kamen, 1991, 177, for the clerical population in 1591, which was eight archbishops, forty-five bishops, and about 90,000 clerics.
6. Defourneaux, *Spain 1469–1714*, 107.
7. Ibid., 112.
8. For saints and their influence, see Casey, 241.
9. Hillgarth, 138.
10. Aulnoy, in Ross and Power, 89; Defourneaux, 110.
11. Defourneaux, 110–112.
12. Ibid., 135ff, for a description of the theater.
13. Casey, 186.

5

The Inquisition

In the view of the Roman Catholic Church it was dangerous for a Christian to look for direct communication with God or to hold views and opinions contrary to established doctrines. Nonconformity undermined the authority and power of the church. Such activity amounted to heresy, and efforts by the church to eliminate this gravest of sins was a driving force in Early Modern Spain.

Dissenters had for centuries been beheaded or burned at the stake for antichurch views, but such cases, generally left up to bishops and their ecclesiastical courts, were nonsystematic and sporadic. To deal with ever larger groups of heretics, more effective measures were deemed necessary. An official judicial tribunal was needed by the church to inquire into such matters and punish the guilty. In short, an Inquisition—a body of ecclesiastics charged with ferreting out heretics, exacting a confession of their sins, and making them atone so that, according to the church, their souls would be saved.

THE MEDIEVAL OR PAPAL INQUISITION

An inquisitorial tribunal was established on 20 April 1233 when Pope Gregory IX issued a bull that conferred on the Dominican order of friars the task of eradicating heresy. Anyone once baptized in the Roman Catholic Church and hence ipso facto a member of the Catholic faith, or adherents to dissident sects that had broken away from it, fell under the Inquisition's jurisdiction. Followers of non-Christian faiths such as Judaism or Islam did not fall into the category of heretic, and they could not be officially persecuted for their religious beliefs.

Dominicans were chosen for the task because their founder, Saint Dominic, had been a leading figure in combating the Cathars (Albigenses) in southern France, against whom a holy crusade had already been launched by Innocent III in 1208. This sect maintained that the corrupt Catholic Church, with its immense material wealth, was the agent of Satan. Two official inquisitors were assigned to the city of Toulouse—a Cathar stronghold—and were given authority to arrest heretics and sentence them to death by burning, with no appeal.

In 1232 papal inquisitors appeared in Aragón as part of the campaign conducted against the Cathars, who had spilled over the Pyrenean mountains into Spain. The inquisitors were not overly ambitious nor were the Aragonese sympathetic to their goals. The papal inquisition in Aragón was mild, and few people were persecuted.

In 1252 Pope Innocent IV officially sanctioned the use of torture to extract the truth of their heresies from suspects. The prisoner was assumed to be guilty and denied defense counsel, and the names of witnesses kept secret. Since the Inquisition was financially maintained by the confiscation of the victim's property, probability of acquittal was slight.

By the fifteenth century the Inquisition in Aragón had nearly fizzled out. In Castilla, on the other hand, it had not yet been established. As the century advanced, clerical zealots and some political officials in Castilla began to clamor for the introduction of an inquisitorial body to deal with the so-called Crypto-Jews, those Conversos, or New Christians as they were also called, who had converted to Christianity to enhance their financial and social opportunities but who secretly practiced Jewish religious rites. They were despised by clergymen for relapses into their ancestral faith and by some of the aristocracy jealous of the Conversos' skills in finance and administration, which carried them to high positions in church and government, often under the protection of the king or high-ranking nobles who relied on their abilities.

THE SPANISH INQUISITION

Three years after succeeding to the throne in 1474, Queen Isabella visited Sevilla where Alonso de Hojeda, a Dominican prior, preached to her about the wickedness of the Jews and their betrayal of Christianity through false conversions. These sentiments were backed by Pedro González de Mendoza, archbishop of Sevilla, and the stern Dominican prior Tomás de Torquemada of Segovia. The three agreed that Conversos throughout Andalucía and indeed throughout all of Castilla were secretly engaged in Hebraic rites, a problem that could only be dealt with

Anonymous. *The Virgin of the Catholic Monarchs.* (Isabella I is on the *right*, Fernando on the *left*. Torquemada, the first Inquisitor General of Spain, is kneeling behind Fernando.) (Madrid: Prado).

by a full-time Inquisition. The Catholic monarchs were persuaded and requested from the pope a bull authorizing an Inquisition in Castilla. On 1 November 1478, Pope Sixtus IV sanctioned the appointment of several priests as inquisitors who were given the mandate to deal with backsliding Conversos. Two years later inquisitorial operations began in Sevilla, where Conversos were reputed to be the most flagrant in practicing Jewish rites.

The coming of the Inquisition and the establishment of its headquarters in the convent of Saint Paul instilled enough fear among the Conversos that many fled the city. Flight was enough to convince the inquisitors that they were guilty of heresy or apostasy, and an edict was published on 2 January 1481 demanding that the landowning aristocracy in the realm of Castilla, to whose lands many had fled, arrest and bring them to the inquisitional prison in Sevilla under pain of severe penalties for harboring heretics. The nobles complied.

On 6 February 1481 the first ceremony of the Inquisition took place in

Sevilla. Six Conversos, leading citizens of the city, were escorted in procession barefoot, clutching unlighted candles, from the prison castle of Triana, where they had been incarcerated, to the cathedral to hear Mass and a sermon preached by Fray Hojeda. They were then taken out of town and burned at the stake. Other victims soon followed. In the ensuing months there were so many burnings that a massive stone platform called the *quemadero* (burning place) was constructed outside the city for the purpose. Thousands of Converso families fled Andalucía, resulting in a decline in commerce, but Queen Isabella was apparently not perturbed.

Meanwhile the Holy Office of the Inquisition was gearing up for its frightening mandate. In February 1482, seven more Dominican friars were appointed to the holy body. One of these was Tomás de Torquemada. Born in Valladolid, Torquemada became a friar in the Dominican monastery there and later served twenty-two years as prior of the monastery of Santa Cruz in Segovia. He became Isabella's confessor after she became queen. Over the next several years tribunals were established in all the major cities of Castilla. On 23 February 1484, thirty people were burned alive in the town of Ciudad Real. In 1485 at Toledo, rabbis under pain of death were ordered to report information about any Converso acquaintances they knew of who practiced Jewish rites. The old papal Inquisition was revived in the kingdom of Aragón, but not all the towns were disposed to have it within their walls. The city of Teruel refused permission to set up a tribunal, and Fernando threatened to enter the city with troops. Teruel capitulated to his demands, and other towns saw the writing on the wall. The tribunals proceeded to set up their offices in Barcelona, Zaragoza, and Valencia and directed their attention to the Conversos, who again (as in Andalucía) began to emigrate. The city of Barcelona complained to King Fernando that the commerce of the city would be ruined if the Inquisition were allowed to do its work; but the complaints fell on deaf ears.

Fernando took vigorous steps to assert his control over the Aragonese Inquisition, taking the matter out of the hands of the pope. In 1486, he reminded his newly installed inquisitors who was in charge: "Although you and the others enjoy the title of inquisitor, it is I and the queen who have appointed you, and without our support you can do very little."[1]

By the time the Inquisition was firmly established in Barcelona, there were few Conversos left to persecute. In 1488 it found only 7 victims to burn and only 3 in 1499. Of the nearly 1,200 people prosecuted between the years 1488 and 1505, most in absentia since they had fled, all but 8 were Conversos.

The papacy meanwhile, in accordance with the demands of the Catholic sovereigns, relinquished control of the Spanish Inquisition, which became an instrument of the state, although churchmen functioned as its officers. In 1488 the separate Inquisitions of Castilla and Aragón were united under the *Consejo de la Suprema y General Inquisición*, or Council of the Supreme and General Inquisition. Presiding over this council known simply as the *Suprema* was Tomás de Torquemada, the Inquisitor General. All the tribunals of the Inquisition throughout Castilla and Aragón fell under his direct control. Torquemada set the rules of procedure. Admired by some, he was feared by all. Between 1485 and 1500, 250 condemned were consigned to the flames in Toledo. The consistent support the Inquisition received from the monarchs assured that it would have a significant impact on Spanish society.

Revenues from victims' confiscated property and the fines set out by the Inquisition went in the first instance to the crown, which then paid out the salaries and expenses of the inquisitors.

It may never be known exactly how much of the seized wealth went to the royal treasury, but it is known that wealth expropriated by the tribunal after a year of persecutions in the small town of Guadalupe paid nearly all the costs of building a royal residence.

Under the Catholic monarchs the institution was totally dependent on the crown for finances. Under Carlos I, absent from Spain much of the time, the *Suprema* became more independent, receiving special stipends from the pope. Nevertheless, a shortage of money often forced the tribunals to seek out victims in order to pay inquisitorial expenses, and they sought dioceses where the pickings looked best. If they did not burn people, they did not eat, states an anonymous letter to the king in 1538. For the next two centuries, confiscation of property and church endowments remained the principal source of revenue for the Holy Office of the Inquisition, which also invested its share of money in property, houses, and annuities to bring in a regular income through rents and interest. Other sources of income were fines imposed upon the victims at any amount the inquisitors desired.

FAMILIARS, NOTARIES, AND OTHER MEMBERS OF THE INQUISITION

Inquisitors, officials of the church, were university trained in law and theology. Their police, called Familiars, were laymen who often dressed in black with the white cross of Saint Dominic on their cloaks. They were charged with the apprehension of the accused, and they protected the inquisitors, in return for which they were sanctioned to bear arms and receive benefits and privileges enjoyed by other officials. The status of Familiar was considered an honor, and its ranks were often filled by nobles.

Conflicts arose between inquisitorial and secular courts over the arraignment of Familiars who had themselves committed offenses. Since they were laymen, the secular branch of justice claimed responsibility for their prosecution, but in 1518 Carlos I sided with the Inquisition in giving it legal jurisdiction over Familiars, further enhancing the Inquisition's already considerable power. The decision gave Familiars license for improprieties, knowing they would be treated lightly by their masters. They gained notoriety for acting as informers and spies, although the majority of denunciations of suspects to the tribunals were made by neighbors or acquaintances and business rivals either as their perceived religious duty or due to personal grudges, envy, or hatred.

A notary was employed by the tribunals to keep records of the proceedings, interrogations of the accused, and confessions freely given or under torture. Records were necessary so that heretics reconciled to the church but who later relapsed could be identified and sent to their death at the stake.

Chosen primarily from the rural clergy, the commissaries (*comisarios*) were generally parish priests who acted on behalf of the Holy Office, supplying it with information about suspects. Their collaboration was essential for the Inquisition to carry out its work in the countryside. Often the priests were men of scant education barely above the level of their parishioners. The bishop of Pamplona complained in the year 1553 that those in his diocese were idiots and had elected to become *comisarios* in order to escape his jurisdiction.[2]

PROCEDURES

From their headquarters in the cities inquisitors visited the rural towns and issued orders in the surrounding villages and hamlets that those people with any knowledge of heresy among their neighbors report it. Familiars sought out those who refused to obey a summons, and the right of asylum in churches did not apply. The testimony of two witnesses whose identities were kept secret was considered proof of guilt, and prisoners were assumed guilty unless they could prove their innocence, a difficult matter to arrange since the charges brought against the accused were not divulged to the prisoner. Inquisitors approached the prisoners in the cells and encouraged them to confess, but it was not uncommon for the detainee not to know what to confess to. Depending on the backlog of cases, or through sheer neglect, the prisoner could remain in the cells for months or years without knowing what the charges were. Some depressed inmates confessed to crimes of which they were not accused, confessions that the inquisitors welcomed. In an extreme case a cleric, Gabrial Escobar, arrested in 1607 on a charge of illuminism (personal religious enlightenment outside the church), died in prison in 1622 still awaiting the completion of his trial.[3]

Unlike its medieval predecessor, the Spanish Inquisition allowed the prisoner to have a lawyer (in the early period, of his own choice, but later nominated by the tribunal). The lawyer could only speak to his client in the presence of the inquisitors, however, while the notary wrote down the conversation. By the mid-sixteenth century these advocates were recognized as members of the Inquisition and, needless to say, did not inspire much confidence in the accused. Their general advice was to confess. Acquittals were few.

PRISONS AND TORTURE

After a search of a house for incriminating evidence such as meat soaked, salted and washed to remove any trace of blood and grease—a sign of the Kashrut rule of Jewish dietary law—the victim was hustled away by the Familiars to the prison of the Inquisition, perhaps not to be seen again for years. The prisons were usually located in the same building as the tribunals, often disused royal palaces and castles. Some buildings were old and run-down, and the cells were at best cold, unhealthy, and dismal. As in secular prisons, chains were employed to further restrict prisoners.[4] A device known as the *pié de amigo*, an iron fork, was sometimes fitted to the chin of a prisoner to keep the head upright and rigid. The discomfort more readily induced confession. When envoys from the tribunal visited Doctor Agustín Cazalla the day before he was burned at the stake in Valladolid in 1559, they found him in a dark cell, loaded with chains and wearing the *pié de amigo*. In the same year, Jacques Pinzon, a French Calvinist, who made a disturbance in the Toledo prison, received fifty lashes and the *pié de amigo*, which was still in place six months later.[5]

From the moment of arrest, suspects were cut off from the world, even from their families, and forbidden to speak, lest they spread their heresies. Prisoners who defied the rule were gagged. Solitary confinement was the norm unless overcrowding dictated several persons to a cell.

Interrogation of the suspect was carried out in a chamber with black drapes covering the windows and black buntings on the walls, the only light from a few candles. The inquisitors, who were not moved by pity or pleas of innocence, sat at a long table in white robes and black hoods, their faces hidden. Questions came tersely and quickly. A notary sitting nearby wrote down all that was said and recorded the subject's gestures and mannerisms as the prisoner nervously answered the artful questions designed to trap the victim in contradictions. From time to time someone was actually released after this initial interrogation if the inquisitors were sure the accused had been a victim of malice or a personal grudge. Anyone released had to take an oath that nothing about the interrogation, or of the prison, would be revealed. Nothing they had seen, heard, done,

Bernard Picart. *Tortures of the Inquisition*. Based on an eighteenth-century engraving by Picart, an imagined eighteenth-century depiction of an inquisitional torture chamber. (Madrid: Biblioteca Nacional).

or not done was to be mentioned. It was as if they had not been there. Penalties for breaking the oath could be severe, such as 200 whiplashes.

If confession did not come readily, the interrogation went on for hours. If still no result the prisoner was returned to a cell, and the process repeated again at a later time. The inquisitors made use of the time studying the secretary's notes for contradictions or signs of fear. If the accused remained stubborn and further interrogation failed to elicit the responses desired by the inquisitors, the next step was the Question, a word used euphemistically for a trip to the torture chamber. Here the accused were stripped of their clothes and introduced to the instruments of torture. This alone sometimes brought about a confession.

There was nothing unchristian about the procedure according to the church, if torture was the only way to bring about a confession, subsequent atonement, and in their view, save the soul. While not actually administering the torture themselves (which was performed generally by public executioners), inquisitors were present in order to hear the confession when the pain became unbearable, and a notary was present to write it down. A physician usually stood by in case of life-threatening complications.

A rapid way to bring on terrible distress and agonizing pain was the *garrucha*. The wrists of the accused were bound behind the back, and a rope tied to them was run through a pulley on the ceiling. Weights were attached to the feet, and the victim was hoisted upward and then allowed to fall back toward the ground, coming to a sudden halt. Amid the screams and moans the inquisitors listened for signs of a garbled confession. The severe jerk stretched and often dislocated the arms and legs and sometimes left the individual permanently crippled. If victims passed out, they were lowered to the ground and returned to the cells to await another bout on the hoist. While one of the rules of the Inquisition stated that a person could be tortured only once, the inquisitors evaded the restriction simply by referring to the time between tortures as a suspension of the same process. Known as the *taca*, the water torture usually got good results. Placed in a prone position on a wooden board with the head secured by an iron clamp and a little lower than the feet, the nostrils of the nose were plugged, the jaws were forced open with a metal prong, and a piece of linen cloth (*toca*) was placed across the open mouth. Water was poured slowly on the cloth, which gradually sank deeper and deeper into the throat while the prisoner felt the terror of slow suffocation. From time to time the cloth was extracted so the victim could confess into the nearby receptive ear of an inquisitor. If the panicky victim moved in the minutes of anguish, the tight cords holding him to the board cut deep into the skin. These cords could also be tightened by twisting them with an iron bar like a tourniquet so that the cords cut through the flesh to the very bone.

The time-tested and effective rack was also present in the torture chambers. This was a wooden frame with movable bars at each end. The prisoner's wrists and ankles were fastened to the bars, which were moved in opposite directions by levers, thus stretching the body until the bones became separated. Those who underwent the ordeal sometimes never walked again. Those who fainted were revived, and the process repeated.

While there were other diabolical instruments of torture including forceps for extracting toenails and fingernails and whips, there is no evidence for the reported and imaginative use of mice placed on the victim's stomach under a bowl. As the bowl was heated the mice burrowed into the stomach to escape roasting. Nor is there evidence that victims' feet were roasted over a fire, with grease smeared on the skin to prolong the agony of burning. Secrecy of the proceedings led to many fanciful and ingenious stories.

No one was safe from the Question. Pregnant women were often al-

Ioan Van Hertz. *An Inquisitional Torture.* (Madrid: Biblioteca Nacional).

lowed to sit while being tortured, but children and women in their nineties are on record as being tortured. Confession made under torture was not considered valid, however, and the accused was called upon to ratify his or her statements after the ordeal. If the victim refused to comply, then the threat to continue the torture, which according to the inquisitors had only been suspended, would be invoked. Self-confession was not the only thing the inquisitors wanted to hear. Pressure was also put on the accused to reveal the names and sins of friends and relatives.

The church condemned taking a human life, and death of the prisoner before confession was not a desirable outcome. As some did die under torture, the inquisitors claimed that the prisoner brought about his own death by refusing to admit guilt.

PUNISHMENTS

Punishment could be light for slight offenses and if the offender readily confessed and asked to be reconciled to the church. A condemned person might be sentenced to fast one day a week, or to recite a given

PORTRAITS DE 3 HOMMES CONDAMNÉES PAR L'INQUISITION D'EPAGNE

1 Habit de celuy qui doit estre Brulé vif.
2 Habit de celuy qui a evité d'estre Brulé en avouant avant que d'estre jugé.
3 Habit de celuy qui a evité le feu en avouant apres son jugement. voyez t. 2. pag. 226.

Anonymous. *Three Men Condemned by the Inquisition.* Note the wearing of the *sanbenito.* (Madrid: Biblioteca Nacional).

number of prayers on certain days, or to show up at the church each Sunday with a halter around the neck as a badge of shame, or to go on a pilgrimage.

When whipping was slated, the prisoner was paraded through town on the back of a donkey preceded by the town crier announcing the event. Accompanied by a clerk to keep tally, the executioner plied a leather strap to the victim's back. Two hundred lashes, the limit, were not unusual, but 100 was more common. Passersby and children hurled stones at the accused to show their scorn. No distinction was made between sex or age.

Equally humiliating was the wearing of the *sanbenito (saco bendito,* or blessed sack), a loose-fitting penitential garment like a tunic, made of sackcloth with a hole in the top for the head. This carryover from the medieval Inquisition hung on the body down to the knees, and penitents were condemned to wear it for a period of a few months to years. It was put on whenever the person stepped out from the house onto the street. When it was no longer worn, it was hung in the local church to cast infamy over the descendants of the accused. Other punishments involved fines, exile, confiscation of property, the galleys, and imprisonment. Those who escaped the death penalty by confession were often sentenced to life in prison, which usually meant about ten years. Prisons were not ideal from the point of view of the Inquisition since the inmate had to be housed and fed. Often they were confined to a monastery or even a private house. Several different punishments could be inflicted at the same time. Alonso Ribero, for example, was sentenced in Granada on 30 May 1672 for falsifying inquisitorial documents and received four years' banishment from the locality, six years in the galleys, and 100 lashes. In another case, Francisco de Alarcón, accused of blasphemy, was given five years' banishment, five in the galleys, 200 lashes, and a fine.[6] Banishment, a common sentence, was handed out to those considered a bad influence in the community.

The ultimate penalty was "relaxation" (a euphemism for being handed over to the state authorities for death by burning). By turning the prisoner over to the secular arm of justice, the church avoided violating its own principles of not taking human life. Two types of people were subject to this ultimate penalty: unrepentant heretics and relapsed heretics. Trials and sentences of the already dead were common where the bones of the miscreant, who may have died of natural causes or in the cells of the Inquisition, were disinterred, condemned, and burned. The majority of those who were "relaxed," at least in the early years of the Inquisition, were burned in effigy, the accused having fled the country or gone into hiding.

AUTO DE FE

Once condemned the accused had to appear at an auto de fe, the act of faith. The ceremony could be in private (*auto particular*) or in public (*auto público*). The crimes and penalties of the accused were announced on these occasions. At first the ceremony was a simple affair involving a procession of the condemned to the local church and the sentences read out. In the first auto de fe, held at Toledo on 12 February 1486, over 750 Conversos were reconciled to the church after accusations of Judaizing. With the men in one group, women in another, all barefoot with heads uncovered in the bitter cold and each carrying an unlit candle, they were paraded through the streets to the church of Saint Peter Martyr, the way lined by spectators. The condemned wept as they trudged along in their public shame. At the door of the church two priests made the sign of the cross on the forehead of each of the prisoners and told them to receive the sign that they denied and lost through being deceived. In the church, with the inquisitors sitting on a makeshift scaffold, a Mass was then said, a sermon preached, and a notary read out the crimes of each individual. When this was over, sentence was passed. The condemned were ordered to go in procession for six Fridays, unshod, bareheaded, and barebacked, while disciplining their bodies with scourges of hemp cord. None could hold any public office or official post for the rest of their lives, and those who already held such offices lost them. They were not allowed to become moneychangers, shopkeepers, or grocers. They were forbidden to wear silk of scarlet or colored cloth of any kind or gold, silver, coral, pearls, or jewelry. They could not stand as witnesses. Lastly, if they fell into the same error again the penalty would be death by burning at the stake. The entire affair was over by two o'clock in the afternoon.

The colorful, flamboyant event, a spectacular pageant, is the one generally equated with the usual conception of the auto de fe. This new style was conceived in the mid-sixteenth century by Inquisitor General Fernando de Valdés, a ruthless, career-oriented prelate who saw heresy everywhere, to reinforce the presence and power of the Holy Office.

The new ceremony took place on Sundays or on church holy days in the public squares in order to attract the largest crowds for a lesson in the fate of heretics. The auto de fe began early in the morning and often went on until nightfall. The one held in the main square of Madrid on 30 June 1680 in the presence of the king and court was announced a month ahead of time with Familiars and notaries parading through the streets of the city heralding the event. The square was prepared for the occasion, with seats constructed for dignitaries, inquisitors, and the public. Condemned were brought in from various parts of the country to enhance their numbers.

On the eve of the appointed day those who were to pay the supreme price for their heresy were told that on the following day they would be burned alive, but in its mercy the Inquisition would allot each of them two priests who would do their utmost to save their souls if they repented, confessed their heresy, and showed great desire for reconciliation with the church. In such cases they would be mercifully strangled before the flames reached their flesh.

At sunrise all the prisoners were summoned forth to gather in the great hall of the prison and ordered to remain silent while ropes were placed around their necks and tied to restrain their arms. The procession to the place of penance began, led by bearers of the green cross of the Inquisition, and followed by a company of Familiars. Then came the priest who was to say Mass, transported in a chair under a canopy of scarlet and gold borne by four sturdy men. He carried the Host, and the crowds along the way kneeled as he passed. Failure to do so could place one under suspicion.

Those who had offended least were dressed in black blouses and trousers and were bareheaded and barefoot. Those convicted of more serious

Bernard Picart. *Procession of the Auto de Fe in the Plaza Mayor in Madrid 1723.* (Madrid: Biblioteca Nacional).

sins were dressed in a yellow *sanbenito* adorned with the blood-red cross of Saint Andrew. Condemned to die at the stake were those who were distinguished by black *sanbenitos* painted with grotesque devils and flames and who wore on their heads a conical pasteboard hat in the shape of a bishop's miter called the *coroza*, a contemptuous allusion to a crown. Each was accompanied by two Dominicans in white robes and black hoods exhorting them to save their souls (but not their lives) through reconciliation to the church.

Behind this column, attached to long green poles, came the effigies of those people absent but convicted of heresy, also dressed in the *sanbenito*. Among this group were also the bones and rotting bodies of those disinterred from the grave, condemned after they had died. Then came the inquisitors accompanied by banners of red silk adorned with the papal arms, those of the Catholic monarchs, and symbols of the Inquisition. Armed soldiers walked along on either side of the procession. Bringing up the rear were the throngs of people anticipating the spectacle.

In the square the prisoners were forced to sit on tiers of benches fes-

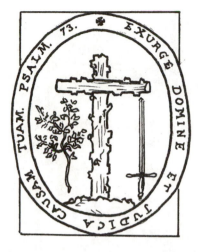

Banner of the Inquisition.

tooned with black crêpe and to remain silent and still so the crowd could have a good view of them, shout insults, and throw garbage at them. (In some places the penitents sat on the ground.) On the benches with the prisoners were friars who continued to exhort them to confess.

In a haze of burning incense, the inquisitors, their assistants, and servants sat on a platform where stood the green cross and an altar with lighted candles. After Mass, and the lengthy sermon was over, the head inquisitor stood and, lifting his arms, recited the oath of allegiance to the Inquisition. The people, on their knees, repeated the phrases after him, swearing they would defend to the death the Holy Office against all adversity.

The crimes of each person from the lightest to the most severe were read out. Now came the time to abandon the condemned prisoners to the secular arm of justice for punishment, as the church could do no more to save their souls. From the altar an appeal was made for the secular arm to show mercy to the guilty. With this formality the Inquisition had done all in its power to save the soul. What happened to the body was not its concern. It was blameless.

Upon completion of the auto de fe, those destined to be burned were strapped to the backs of mules and taken off to the *quemadero* outside the city, where prepared stakes and firewood at their base were overlooked by a white cross. Before being tied to the stakes the prisoners were again asked if they wished to be reconciled with God and receive mercy from the fire by strangulation. The honor of lighting the torch was given to a dignitary, and once lit it was used to set ablaze the firewood at the base of the stakes to which the victims were tied. If any members of the royal family were present, they were given a piece of wood enveloped in green ribbons (the Inquisition preferred color) to toss on the

Goya. *Aquellos Polvos*. Goya's depiction of a convicted penitent during an auto de fe. (Madrid: Biblioteca Nacional).

fire. The church bells tolled, monks chanted, and the air took on the heavy sweet, sickly odor of burning flesh as the greasy smoke drifted upward toward the heavens. The ashes of the condemned were scattered in the fields or in the rivers to obliterate all traces of them. The *sanbenitos* that had been removed before the burning were sent to the parish church of each victim as a reminder of what happened to heretics.

ALUMBRADOS AND LUTHERANS (PROTESTANTS)

The Inquisition was highly suspicious of private devotional life outside the established structures of the parish church or the religious orders, but some nuns and monks believed in a mystical method of worship and became known as *alumbrados*, or "the illuminated ones." They were not opposed to trying to communicate with the Supreme Being directly by contemplation and self-denial and without benefit of priest or idols. Many *alumbrados* were under the patronage of the high nobility who found merit in their search for a purer spiritual life. The Inquisition was hesitant and inconsistent about persecuting such people. Great mystics, such as the Carmelite nun Santa Teresa of Avila, spoke of direct communication with God that occurred while she was in a trance. The In-

Goya. *No Hubo Remedio*. The procession whereby the convicted prisoner is being escorted to the place where he is to be put to death. (Madrid: Biblioteca Nacional).

quisition took note but never prosecuted her. Her contemporary Juan de la Cruz lived a solitary and contemplative life and opposed the clothing of holy statues in the luxury and fashions of the profane world, reducing true devotion, he said, to the mere dressing up of dolls. He also was never summoned before the Inquisition. A few other *alumbrados* got off with light sentences. The Basque priest Juan López de Celaín, connected to the *alumbrados* of Guadalajara, however, was arrested in 1528, tortured, and burned at the stake as a Lutheran (whose religious ideas were often similar) two years later in Granada.

Spaniards generally had little contact with Lutherans (also known as Protestants), but in some cases the inquisitors leveled charges that the accused had been to a country of heretics, which meant any country not under Spanish control. Lutheranism, a sect that had broken away from Roman Catholicism in Germany during the sixteenth century, believed that salvation could be achieved by faith alone—hence, without the aid of priests—and any association with them was suspect. When Alonso de Virús, a Benedictine and confidant of Carlos I, was arrested in 1533 and confined to prison in Sevilla, accused of heresy based on contacts he had with Lutherans while abroad, Carlos I made great efforts to secure his release. Not until May 1538 did the king manage to obtain a bull from

Bernard Picart. *Burning of the Condemned after an Auto de Fe in Lisbon.* (Madrid: Biblioteca Nacional).

the pope annulling the sentence. Virús was restored to favor and became bishop of the Canary Islands in 1542. The powerful Inquisition could thwart the will of kings but dared not defy the pope.

Foreign visitors who showed disrespect for the religious rituals of the church, such as failure to remove one's hat if the sacrament passed by in the street or making derogatory remarks about the church, were subject to arrest by the Inquisition. Cases of alleged Lutheranism that appeared before the tribunals before 1600 numbered 1,995, of which 1,640 concerned foreigners.[7]

The most likely city in Spain for contact with Protestants was Sevilla, a center of international trade and book smuggling, much of which was destined for the New World. A small Protestant movement, consisting of about 120 people, perhaps sympathizers more than practitioners, began in Sevilla. It was exposed in 1557 when some members were arrested for bringing Protestant books into the country from Geneva.

About the same time another group of Protestants appeared in Valladolid. Their numbers were also small, perhaps about fifty-five or sixty, and mostly aristocrats. Here they seem to have been truly immersed in the new religion rejecting most of the Catholic dogma. A wave of arrests took place as stringent repression was set in motion in both cities. The result was a series of autos de fe of the new style, the first held in Valladolid on Sunday, 21 May 1559, with the regent Juana and her court in attendance. (Juana, sister of the king, acted as regent when Felipe II was out of the country.) Thirty people were accused, and fourteen of these were burned at the stake. Another auto was held six months later with the king present. Thirty more Protestants or their sympathizers were accused, and twelve, including four nuns, were burned. Sevilla was next.

On Sunday, 24 September 1559, seventy-six stood accused in Sevilla of crimes against the church, and nineteen were condemned to the flames as Protestants (*Lutherans* was the term employed by the inquisitors).[8] This, too, was soon followed by another auto on 12 December 1560 in which of fifty-four accused, fourteen were "relaxed," including two English sailors, William Brook and Nicholas Burton, the latter a ship's master. His cargo was appropriated by the authorities. Another Englishman by the name of Frampton sent out to try to recover the ship and its merchandise, also fell afoul of the Inquisition. Under torture he promised to embrace Roman Catholicism and received only a year in prison. Also among the condemned was a lady of Sevilla, Leonor Gómez, along with her three young daughters.

More autos followed over the next several years, and organized Protestantism ceased to exist in Spain. From time to time a carelessly outspoken Englishman, Scot, or Dutchman was apprehended by the inquisitorial police and sentenced for heresy. Some were relaxed; others abjured and suffered lesser punishments. The English sailor Richard Hasleton of Braintree, captured by Barbary pirates in 1582, was a galley slave for several years, escaped, and was rescued by a Genoese vessel. Upon learning that he was a Protestant the captain of the vessel turned him over to the Inquisition in Mallorca. Incarcerated in the dungeon of the castle and tortured, he escaped to North Africa, where he spent another ten years as a slave among the Saracens before he managed to get himself back to England. Concerning his experience with the rack and water torture of the Inquisition, he wrote later that he "would have no feeling of any limb or joint" but "lay in a most lamentable and pitiful manner for four or five days having a continual issue of blood and water forth from my mouth all that space, and being so feeble and weak, by reason of my torments, that I would take no sustenance."[9] His story of the Inquisition, along with those of other compatriots who suffered its jails and torture chambers, helped fuel the Black Legend that contributed in no small measure to the image of the Inquisition in northern countries. Wildly imaginative accounts in books and pamphlets circulated in Protestant lands greatly exaggerated the sadistic bent of the Inquisitors, and denigrated the achievements and character of the Spanish people.

OTHER OFFENSES

The great witch-hunts that consumed Europe were relatively muffled in Spain in spite of the fact that many churchmen believed in the reality of pacts with the devil and witches' curses. During the sixteenth century, the concerns of the Inquisition about witchcraft were of less importance than sins of heresy. Men or women who claimed to have magical power to heal and to assist in love matches by casting spells over one or the other of the parties involved accompanied by the use of charms, potions, and advice were not greatly molested by the Holy Office. The medieval Inquisition had left the punishment of such matters as sorcery and witch-craft up to the secular courts and remained noncommittal since it was not clear if heresy was involved in these acts. The notions that witches flew through the air, copulated with the devil, and could change into the bodies of animals were considered delusions of ignorant people more to be pitied than punished. The Inquisition simply regarded them as pawns of Satan who made them think they had extraordinary powers. If a sorceress invoked the name of the Holy Trinity in the process of conjuring up a spell, however, then the Inquisition took a dim view. Construed as a mild form of heresy, the sentences were generally light, amounting to whippings or banishment. If there was no evidence the suspect worshipped the devil or employed Christian objects such as cru-cifixes or communion hosts in magical rites, sentence was light or the case was dismissed.[10]

Freemasons, the fraternal order derived from medieval guilds of stone masons, were hounded and persecuted throughout Europe by the papal Inquisition. In 1738, the year of the Vatican declaration of war on the Masons, the Spanish Inquisition raided a lodge in Madrid and arrested the members, eight of whom were sent to the galleys. Ten years later, a detailed four-year investigation of the lodge's activities was completed, concluding that Freemasons acted contrary to the purity of the Holy Roman faith (one of their basic tenets, at odds with Catholic dogma, was that religion was solely the concern of the individual) and to the public safety of the realm. In 1751 the Inquisition obtained a decree from Fer-nando VI that sanctioned the automatic death penalty without the right of trial for all Freemasons. At the time, one inquisitor, Father Torrubia, joined a lodge in order to spy and denounce its members. His reports indicate that there were ninety-seven lodges in Spain.[11]

Punishment for homosexuality, the unspeakable crime of the Middle Ages, in Spain entailed castration or stoning to death. Under the Catholic Kings the punishment was changed to death by burning and confiscation of property. Leniency was shown to the clergy, who formed a high pro-portion of the offenders, and in some cases to the high nobility, who could afford a large fine. In the years 1570 to 1630, the inquisitional tribunal of Zaragoza examined 543 cases of homosexuality and executed 102 persons.[12]

The Inquisition eventually assumed authority over many other types of misbehavior, usurping the authority of civil courts. Bigamy, for ex-ample, was added to the catalog of religious sins since having more than one wife or husband defied the authority of the church. The offense was treated lightly, however, if the penitent confessed his sin, declaring he was overcome by passion for the second, or third, mate. If the accused expressed contempt for marriage itself, a church sacrament, he or she was then close to heresy and would be treated accordingly.

Adultery and unmarried sexual intercourse were more thorny problems. Priests, bishops, and even the pope indulged in the practice. Such matters were ignored, therefore, unless those so engaged embraced the view that there was no sin involved in such actions. This belief would then be contrary to church principles and the sinner subject to a charge of heresy. Blasphemy was also a crime in which the misuse of sacred liturgy or offensive use of the names of God, the Virgin Mary, or the saints was punishable.

The moral behavior of the clergy was of concern to the religious establishment. Besides keeping concubines, priests often abused their privileged position to seduce parishioners. For the most part the Inquisition was interested in solicitation during confession. The contact between priest and female penitent was close and intimate. (The confessional box did not begin to appear until the late sixteenth century.) The Inquisition treated such matters as heresy through misuse of the sacrament of penance.

The actions of priests were watched closely. Fray Lucas de Allende, guardian of the Franciscan convent of Madrid, busied himself with writing down the dreams of Lucrecia de León, who claimed to have conversations with God and the saints in her dreams. Allende was arrested and lay in prison from 1590 until 1596 when he was sentenced to a reprimand and a warning not to meddle in such affairs.[13] Other matters involving priests pertained to what they said. The tribunal of Barcelona, for example, prosecuted a priest in 1666 for declaring that he would rather be in hell beside a Frenchman than in heaven next to a Castillian.[14]

THE LAST VICTIMS

By the end of the seventeenth century the auto de fe no longer held the same appeal for the masses. People were becoming indifferent to the all-day event, and by the early eighteenth century, the lack of victims and the rising costs meant that the public ceremony was becoming a thing of the past. Mass persecutions ended. By the second half of the eighteenth century only private autos were employed.

That the Inquisition was winding down is evident from the number of cases tried. The tribunal in Toledo heard some 3 to 4 cases a year in the late eighteenth century, compared to over 200 in the mid-sixteenth century. During the eighteenth century the Inquisition heard about 4,000 cases, but of these, only about 10 percent were concerned with Judaizing, the original primary preoccupation of the Inquisition, or Protestantism. Cases that were once hardly considered, involving such matters as magic or sexual aberrations, now occupied more of the inquisitors' time.

A young lawyer, Pablo Olavide,[15] who had been in France and had met both Rousseau and Voltaire, corresponded with them upon his return to Spain. Denounced to the Inquisition as an atheist who did not believe in miracles or in the exclusive salvation of Catholics, Olavide was found guilty and sentenced in 1778 to eight years' confinement in a monastery. His property was confiscated, and he and four generations of his descendants were barred from public office. Some years before, death at the stake would have been his punishment. Only on four occasions during the eighteenth century did burning take place after an auto de fe. The last victim, the visionary María de los Dolores López, who claimed to have direct contact with the Virgin Mary and to have been the prime mover in the release of millions of souls from purgatory, was burned alive in 1781.[16]

In 1790 the government intervened in the case of a friar, Augustín de Cobades, who was found guilty of molesting female penitents and conspiring to deceive the Inquisition. His conviction in Valencia was overthrown as a result of intervention from friends in high places in Madrid. The *Suprema* could no longer stand up to the government.

Following the French Revolution in 1789, the subsequent war with France in 1793 further weakened the Inquisition. In Valencia, for example, call-up papers to serve in the army were issued by the local authorities to the tribunal's police, the Familiars, ending their privileges and depriving the tribunal of its agents. The cost of the war also forced the government to sell off properties of public corporations including those of the Inquisition. On 27 February 1799, a royal decree proclaimed the sale by auction of the immovable property of local tribunals. The loss of property brought an end to some of the financial independence of the Inquisition and accelerated its downward spiral.

After Napoleonic armies had overrun Spain in 1808 and Joseph Bonaparte sat on the throne in Madrid, the French authorities increasingly interfered with the activities of the Holy Office. In Córdoba, the royal castle and headquarters of the Inquisition since 1480 had already been ransacked by French troops on 7 June 1808 and part of the archives lost— blown away down the Guadalquivir River. On 4 December 1808 Napoleon himself arrived at Chamartín, now a suburb of Madrid, and among the decrees he issued, one of them abolished the Inquisition and all its tribunals on the grounds they were a threat to civil authority. The Inquisitor General resigned. But the institution was not easy to dispatch. The decision rested with the Spanish Cortes, which had assembled on 24 September 1810 at Cádiz outside of French control.

The conservatives in the assembly pressed for a continuation of the Inquisition, but a liberal committee working on a constitution for the country concluded that the Inquisition was incompatible with the new constitution, and on 22 January 1812, the Cortes agreed by ninety to sixty votes to abolish it. The Holy Office now reverted to its medieval form. On 26 January 1813 a passage of the thirteenth-century legal code was restored, giving jurisdiction in cases of heresy back to bishops. This, of course, could only be instituted in regions not under French authority. After the French were expelled from Spain, reinstated Fernando VII denounced the Cortes and the constitution. He restored the Inquisition to its full functions. In further edicts he gave back to the tribunals their property, rental income, and prebends. A new Inquisitor General, Francisco Javier de Meir y Campillo, was appointed, and the regional tribunals set to work to recruit new Familiars and theological advisers. During Lent of 1815 an edict was published in Madrid that called upon the people to denounce not only Jews, Muslims, and Protestants but also those associated with modern rationalist philosophy, that is, anyone exposed to the concepts of the Age of Enlightenment.

In 1820 a military uprising forced Fernando VII to accept the terms of the Cortes, and once again the property of the tribunals was seized and sold at auction and the Inquisition abolished. Then, with the help of a new French army, Fernando again gained the upper hand supported by the church, and the Inquisition was restored.

The last death sentence for heresy was pronounced in Valencia in 1824. A schoolteacher, Cayetano Ripoll, while in prison in France during the Peninsular War had become a Deist, a follower of the Rationalist religious philosophy that flourished at the time and that held that natural religion is inherent in each person and accessible through the exercise of reason. Charges brought against Ripoll included failure to attend Mass and his insistence that the Ten Commandments were all that was necessary in religious teachings.

Ripoll refused to recant despite two years in prison. Deemed a heretic and turned over to the secular high court of Valencia, he was hanged on 26 July 1826. The extent of changed public opinion by this time is evident in the fact that his body was only symbolically burned. It was placed in a barrel with flames painted on it and buried in unconsecrated ground.[17]

On 15 July 1834 Queen María Cristina, widow of Fernando VII and acting regent for the young Isabella II, definitively abolished the Inquisition. What had begun in the reign of the first Isabella nearly three and a half centuries before ended in the reign of the second.

IMPACT OF THE INQUISITION ON DAILY LIFE

Fear hung over the heads of people of minority groups, and many of those most at most risk, the Conversos, left Spain for foreign lands. Others blended in to the Spanish tapestry. Moriscos, after much persecution, were expelled.

Among old Christians the Inquisition generated a climate of suspicion.

Criticism of it was a crime, and any utterance, in jest, trivial or careless, denigrating the Holy Office or the church had to be guarded against, lest it be heard and denounced to the tribunals. Even among members of a family it was the sacred duty of parents and children to denounce each other if heresy was suspected.

Abuses of authority by inquisitors and Familiars were common and led to conflicts. Members of tribunals demanded to be served first in the marketplace and obtained the best provisions. An extreme case occurred when a hidalgo in Córdoba bought a fish and refused to give it up to an acquaintance of a servant of an Inquisitor who demanded it. The hidalgo was punished with 200 lashes and sent to the galleys.[18] Local tribunals could do as they pleased, knowing that even their most arbitrary acts such as seizing the houses of residents in the town of Llerena for their own use would be supported by the all-powerful *Suprema*.[19] Arrogant inquisitors with unlimited power and their assistants, ignoring municipal ordinances that applied to others, incurred the animosity of all levels of society—a society that at the same time thought the Inquisition necessary to defend the faith.

Cataluña was an area where it was difficult for the Inquisition to make inroads. The people of Barcelona held the tribunal and its methods in disdain, and the inquisitors there complained that the city officials never came to the autos de fe. In the high Pyrenean Valleys no inquisitor ever came. In those villages that were visited, the inquisitor, a total stranger in the midst of suspicious, distrustful farmers, was often met with a wall of silence to his probing questions. Similarly, hamlets in Galicia and Asturias had never seen a real inquisitor. Nevertheless, fear of his visit and the name of the Holy Office could conjure up anxiety. Stories were told of inquisitors stealing quietly into villages in the dead of night on silent horses with padded hooves, to listen at the doors and windows of the houses for a blasphemous word or heretical pronouncement from inside. Children were frightened by these tales of nocturnal specters who came to snatch people away and burn them alive.

NOTES

1. Kamen, *The Spanish Inquisition*, 137.

2. Ibid., 148.

3. Ibid., 197.

4. The extent of the use of chains is unknown, but for examples of prisoners who were fettered, see Lea, *History*, 2: 511.

5. Ibid., 2: 512.

6. Kamen, *The Spanish Inquisition*, 202.

7. Ibid., 277, for these figures.

8. The term *Protestant* was given to the Lutheran movement after Lutheran protesters at the Diet of Speyer in 1529.

9. Roth, 96.
10. Kamen, *The Spanish Inquisition*, 269–276.
11. Baigent and Leigh, 169.
12. Kamen, *The Spanish Inquisition*, 268.
13. Lea, *History*, 3: 96.
14. Kamen, *The Spanish Inquisition*, 265.
15. Edwards, 123.
16. Lea, *History*, 4: 89.
17. Edwards, 132.
18. Lea, *History*, 1: 533.
19. Ibid., 1: 527.

6

Jews and Conversos

It is not clear when the first Jews arrived in Spain, but Hispano-Jewish communities were clearly established in the sixth and seventh centuries during Visigothic domination and were persecuted by these Germanic-Christian warriors who then ruled the Iberian peninsula.[1] Relief from oppression came about in the year 711 when a Moorish invasion from Morocco overthrew the Visigothic kingdom. Jews prospered economically and socially under the Muslim caliphate of Córdoba.

During the centuries of Reconquest, when Christian communities of the north pushed southward to gradually repossess the land, Muslims (who had remained in the reconquered towns), Jews, and Christians co-existed, if not in perfect harmony at least in a state of mutual tolerance. The use of municipal bathhouses in the frontier towns, for example, were organized on the basis of gender and religion. Christian males used the baths on certain days and Jews and Muslims on others. At different times from the men, women, regardless of faith, shared them. Such customs differed somewhat from town to town and from time to time. During the thirteenth century in the reign of Alfonso X of Castilla, the church of Santa María la Blanca (which still stands in Toledo) was used by Muslims on Friday, Jews on Saturday, and Christians on Sunday. The court at Toledo was a center of learning attracting learned scholars from all over Europe, and Jewish scholars there were instrumental in translating Arabic texts, originally from Greek classics, into Latin. Jews served as financial advisers, councilors, and physicians, whereas others followed occupations such as shopkeepers, grocers, butchers, dyers, weavers, cob-

Sign at entrance to the Jewish Quarter.

blers, blacksmiths, chemists, jewelers, and silversmiths. Jewish women often worked as laundresses, midwives, and spinners. Tailors were typically Jewish; there were thirty in Murcia in 1407.[2] In Logroño they were often leather workers. Some Jews were wealthy and influential, but most were poor and humble.

It was not uncommon for Jewish craftsmen to work for Christian employers or for Christians to seek the aid of a Jewish doctor or a Jewish advocate to represent them in secular courts. Not all Jews were town dwellers. Some lived in the villages that dotted the medieval countryside where they farmed, bred sheep, or tended vineyards and orchards. However, the always present fundamental religious differences between Jews and Christians began to be more acutely felt as the Middle Ages neared their close.

ATROCITIES AGAINST JEWS

Under the leadership of strong and aggressive popes in the thirteenth century, the Roman Catholic Church asserted its dominion over all of Christendom including kings and emperors, and as the church grew more arrogant and powerful, the Jewish communities became more sub-

Etching after a drawing by Jean-Baptiste Vanmour, 1714. *Jew.* (The Israel
Museum, Jerusalem).

ject to anti-Semitic sentiment and more vulnerable to discriminatory laws
and acts of violence.

Some Jews who held high public office under aristocratic protection
of the king, owing, for example, their learning and expertise in medical
and fiscal matters, lived like wealthy Christians, which inflamed envy
among the poorer Christian multitudes. When the church declared in
1179 that money lending for interest was a sin for Catholics, Jews, with
their own strict moral code, filled in the void. This also fueled resentment
among the masses toward Jews.

While some nobles were jealous of the achievements of the Jews, the
general Christian populace of the cities and towns resented the wealth
of Jewish families because they felt it came at the expense of the common
people. The more ignorant saw the Jews as betrayers of Christ and fed
on malicious rumors of Jewish atrocities against Christians.

With the church leading the crusade, the nobility and even kings in
many parts of Europe turned against the Jews. City councils began to
pass laws restricting their activities. In 1235, the Council of Arles in
France ordered all Jews to wear an identifying yellow patch over their
hearts; in 1290 England expelled all its Jews from the kingdom, and in
1306 France did the same. Many found refuge in Spain. Of the three

Etching after a drawing by Jean-Baptiste Vanmour, 1714. *Jewish Woman Bringing Her Merchandise for Sale.* (The Israel Museum, Jerusalem).

great religions there—Christianity, Islam, and Judaism—the Jews were the smallest and the most vulnerable to discrimination. On the Iberian peninsula an early foretaste of the fury to descend on them came in 1328 when the Franciscan preacher Fray Pedro Olligoyen stirred the populace to rise up against the Jewish quarter of Estella in Navarra. The houses were pillaged and the inhabitants massacred. Neither man, woman, nor child was spared, and the venom spread throughout the kingdom.

With different dietary requirements from Christians and different religious practices, the Jews were often under suspicion as some kind of subversive element. Jewish communities generally were forced to live in separate quarters of town. In Spain, these ghettos, called *aljamas*, maintained their own officials and were generally exempt from municipal obligations except the duty to defend the town in case of attack. These communities were under the direct control and protection of the king, who considered the Jews his personal property. The concern of King Juan is stipulated in a document of 6 April 1443 in which he chastises individuals and towns for causing distress to his Jewish and Moorish subjects.[3] The *aljamas* paid taxes directly to the crown and not to the town of which they were a part. Taxes were negotiated between king and *aljamas* through representatives of both and could take various forms such as a poll tax, that is, a certain amount of money for each individual, as was the case in Castilla, or a household tax established in Aragón.

If the Jewish population of a town was small the affairs of the Jewish quarter were conducted at an open meeting of all the inhabitants. In larger and more typical *aljamas*, a number of important men were regarded by general consent as the heads of the community and entrusted with matters of public interest. In the largest of the townships such as Barcelona, Toledo, and Zaragoza, officials were elected.[4]

Nevertheless, in spite of royal protection, the crown was hard-pressed to protect its Jewish subjects from hostile Christian municipalities, some of which began to pass arbitrary laws confining Jewish activity more and more to their own quarter, and others went even further. Some municipal laws forbade them to shave or cut their hair in order to be more readily recognized. In some places they were not permitted to farm the land or to become doctors, surgeons, or bankers or indeed to hold any position that would give them authority over Christians. In other areas they were not allowed to ride a horse since that would place them physically above Christians who were on foot, nor could they wear fine clothes but, rather, had to go around in coarse, colorless garments. Restrictions, differing from town to town, increased in the fourteenth century.

Andrés Bernáldez, a parish priest of Los Palacios near Sevilla, denounced Jews for being merchants, tailors, shoemakers, smiths, jewelers, weavers, and tanners as well as tax-gatherers and officials. None tilled the soil as a farmer (this was not strictly true) or became a mason or carpenter, the implication being that Jews preferred occupations that made money but preferred not to dirty their hands with hard work. The fact that the Jews in the ghettos were cut off from the soil and other trades because guilds would not accept them seemed to escape the priest's notice.

Excluded in both local municipal legislation and in the minds of the common populace from many of the ordinary jobs, Jews were compelled to seek their livelihood in professions where they could benefit from the favor of the upper classes. As financiers, administrators, stewards, tax-gatherers, and retailers, both Jews and Conversos could make a comfortable living. It is somewhat ironic that Jews were often disliked for not doing the jobs that they were not allowed to do.

Where the Jewish communities lived had a bearing on their treatment. The crown of Castilla might act in one way and that of Aragón in another. Some towns imposed their own anti-Semitic statutes, whereas others did not. Nevertheless, repression of the Jews, even if uneven geographically, grew throughout the country until, in the fourteenth century, atrocities against them became commonplace.

Ferrant Martínez, archdeacon of Ecija in Andalucía, was loud and fervent in his bitter denunciations in the late fourteenth century. A man of fierce passion but seemingly little learning, he harped on the message that the Jews had murdered Jesus Christ, thus committing the most heinous crime in history. He attacked their personal habits, claiming they were not clean, cooked their food with too much oil, and smelled bad.[5] Whatever hatred he spouted, there were ample simple minds to absorb it. In June 1391 his condemnations bore fruit. Angry rioting mobs in Sevilla murdered hundreds of Jews in their homes as the *aljama* was destroyed. The contagion spread rapidly. The fiery oratory of the zealous Dominican Vincent Ferrer (canonized in 1455) led to violence in Valencia, where 250 Jews were slain, and to Barcelona, where 400 met the same fate.[6] Later on, Ferrer's arrogant and contemptuous crusade throughout the country in which he entered synagogues with a crucifix in one hand and a scroll of the law in the other, backed by ugly, obstreperous mobs, led to the anxious conversion of thousands of Jews who wanted to escape persecution.

While the major Jewish quarters were reduced to rubble and ashes, some of the residents found shelter from the vicious mobs in remote towns or even in castles of the nobility; but those unprotected converted to Christianity or paid for their resistance with their lives. The converted swelled the ranks of the Converso communities whose apostasy until then had been more or less voluntary and relatively insignificant in numbers. Even these New Christians were still not safe among an anti-Semitic population who regarded them with suspicion and referred to them as *marranos*, a derogatory term.

The mass conversions of 1391 and shortly thereafter reduced the Jewish population of Aragón to a quarter of its former size. The *aljamas* of Barcelona, Valencia, and Mallorca had disappeared completely, and in smaller towns it was much the same. Gerona, north of Barcelona, once a thriving Jewish community, was reduced to a fraction of the former families. Nor was the situation any different in the cities of Castilla where, along with that of Sevilla, the Jewish ghettos of Burgos and Valladolid, among others, were destroyed.

A Castillian decree issued in 1412, motivated by Vincent Ferrer and others, deprived Jews of the benefit to hold office or possess titles while at the same time preventing them from changing their domicile. For good measure they were excluded from the trades of grocer, carpenter, tailor, and butcher, and they were prohibited from bearing arms or employing Christians to work for them. The ban went further: They were restricted from eating, drinking, bathing, or even talking with Christians. In some places they were required to wear, as in Arles some years before, a yellow patch four fingers wide on the front of their garments (a device employed in the twentieth century by the Nazis). Easily identified as

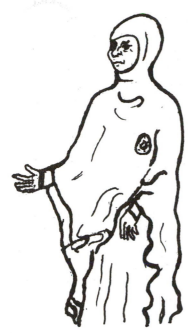

Jew with identifying patch.

Jews, they were constantly insulted in public. This widespread and excessive legislation was unenforceable, however, and was largely ignored.

DEBATES IN TORTOSA, 1413

In February 1413 Jewish communities were ordered to send delegates to the town of Tortosa, ostensibly to debate the merits of Christianity and Judaism. The conference was organized by Ferrer and attended by the Aragonese pope, Benedict XIII.

Besides the pope, cardinals, archbishops, and bishops were there in great numbers, dressed in gold vestments, along with nobles and burghers in all their finery. The pageantry went on until November 1414 and was less a debate than a series of lectures on the virtues of Christianity and a condemnation of the Jews. It was meant to intimidate Jewish leaders and was successful. The chief spokesman for Christianity was the learned and brilliant Converso Gerónimo de Santa Fé (Joshua ha-Loqui converted by Ferrer in 1412). The Jews had no outstanding speakers, but little difference would have resulted since the conference was not meant to listen to them but to instill the values of the "true faith." During the debates some key members of prominent Jewish houses, such as the Caballería, Benveniste, and Bonifos, converted and entered the king's service. When the news spread that the Jewish delegates had been soundly defeated in the discussions and influential Jews had converted, there was another rush throughout the country to undergo baptism.

On the brighter side the new king of Aragón, Alfonso V, who ascended the throne in 1416, taking advice from the now Christian Caballería family, reversed anti-Jewish legislation initiated by Ferrer. The Aragonese crown protected the Jews and Conversos from scurrilous attacks for the next seven decades. This was not the case elsewhere.

TOLEDO

An attack on the dwelling of a Converso tax collector in Castilla's then-leading city Toledo was followed by a more general assault on the large Converso community of the city. The leaders of the uprising, Pero Sarmiento and Marcos de García Mora, incited mobs to riot and issued a statute (*Sentencia-Estatuto*) in 1449 forbidding Conversos to hold public office due to their Jewish ancestry. The ordinances were based upon *limpieza de sangre*, and the preamble read:

We declare the so-called *conversos*, offspring of perverse Jewish ancestors, must be held by law to be infamous and ignominious, unfit, and unworthy to hold any public office or any benefice within the city of Toledo, or land within its jurisdiction, or to be commissioners for oaths or notaries, or to have any authority over the true Christians of the Holy Catholic Church.[7]

As Conversos were Christians, religion had become almost irrelevant; racism was paramount. Condemned by Pope Nicholas V, the Toledo statutes were, nevertheless, approved by the king in 1451. A century later *limpieza de sangre* was an official requirement to public office, and descendants of Jews were barred in many places from positions of authority in the church, universities, the municipalities, and the army, although once again such edicts were to a large extent ignored except by the most zealous anti-Semites.

TAX COLLECTORS

To travel the dusty or rain-soaked roads of the countryside from village to village, demanding taxes owed, or knocking on the door of an upper-class urban dwelling to inquire why the occupant had not paid his due to the crown treasury, was not a desirable occupation. It was not unknown for a tax collector to go out on the job in a remote corner of the country and never return. No doubt a few absconded with the king's money, but others were murdered, occasionally by bandits, more often by the subject of the inquiry. The tax collector was universally hated, and not everyone was willing to undertake the task. An added danger lay in the bookkeeping. If the accounts did not tally and the money came up short, the collector had to make up the difference. It was a hanging offense to cheat the king. This was a job still open to Jews, however, and with few other options, many took it. In the city of Burgos it was reported in 1367 that collecting of revenues was farmed out to Jews because no one else bid for it. Still, the number of Jewish tax collectors overall was not large in proportion to the number of Christians who did the same job.

PERSECUTION OF CONVERSOS

In 1465, a manifesto drawn up by a group of aristocrats demanded the introduction of an Inquisition in Castilla. They were not so concerned with the Jews who were already suppressed but with Conversos who had similar opportunities to advance socially and economically as themselves. Short of inquisitorial tribunals, the nobles wanted the bishops to take more vigorous action to root out Conversos engaged in Judaizing, such as observing the Sabbath or other non-Christian practices.

Threatened by this demand, New Christian Conversos sometimes acted precipitously. For example, on Sunday, 19 July 1467, an armed band of Conversos entered a house of worship in Toledo during the High Mass and accused the congregation of not being true Christians. A major riot soon followed, and the anger spread to neighboring towns such as Ciudad Real. Conversos were ejected from their posts and offices. In June 1468 a royal decree confirmed all Old Christians in posts that had been seized from the Conversos themselves. The following month, the monarch granted Ciudad Real a statute banning Conversos from municipal offices. From the pulpit, preachers capitalized on such incidents.

In spite of miserable and humiliating conditions many Jews, out of religious conviction, were unwilling to become marginally better off New Christians. When, in about 1470, a Jew in the town of Calatayud, Judah Benardut, was asked why he did not convert to avoid having stones thrown at him and to stop being called a Jewish dog when he could get offices and a thousand other honors, he replied:

I . . . do not wish to become a Christian, neither for those honours nor in order to escape insults. I hold fast to my religion and I believe that I will be saved in it, and the more humiliations I have to endure to sustain my religion the more shall my soul be saved.[8]

While a statue of the Virgin Mary was being carried through the streets of a predominantly Converso neighborhood in Córdoba, a young girl, probably accidentally, dropped some liquid that may have been water from her balcony onto the statue. It was immediately taken as a grave insult by those below, who went on a rampage looting, wrecking, and burning Converso houses and murdering the occupants. Many Conversos fled the city for safer country towns, whereas others left the country by ship for foreign lands. Tension ran high and rumors were rife. It was said that Jewish doctors kept a special poison in their fingernails to kill Christian patients and that Jews kidnapped and killed Christian children in order to drink their blood. The fact that Jewish dietary laws as set out in the book of Leviticus in the Torah (the Jewish Bible) condemn the consumption of any kind of blood seems not to have been sufficient to deter that which the Christian populace wanted to believe. Rumor, gossip, and hearsay were important ingredients to arouse the wrath of Gentiles against Jews. The Black Death was thought to be brought on by Jewish curses or poisoning of the water.

When Isabella succeeded to the throne of Castilla the religious climate was such that an Inquisition, at least in the minds of many, might bring some harmony to the turbulent situation. Jews and Conversos of the court were in favor of the marriage between Isabella and Fernando, hoping it would bring a more stable government and consequently less persecution. The expectation was at first fulfilled as the Catholic Kings gradually restored order to the two kingdoms. They protected the Jews and took their side in civil disorders against them. When Bilbao prohibited Jews from spending the night within its walls, they intervened on behalf of the Jews. Isabella, in fact, stated in 1477 that all the Jews in her realm were hers and under her care and protection, and it belonged to her to defend and aid them and keep justice.[9]

Nevertheless, the Catholic Kings became alarmed by constant reports of the alleged Judaizing activities of Conversos. Priests in Sevilla climbed the tower of the Cathedral on Saturdays to look out over the city in order to see which chimneys did not issue forth smoke, a sure sign that the Sabbath was being observed in the house. Alonso de Hojeda warned Isabella repeatedly of numerous relapses into Jewishness, asserting that only an Inquisition could put an end to it, and he had his way. The Inquisition was initiated by the crown to halt the perceived threat to Christian unity.

EXPULSIONS WITHIN SPAIN

Isabella and Fernando were persuaded by church leaders and the Inquisition that the separation of Jews from Christians was the only solution to prevent the New Christian Conversos from indulging in Judaic rituals. In order to minimize contact between the two groups, Jews were expelled in 1483–1484 from the dioceses of Sevilla, Córdoba, and Cádiz but allowed to settle in other areas of the country. At the time royal troops were engaged in a war with the Muslim kingdom of Granada, which may also partially account for the expulsions through fear of Jewish collaboration with the enemy. Typically, the expulsions were erratic, poorly coordinated, and never fully carried out. Nevertheless, the Jewish communities were kept in a constant state of anxiety wondering what would happen to them next. In 1486 the Inquisition issued an order expelling Jews from some dioceses of Aragón, such as Zaragoza. It was then postponed and finally rescinded, but some towns, ignoring the crown, carried out their own expulsions.

After some ten years the local expulsions had failed to stem the alleged heresies of the Conversos, and the Catholic Kings now became even more convinced by the arguments of various Christian prelates of the need to separate Jews and Christians. In spite of previous efforts to protect the rights of Jews, they now initiated the most dramatic expedient of all to solve the problem of Jewish influence on the New Christians—a total expulsion of all Jews from the entire country.

In 1491 the matter of expulsion was given more urgency by the alleged ritual murder of a young Christian boy at La Guardia in the province of Toledo. Many unauthenticated stories circulated about Jewish conspiracies and atrocities against Christians, but this one inflamed the imagination of all. A Converso, Benito García, according to the story, had been arrested with a holy wafer in his knapsack. Under torture he revealed the names of others, who were promptly taken into custody. The six Jews and five Conversos involved were accused of kidnapping and crucifying a Christian child on the eve of Passover and cutting out his heart to be ground up and mixed with a holy wafer, which, according to the accusation, they would use to poison the Christian water supply throughout the land.[10]

After a prolonged trial and torture by the Inquisition in which Torquemada took a personal interest, the culprits "confessed" and were burned or strangled at the stake in Avila. Three who had already died in prison were burned in effigy. No missing child was ever reported; no remains or grave was ever found. It was assumed by the Christian populace that the little martyr had been taken directly to heaven. At the moment of his death, his blind mother supposedly regained her sight, adding another miracle to the story.

With the fall of Granada to the Christians on the second day of 1492, the time was ripe for the order of expulsion, well prepared by vicious rumors of Jewish crimes. Thus, while Isabella and Fernando's tolerance of Jews and Conversos was well known, they succumbed to the anti-Semitic strain that manifested itself in atrocities against Jews in various cities and to the extreme zeal of prelates of the Christian church.

EXPULSION FROM SPAIN

On 31 March 1492, the edict of expulsion was issued by the royal couple from Granada. It gave the Jews of both realms, Castilla and Aragón, until 31 July to accept baptism or leave the country. The decree gave as justification the "great harm" suffered by New Christians or Conversos, by contact, intercourse, and communication with Jews who, it claimed, attempted to seduce faithful Christians from the Holy Catholic Church.

When the news spread, a deputation of Jews led by Isaac Abravanel, the chief Jewish spokesman, solicited and received an audience with the king. Their pleas were not successful, and so at a second meeting they offered Fernando a large sum of money to reconsider and allow them to remain in Spain. At a subsequent meeting between the king and the Jewish delegation, Fernando was adamant. He was determined to be rid of them, and the queen supported his decision.

While the ultimate decision and responsibility for the ousting of the Jews rested with Fernando and Isabella, the proposal to expel them from the country came originally from the Inquisition, as stated by Fernando in a letter he sent to the duke of Aranda.

The Holy Office of the Inquisition, seeing how some Christians are endangered by contact and communication with the Jews, has provided that the Jews be expelled from all our realms and territories, and has persuaded us to give our support and agreement to this, which we now do, because of our debts and obligations to the said Holy Office: and we do so despite the great harm to ourselves, seeking and preferring the salvation of souls above our own profit and that of individuals.[11]

Not all Jews were under the jurisdiction of the crown, but the king explained to the nobles, for example, to the Catalan duke of Cordona, who had assumed that his Jews were not included in the edict, and to the duke of Alba in Salamanca, that everyone was to be expelled. The nobility could compensate themselves for the loss by acquisition of Jewish property.

The monarchs may have thought that most Jews would prefer conversion to exile. The rabbi of Córdoba had undergone baptism in May not long after the expulsion order, setting an example, and in June the chief judge of the *aljamas* and treasurer of the crown, the eighty-year-old Abraham Seneor, had followed the same path in Guadalupe with the two monarchs in attendance. He had rendered faithful service to the crown and was soon made city councilor of his home town, Segovia, and appointed to the royal council. Isaac Abravanel, his friend and colleague, remaining faithful to his beliefs, began the dismal negotiations for the process of emigration.

No exact figures for the number of people expelled from Spain are available, but recent research, based on tax returns in the Jewish communities, places the total number of Jews in Spain in 1492 at over 80,000. There seems to have been somewhat less than that number in Castilla, about 9,000 in Aragón, in the province of Valencia about 1,000 (almost all in the town of Sagunto), and in Navarra about 250 families.[12] Many of these converted and did not depart the country. The richer Jews often helped others who were less wealthy to undergo the journey into exile, whereas the very poor, very old, or infirm had little choice but to convert. Many who could not bear to lose all they had worked for also submitted to the Catholic Church. About half of the Jewish population became New Christians.

It was useless for Jews destined for exile to sell their valuables or other possessions for gold and silver since they were forbidden to take these metals out of the country. They traded houses and property for a mule to carry them to the ports of embarkation and a vineyard for a little cloth or linen. Thousands walked along the hot dusty roads with no idea where they might go once they reached the ports or the frontier of Portugal. They left by cart, on foot, on the backs of donkeys or mules; some were born on the roads—others died there; they were mugged, fell from sickness; and all who saw them exhorted them to convert to Christianity to save their souls.

Some wealthy Jews who could pay for favors managed to take their portable possessions (including jewels) with them. A few, such as Abravanel who had done service for the king, were allowed to take their personal wealth. But most took only what was allowed and transferred their assets to Conversos, especially relatives. Individuals and corporations that owed money to Jews benefited largely from the deportations.

Where to go was a major problem. About 10,000 set out for Italy. Most Italian cities barred them from entering, but others such as the town of Ferrara had more enlightened rulers and gave them shelter. Those that found refuge in Naples or Venice were later expelled, and even Ferrara eventually turned on them. Livorno was an exception and allowed them to remain.

Many Jews from Castilla went to Portugal and were allowed a stay of eight months for a hefty fee. Those arriving and unable to pay for the permit were sold into slavery. Those who chose Portugal were engulfed in a double tragedy, for five years later they were given the same options—conversion or exile. Some Spanish Jews went to the then-independent state of Navarra where they were accepted but only for a short time before forced conversions were enacted there.

Some Jews from Andalucía crossed the Mediterranean to North Africa, but there are no records as to how many succumbed en route or were lost at sea. Once word circulated that the tens of thousands of Jews were searching for a new homeland, boats and their captains from Genoa, Venice, Naples, North Africa, and Spanish ports gathered at the points of embarkation like hovering vultures to take on board the refugees who paid dearly for passage. The captains of the ships crowded them on the decks in unseaworthy numbers and then, too often, tried to sell their passengers to the Barbary pirates as slaves and seize their belongings. The ships they boarded were not only overcrowded but filthy and dangerous. When they reached the open sea, some were driven back by storms, forcing hundreds to accept baptism and remain. Other overloaded ships capsized, and their passengers drowned. Some perished on ill-managed ships engulfed in flames. In some cases, when sickness broke out the captains abandoned the ships and left the passengers to die of thirst or hunger on the high seas or cast them on deserted shores where a similar fate awaited them. Jews arrived in North Africa only to be robbed and murdered on the beaches or in the port towns for their few possessions. Some returned willingly from the strange, inhospitable land to the home they knew and accepted their new status as Conversos.

Independent sheiks of the North African coast who let them come ashore denied them access to the interior, but the king of Fez allowed them to settle outside the city walls and many headed there. But many who set out for the safe haven of Fez were robbed and beaten on the way. Some Jews made it to Oran and managed to settle in.

More than a few coastal cities closed the gates to Jews for fear of the plague, which was again appearing on the scene. On 29 August 1492 nine caravels with plague-ridden Jewish passengers put into the Bay of Naples after sailing from port to port where they were refused entry. Witnesses reported they appeared like skeletons out of hell. Some reached Marseilles in France, where the local community of resettled Jews had to buy them from the ship's captain who threatened to sell them to pirates.

Conditions were bad enough in North Africa and some places in Italy that many wandered on toward the east to find shelter in the Ottoman Empire. They were welcomed in the Turkish lands where their talents were appreciated. Many arrived in Salonika to mingle with Turks, Greeks, and Jews already living there and were cordially received. Others went on to Istanbul.

The refugees all had in common terrible suffering both physical and psychological, and almost wherever they went they found exploitation, maltreatment, or indifference. Those that left Spain never to return seem to have numbered about 40,000. How many of them died along the way will never be known. Exiles who did go back had their property restored if they converted. In at least one case in Ciudad Real an official was obliged to return some houses that he had bought at bargain prices when the deportee reappeared.

CONVERSO WOMEN

Conversos who secretly practiced Jewish rites but lived openly as Catholics were known as Crypto-Jews or secret Jews. They kept holy days, especially Yom Kippur, baked unleavened bread at Passover, and slaughtered animals according to Jewish dietary laws. Women performed ritual slaughter of fowl. They would not use the local abattoir (slaughterhouse) of the town or buy meat from the local butcher. On Fridays before the beginning of the Sabbath, Jewish women would put a vessel full of water on the window sill so the wandering soul could come and cool itself.[13] These and other religious activities aroused the suspicions of the Old Christians and the Inquisition.

Because Jewish men were afforded a wider range of commercial, business, and social opportunities through conversion, they were less likely to remain loyal to their original beliefs than their women.

Converso women in the postexpulsion period played a large role in the perpetuation of Judaism. With no Jewish community left in Spain to provide rabbis, teachers, schools, and texts, the family and the home became the center of Crypto-Jewish activity. The women taught their children Jewish rites and prayers, maintained the dietary laws and the Sabbath, and celebrated Passover as best they could. Some suffered torture, life in prison, and even burning at the stake when household servants reported the non-Christian irregularities of their employers or neighbors suspected unusual activity and reported it to the Inquisition.

Converted Jewish women (Conversas), practicing Crypto-Judaism, were sometimes caught up in mystical experiences involving visions and messianic prophecies. Mari Gómez of Chillon and a twelve-year-old girl, Inés of Herrera, claimed to have seen prophetic visions. The news created heightened excitement in the Converso communities of Extremadura and La Mancha. Between 1499 and 1502 the visionaries inspired a renewal of Jewish observances with special emphasis on fasting and an intense expectation of the arrival of the prophet Elijah and the Messiah, heralding a return to the Promised Land. The movement and its optimism were quickly extinguished by the Inquisition, and little Inés was burned at the stake while Mari managed to flee to Portugal.[14]

Slender was the proof needed by the Inquisition to convict a Converso of being a Crypto-Jew. Avoidance of pork (in keeping with Jewish dietary laws), observance of the Sabbath on Saturday, killing of fowl according to Jewish rituals, keeping of fasts on Jewish fast days, eating meat during Lent—all such lapses were eagerly reported to the tribunals by Old Christians who kept careful watch on their neighbors.

Elvira del Campo, of Converso descent, was tried at Toledo in 1567. She gave all the outward signs of being a good Christian, going to Mass and Confession, and was kind and charitable. But she would not eat pork and handled it with a rag when she cooked it for the household and her husband, an Old Christian. She justified this by saying pork disagreed with her, and handling it made her hands smell bad. The chief witnesses against her were two of her husband's employees who lived in the house. Since she was unwilling to confess any wrongdoing, she was strapped naked on the rack and stretched in order for the inquisitors to learn more about her Jewish behavior. Days were allowed to pass between sessions so the joints would stiffen and the next bout became more painful. She was also subjected to the *toca*. All the while, as recorded by the notary, she repeatedly begged to be allowed to confess but didn't know what to say. If told what to say she would say it. Ultimately she confessed to Judaism, repented, and was reconciled with the Catholic Church.[15]

Age was not a factor. According to inquisitional records, girls and boys as young as eleven and twelve were sentenced to life in prison for observing Jewish rites.[16] The oldest of the victims in Spain appears to have been María Barbara Carillo, who was burned alive at Madrid in 1721 at age ninety-six.[17]

The Inquisition had a long memory. In 1485 Gómez García confessed to observing Yom Kippur (day of atonement in Judaism), removing fat from meat, wearing a clean shirt on the Sabbath, and allowing his wife and daughters to follow Jewish laws. His wife confessed to the same observances. The eldest daughter, Mayor, who was thirty years old at the time of her parents' confessions and reconciliation to the church, admitted she had fasted on Yom Kippur and had seen her mother and sisters light candles on the Sabbath. She said she gave up Jewish practices when she married in 1479.

The Inquisition recalled Mayor in 1530 when she was seventy-five years old and accused her of giving false testimony and of observing Jewish law after she married. Mayor was subjected to torture to discern the truth. She revealed nothing and was not severely prosecuted.[18]

Until 1570 in Lima and 1571 in Mexico there were no tribunals of the Inquisition, a fact that made these and other places in the Americas desirable destinations for people of Jewish origin. Castillian laws prohibited mass migrations of Conversos to the New World, but many individuals managed to secure passage.

NOTES

1. Persecution is evident in the works of the greatest churchmen of the day, Saint Isidore of Sevilla, for example, and by the laws enacted by various Visigothic kings. For more detail, see Lea, *History*, 1: 39ff.

2. Kamen, *The Spanish Inquisition*, 8. See also Angus Mackay, "The Jews in Spain during the Middle Ages," in Kedourie, chapter 1.

3. Neuman, 1: 185–190.

4. Ibid., 1: 34.

5. Lea, *History*, 103.

6. Kamen, *The Spanish Inquisition*, 10.

7. Gerber, 127.

8. "Towards Expulsion 1391–1492," in Kedourie, 56.

9. Kamen, *The Spanish Inquisition*, 16.

10. Lea, *History*, 1: 134.

11. Kamen, *The Spanish Inquisition*, 21.

12. Haim Beinhart, "The Conversos and Their Fate," in Kedourie, 110.

13. Ibid., 23.

14. Baskin, 127–128.

15. Lea, *History*, 3: 24, 233.

16. Ibid., 3: 161, for cases of incarceration of children.

17. Roth, 126.

18. Le Beau and Mor, 24–25.

7

Muslims and Moriscos

With the termination of the 1482–1492 war with Granada, the Moorish Nasrid dynasty of King Boabdil, the last of the Iberian Islamic states, was no more. By the conditions of the surrender the inhabitants were allowed to remain, keep their houses and other possessions, abide by their own laws and religion, and pay no extra taxes. A few thousand, including Boabdil, departed for North Africa, but the majority stayed on.

The period of tranquility in Granada lasted only half a dozen years before the promise made by the Catholic Kings, who had assured the Muslims freedom of worship, was broken. In 1499, transforming the mosque into a Catholic church, the zealot archbishop Jiménez de Cisneros began a program of conversion through intimidation, persecution, and bribery. Muslims soon lined up at the baptismal font. As pressure increased, those wishing to convert turned into a deluge that was baptized by water hurled from a large mop revolving overhead. Converted Muslims, like the converted Jews, referred to as New Christians, were commonly called Moriscos in reference to their Moorish North African background. Cisneros held the view that all Muslims should be converted and enslaved. Although once baptized, Moriscos were promised the same privileges as Christians, they were not allowed to carry arms and were continually coerced to abandon their traditional colorful clothes, music, dances, and eating habits.

In 1501, the aggressive archbishop, armed with a royal decree, gathered up all the Arabic books he could find, including the Koran, flung them into a gigantic pile in the public square, and set fire to them. Om-

Muslim resident of Granada.

inous threats were issued to those who had not yet come forward to give up Islam, while overt objection to the policy was met with a trip to the local prison.

With Granada now in the Christian fold, Queen Isabella was not inclined to abide Muslims in the rest of her realm. In 1502 a royal edict proclaimed either baptism or exile for all Muslims in Castilla. Several hundred of those of the Islamic faith who could pay the large sums of money required left for North Africa, whereas the remainder submitted and became, at least nominally, Christians. The Islamic religion now no longer existed officially in Castilla, but such was not the case in Aragón where Muslims were still permitted to follow the teaching of Mohammed. By far the largest numbers of remaining Mudéjares (Muslims under Christian domination) inhabited the old kingdom of Valencia where they made up about a third of the total population. A few converted to Christianity, and some prelates made great efforts to baptize others; but on the whole they remained true to their faith.

Besides involvement in agriculture, Moriscos and Mudéjares made their living from handicrafts, cartage or transport using donkeys or mules, and small-scale commerce. There were a few wealthy traders, but generally the people were poor and illiterate. Popular prejudice against Moriscos was rampant and reinforced by men of the church such as Juan de Ribera, archbishop of Valencia who, after a period of concern about

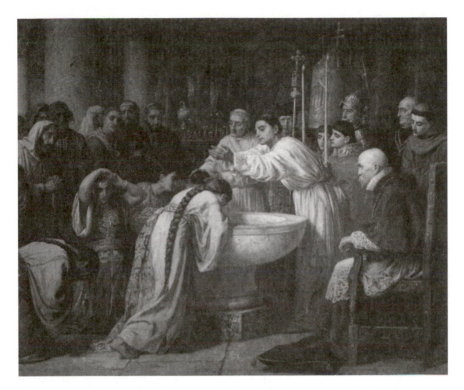

Edwin Long. *The Moorish Proselytes of Archbishop Ximenes, Granada, 1500.* (Russell-Cotes Art Gallery and Museum, Bournemouth).

Morisco welfare, turned into their implacable enemy. Their cheap labor was one of the major grievances that stimulated popular enmity, and he accused them of working for smaller wages and hence costing Old Christians jobs. They were accused of amassing money but spending little. They bought no bread, wine, or meat, depriving the king and local communities of excise taxes that then fell more heavily on Old Christians. Moriscos were also denounced because they did not put their children in religious schools and paid nothing for their education. More threatening had been the rapid rise in Morisco population, generally outstripping population growth among the Old Christians, partially a consequence of the fact that Morisco girls married at a younger age than the daughters of the Old Christians. The bishop of Segorbe, Martín Salvatierra, had wished to solve this vexing question by castrating Moriscos; others suggested forbidding marriage. Population increases were also due to the fact that the men did not serve in the army where fatalities were often great, and neither did they emigrate to the Indies, as did many young Christian men. For some Old Christians, the country was being peopled with heretics, overwhelming the faithful.

Ostracism from hostile Christian society forced Moriscos to adhere more strongly to their own customs and to marry within their own group. At baptism they took Christian names as required but continued to use Muslim names in private. They attended the compulsory Catholic Mass without enthusiasm and often preferred to die without the Christian sacraments, calling for the priest too late, asserting the death had been sudden.

The majority of Mudéjares still living in Aragón and Valencia consisted of peasants who were tied to a harsh semifeudal regime and who supported their Christian noble masters with their toil. In return, they were given protection from arbitrary legislation and from the hatred and violent acts of the intolerant populace. In short, the power of the landed aristocracy that relied on cheap Mudéjar labor on their estates maintained the status quo. To placate them, Fernando ordered the Inquisition of Aragón not to resort to forced conversion.

In 1520, class conflict among Old Christians arose in Valencia between urban bourgeois and artisans, on the one hand, and the aristocracy, on the other, resulting in open warfare. The urban rebels terrorized the Mudéjar vassals on the estates of the nobles and forced thousands of them into mass baptism. This in effect freed the vassals, now New Christians, from their lords, constituting an attack on aristocratic power.

The insurgents lost the struggle with the intervention of royal troops, but the Moriscos (as the vassals had now become) were not allowed to revert to Islam. Obligatory baptism was invalid in the minds of some people, but church authorities and especially the Inquisition argued that compulsion to convert had not occurred since the Mudéjares had a free choice; they could have chosen death over conversion, hence baptism was valid. Like the Muslims of Granada, followed by those of Castilla, many of those of Valencia were now officially New Christians or Moriscos. The net was about to be cast wider.

In 1525, in spite of continued objections of Aragonese nobles to the arbitrary treatment of their vassals, Carlos I issued a decree ordering the conversion of all Mudéjares remaining in Valencia and all those under the crown of Aragón by the following year. By 1526 there were no longer any official followers of Islam in Spain. All Mudéjares (or Muslims) were now Moriscos (or New Christians).

When Carlos I visited Granada in 1526 he was informed that numerous Moriscos still adhered to the Muslim faith and in the years since their conversion almost none became true Christians. In both Granada and Valencia they tenaciously held on to their beliefs and customs. Old Christians were irritated by this persistence in which Moriscos still slaughtered their animals ritualistically for meat; did not eat pork, as was the Spanish custom, nor drink wine; and cooked with olive oil instead of lard or butter. They still said their Muslim prayers and observed fasts and ablutions and the practice of circumcision.

In 1526 Morisco leaders in Valencia managed to obtain from Carlos I and from Inquisitor General Alfonso Manrique, cardinal and archbishop of Sevilla, a secret agreement by which, in return for a substantial amount of money, the Moriscos would be free of inquisitorial interference for forty years. Meanwhile, in the same year, the authorities convoked an assembly in Granada to deal with the problem there. The cultural features of the Moriscos were assailed: their style of dress condemned along with the use of the Arabic language and Arabic names.

In 1533 the Cortes of Aragón meeting at Monzón a little northeast of Zaragoza raised objections that the Inquisition confiscated lands of the Moriscos who it found guilty of backsliding to the detriment of the feudal owners who had leased the land to them in the first place. The Inquisition mostly ignored the complaints. Fearful of losing their vassals, the nobility of Aragón persuaded the Inquisition in 1556 to allow the Moriscos to pay an annual tax to the tribunal of Zaragoza, provided that their property would not be seized due to a conviction for heresy. All benefited. The Inquisition received an annual income, the Moriscos preserved the property for their progeny, and the landowners retained their leases.

In some places where Moriscos owned land, local authorities demanded that they show proof of ownership; if they could produce none, they were fined. If they could not pay the fine, the land was confiscated and sold. Thousands of hectares passed into the hands of Christian officials in this manner. Similarly, Moriscos also lost their silk manufacturing businesses to Christians, causing many to become destitute. But there was worse to come.

Churchmen considered cultural differences between Christians and Moriscos the leading cause of preventing effective assimilation, and when the forty-year grace period allowed by Carlos I neared expiration and the Moriscos of Valencia sought to renew the agreement, Felipe II, now on the throne, refused. In 1565, when the clergy held a synod in Granada, they advised the king that patient and gradual evangelization of Moriscos was ill-advised, and drastic measures should be taken.

A royal decree published in 1567 prohibited the Moriscos from using any language other than Castillian, from performing their traditional dances and wearing traditional dress, reading their own literature, and from observing any rites they had followed in the past. Frequent bathing was considered unchristian and could only be associated with Muslims and Jews. In 1576 Felipe II banned the public baths, until then found in the smallest of the Moorish towns, for to bathe was clear evidence of apostasy. Inquisitional records often show the phrase "the accused was known to take baths."[1]

Spanish monks, according to their practice of establishing principles opposite to the infidel, considered physical dirt as the test of moral purity and true faith. By dining and sleeping year in and year out in the same unchanged woolen frock, they arrived at the height of their ambition—the odor of sanctity.[2]

Muslim houses were to be kept open on feast days (Fridays and Saturdays) and during weddings to prevent non-Christian ceremonies. Muslim women were forbidden to appear in the streets veiled, as was their custom. Morisco leaders protested, to no avail. Instead they were confronted with severe penalties for anyone who defied the new laws. Ruthless persistence to eradicate all traces of Islamic beliefs and customs finally led to a bloody confrontation in Granada.

REBELLION OF 1568

It seemed to the Christian authorities that a national threat was at hand. Moriscos had connections with both Morocco and Turkey, the great Islamic enemies of Christendom, and prophecies of doom foretold another conquest of Spain by the followers of Mohammed. Muslim bandits were thought to circulate in the mountains along the eastern seaboard of the country, giving shelter and succor to North African pirates along the coast. An attempt to disarm the rural Moriscos met with little success, and tensions grew, finally erupting in a massive rebellion on Christmas Eve, 1568.

The hopeless state of affairs for the Moriscos is clear from their desperate act of defiance. Led by the wealthy Aben Humeya (his pseudonym), a town councilor of Granada, at the time under house arrest for pulling out a dagger in council, the villages of the mountainous Alpujarras, south and east of the city of Granada, broke into open warfare, although there was little support from the Morisco quarter of the city of Granada, which was tightly controlled by Christian officials.

Numbering only about 4,000 men at the beginning, the insurgents murdered the few Christian families and priests who lived in their villages and smashed and burned churches and sacred images. The rebel forces quickly grew to about 30,000. Aben Humeya was himself killed by rivals, but the struggle spread, and for two years the region was inflamed in warfare.

The government lacked trained soldiers on hand to stem the uprising in the Alpujarras, so the great lords of the realm were ordered to mobilize their vassals and the towns to assemble their militias. The irregular Christian forces were a far cry from the caliber of the elite Spanish troops away in Flanders and Italy, and the skirmishes, sieges, and atrocities ranging over the vast and trackless mountains of the Sierra Nevada dragged on. The twenty-three-year-old Don Juan of Austria, the illegitimate half brother of Felipe II, was sent to quell the uprising with about 20,000 soldiers mustered in short order. The fighting was fierce and bloody. The little town of Galera northeast of Granada bravely resisted the royal troops, but when it fell, the 2,500 or so inhabitants were slaughtered down to the last baby. The town was razed to the ground and the earth salted to prevent future settlement and farming.

The king gave the royal troops the right to plunder at will (*campo blanco*), adding fuel to the conflagration. Everything of value was looted, stolen, or destroyed. Quests for bales of silk, animals, money, jewels, and slaves by marauding soldiers became routine wartime activities. Moriscos sold their prisoners to the Barbary pirates at Saldas near Almería, often trading them for a musket, while the militiamen gathered their prisoners, now slaves, in the city of Granada to sell or trade. The Moriscos in the city lived in anguish in expectation of an Old Christian descent on their homes and the loss of their property and their lives as the entire region remained gripped in fear and hatred.

Don Juan went about his task with grim efficiency, but even before the brutal battles began to wind down with mass surrenders of Moriscos in 1570, a solution to the problem of Granada was put into practice.

To integrate Moriscos into Spanish society, Felipe II ordered them forcibly dispersed throughout Castilla, where, he hoped, they would forget their traditional ways and cease to be a threat to the Christian faith or to the security of the kingdom. On 1 November 1570 the Moriscos of Granada were assembled under guard, chained, and placed in convoys and sent north in a pathetic exodus of wagons, mules, and straggling women with babies in their arms. It has been estimated that about a quarter of these died under the deplorable conditions of their journey. Except for those bands of Moriscos sheltering in the mountains, the rebellion was effectively over, and their possessions were sold off to monasteries, noblemen, and churches at considerable profit to the royal treasury. Within the month some 50,000 Moriscos were expelled from their homes and resettled in Castilla. About 12,000 peasant families consisting of Castillians, Asturians, and Galicians now flocked southward to Granada to take over the deserted towns, villages, and houses of the former Morisco occupants. Old Christian carpetbaggers came also from other areas of Andalucía and Extremadura to collect the spoils.

According to the king's demands, the Moriscos were to mingle with the Christian population and not live in their own enclaves. Appearing in Castilla, rootless and scattered among the villages, they soon gravitated to the towns where they took up menial tasks and flocked together in their own quarters. They were still disliked by the Old Christians, and hatred was soon whipped up against them by the clergy and officials.

The expulsions continued for years, however, and Granada lost some 120,000 Moriscos. The province lay torn and desolate, about one third of the 400 towns abandoned. The Old Christian settlers lacked the technical farming skills of the previous occupants. A Jesuit priest who worked among them criticized the newcomers as shiftless and devoid of the moral attributes of the previous population.

In their new homes the Moriscos became an unassimilated minority among suspicious, hostile neighbors. Whereas Castilla had about 20,000 Mudéjares at the beginning of the sixteenth century, by the end, there were roughly 100,000 Moriscos. The tensions and conflicts between Old Christians and former Muslims that were once mostly restricted to the south of the peninsula were now widespread throughout Castilla. Co-existence was often shattered by violent incidents between the two communities. In a few cases around Valladolid, Moriscos turned to banditry. The problem of Granada, as perceived by the authorities, had now shifted to become the problem of Castilla. The cities of Sevilla, Toledo, Córdoba, and Avila began to experience the enmity and jealousy of the Old Christians as some Moriscos were becoming rich through hard work and skill in commerce. Before, this had been mostly absent. Open rejoicing by Moriscos upon the news of the total destruction of the Portuguese army in Morocco led to violent confrontations with Old Christians. Tensions increased when a subversive plot was uncovered in Sevilla among Moriscos and their accomplices in Morocco advocating an invasion and later when Moriscos were found to be plotting with Protestants in France.

EVENTS IN TOLEDO

The cardinal of Toledo, with a seat on the Council of State, passed on to the council the views of Juan de Carillo, the commissioner of the Inquisition of Toledo. It was reported that the colony of Moriscos in that city had been heavily reinforced by the refugees from Granada in 1570 who brought their Islamic beliefs, their bitterness, and their hatred of Castilla with them and continued to speak Arabic among themselves. They never went to Mass, never accompanied the holy sacraments through the streets, and were only prompted to go to confession through fear of sanctions against them. They married exclusively among themselves and hid their children to avoid having them baptized. Circumcision was common, and *alfaquís*, Muslim clergy, still moved about among the inhabitants. Extreme Unction was seldom requested. Many Old Christians felt that the Council of State must act quickly against the rapidly multiplying nonbelievers.

Anathema for many Moriscos were the doctrines of the Trinity, the divinity of Christ, and the sacraments of Baptism, Penitence, and the Eucharist. Many loathed the priests and maintained the practices of Islam such as prayers toward Mecca, Ramadan (the holy month of fasting ordained by the Koran), ritual ablutions, and certain dietary restrictions.

The statutes of the *limpieza de sangre* were applied to the Moriscos as they were to the Conversos. By the latter half of the sixteenth century, Moriscos could not become Familiars of the Inquisition, and they could not enter the priesthood, no matter how good a Christian they were. They were denied access to public positions and professions (a very few became doctors) and hence to any sort of status. Many turned to commerce and industry, the few avenues left open to them, but the vast majority of those in the region of Aragón were poor peasants. A precious few in Granada and Castilla were well off and some even rich, but even so, it may be surmised that they lived anxious lives in fear of the unheralded and dreaded knock on the door by the Familiars.

In remote areas, Moriscos were able to establish thriving communities such as in Hornachos in Extremadura, a town of 4,800 people in 1580. Ten years later, in 1590, the town purchased its own jurisdiction from Felipe II. It was tolerated by its neighbors, and the occupants prospered and some even grew wealthy.

On 29 November 1588, the Council of State acted on the advice of the cardinal of Toledo. The Inquisitors were ordered to make all inquiries possible about Moriscos and draw up a census of Morisco inhabitants throughout the country. Citizens of Sevilla expressed fears that the numerous Morisco enemy within would give assistance to the English who were raiding Spanish Atlantic coasts in 1589, while in Valencia the Old Christian inhabitants of the city were concerned about continued Morisco contacts with Muslim pirates and raiders along the coast. In 1590, the king was presented with several proposals.

One of them was to subject the Moriscos to serve in the galleys, with pay, for a period of time to be determined. Such a measure would inhibit their high birthrate. A more radical proposal by the marquis of Denia advocated that all males between ages fifteen and sixty be sent to the galleys for life, the women and old men shipped off to North Africa, and young children kept in Spain for a proper Christian education.

Another proposal separated the Morisco children from their parents, to be raised in noble families or by the church or even by artisans to ensure a good Christian upbringing. It was also a consideration to send those from Granada back to that region in order to remove them from Toledo, which was so near the heart of the realm. They should also be forced to live in the countryside away from towns, and the most dangerous of them would be executed. Another option was total expulsion from Spain. This drastic measure had worked against the Jews and had even brought the Catholic Kings acclaim from other European states and from Rome. It would clearly solve all these problems at once.

MORISCOS AND THE INQUISITION

The Inquisition had a new target besides the Conversos, but Moriscos were not often wealthy, they offered little economic threat to the upper classes, and many lived in remote farming areas outside the major cities. Consequently they were not at first so readily assailed for heresy when they tended to backslide as were the converted Jews; but this was soon to change.

The tribunal of the Inquisition in Granada intensified its activity after the Morisco uprising in 1568. Out of 917 Moriscos appearing in autos de fe between 1550 and 1595, 20 were burned at the stake.[3]

Moriscos were tried, as were others, for uttering offensive statements such as that everyone should be allowed to practice their own religion. One was so bold as to say that Jews and Muslims could be saved by their own laws.[4] The views of inquisitors were not unlike those of most Spaniards of the time. They referred to the Arabic language as profane, one that tainted anything translated into it—and hence opposed a translation of the catechism or other Christian works that might be beneficial to the Moriscos in trying to cope with their new religion. To prefer water to wine or beef to pork were matters of great suspicion. Spying on one's compatriots was encouraged. A little group of Moriscos in Toledo in 1538 were arrested by the Inquisition on charges of getting together and playing their musical instruments at night and performing *zambras*, or Moorish dances. A most damning accusation was that they ate couscous, a North African dish of steamed semolina.[5] Such acts usually warranted a fine and an appearance at an auto de fe. By the time of Felipe II, sterner measures were used, and a Morisco could face severe penalties for trivial matters classified by the tribunals as heresy.

In 1591 Isabel Ruiz, a Morisca, appeared in an auto de fe for putting clean linen on the corpse of her husband and was fined 10,000 maravedís.

Bartolomé Sánchez appeared in the 1597 auto de fe on suspicion of heresy for cleanliness. He confessed to bathing and was sentenced to three years in the galleys, perpetual imprisonment, and confiscation of his property. Another Morisco, Miguel Cañete, a gardener, was tried in 1606 for washing himself in the fields where he worked. He stood steadfast under torture, but as he revealed no further information and there was nothing else against him, he was released.[6]

In early summer of 1588 in Aragón, minor outbreaks of street violence in clashes between Moriscos and Old Christians became the subject of debate in the Council of State. The king was urged not to repeat the performance of Granada twenty years before but to take drastic measures immediately.

When it was economically expedient the "sins" of the Moriscos were overlooked. As late as 1594, the king, short on gunpowder for the military, ordered the Inquisition to remove restrictions on Morisco employment in Aragón so they might be engaged in making gunpowder, one of their traditional occupations. On previous occasions, civil and religious crimes were sometimes dismissed if a qualified Morisco offender was willing to work in the silver mines of Guadalcanal or the mercury mines of Almadén.

The country was financially impotent to act with haste concerning the Moriscos. Problems with the English and French and continuing involvement in the Netherlands had a dampening effect on other proposed major enterprises. A report to Felipe II in 1596 comments on the lack of government action with regard to the unbelievers and draws the king's attention to the fact that some Moriscos had become rich, a matter that ought not to be tolerated. The report suggested the king have Francisco Toledano (the wealthiest Morisco iron merchant living in Madrid, who carried on extensive trade with the Basque country) arrested without delay. In 1599 the Council of State again took up the Morisco question, urging the king to make up his mind and do something before the realm was overrun by their increasing numbers and growing financial influence. The return of peace to Spain finally allowed the government to concentrate on the Morisco problem. The failure of cohabitation of Islam and Christianity, of Old and New Christians, was about to come to its abject end. Social and religious tensions had rendered coexistence and integration of these two cultures impossible. By the end of the sixteenth century, Morisco banditry and plots with the Turks and with Protestants, as discovered in intercepted letters, made the matter of national security urgent.

Juan de Ribera, who had made strenuous efforts to apprise the Morisco population of the ways of the church, came to support the idea of expulsion. He was backed by some high-ranking aristocrats at court, but others, concerned about the resultant economic problems from the loss of so many productive people, were not in favor of such a drastic move. The arguments went on for years. The views of the army, concerned about the military danger if the Moriscos supported a Turkish invasion on the coasts of Spain, carried weight. The attitude that finally prevailed was for expulsion. Felipe III convened a committee to look into the matter, and supported by the church, the decision was made to rid the country of this unwanted segment of the population. Considerable opposition from the nobles of Valencia who did not wish to lose their vassals failed to move the pious king or the church authorities.

EXPULSION

When Felipe III came to the throne in 1598 it was clear that many high-ranking nobles rejected expulsion of the Moriscos, such as the duke of Lerma and the king's confessor who in 1602 agreed that it would be wrong to drive baptized people into the lands of Barbary (in North Africa) where they would be forced to become Muslims once again. However, by 1609 the duke of Lerma and others had changed their minds. The aristocracy of Valencia where the duke's lands lay came to the conclusion that since Moorish rents had stagnated and costs were rising, they would support the expulsion if compensated by the acquisition of Morisco land.

On the eve of expulsion the Morisco population of Spain stood at about 319,000. More than 60 percent of them were concentrated in the southeast, with Valencia showing the greatest density of about 135,000, whereas in Aragón they formed about 20 percent of the total population with numbers of about 61,000. Moriscos in Castilla numbered about 115,000 or so.

Preparations were made in secret. Galleys were prepared; the Atlantic fleet was alerted and ships were positioned in the Mediterranean ports; and the *tercios* (army regiments) were mobilized, with some units recalled from Italy, and stationed in strategic positions around Valencia, whose Morisco inhabitants would be the first to go.

The expulsion was eventually decreed on 4 April 1609 in the Council of State and was published in Valencia in September. It exempted those certified by the parish priests as good Christians and children under the age of first four, then fourteen, whose parents consented to their remaining behind. The view of Archbishop Ribera that all Morisco children should become slaves was rejected.

The Moriscos were rounded up by the army, carted to the ports, put on waiting vessels (many of foreign origin that expected to profit from the bonanza since the Moriscos were compelled to pay their own passage), and escorted across the sea by Spanish warships to the beaches of North Africa, where they were dumped. They were allowed to take their money and jewelry, and those that made it to Tunis were reported to have been well received. Thousands of others making their way inland from Spanish-held Oran into the Barbary States were stripped of all their possessions and some murdered by marauding North African tribesmen, their women and children sold into slavery. Many more died of privation, exposure, and disease. Those who arrived at Tetuan (Morocco) clinging to their Christian faith and refusing to enter the mosques were put to death, sometimes by stoning.

Of the 25,000 or so resisting deportation, banding together in the mountains and coastal wilderness, most perished at the hands of Spanish soldiers. Some 13,000 from Aragón were sent over the Pyrenees into France, but French officials shepherded them to the port of Agde, charged them for transit duties through France, and shipped them out to Tunis after collecting fees for their sea passage.

Further decrees extended the deportation orders to the remainder of Spain, which took place in stages up to 1614 when the last stragglers were rounded up. In spite of objections of many local authorities in Aragón and Murcia, among other places, the deportations, begun in Valencia, eventually totaled close to 300,000 Moriscos.

The loss of these people was insignificant in Cataluña, Cantabria, and other northern areas where their presence had been minimal and where the expulsion passed nearly unnoticed. In the towns of Córdoba, Sevilla, and Toledo where there had been larger numbers of Moriscos, the damage to the economy was relatively severe. In the southeast it was a disaster. Valencia lost a third of its population and was faced with major economic problems. Murcia and regions of Aragón suffered similarly.

Agricultural output fell sharply with the departure of so many working hands, tax returns declined, the cost of cartage went up without some 5,000 Morisco muleteers, and even the Inquisition faced a troubling future. The tribunals of Valencia and Zaragoza complained that the loss of these people had resulted in their bankruptcy. Land once rented out to Morisco farmers and from whom they gained nearly half their income was losing money. The Spanish Inquisition had taken no overt active part in the expulsions; it had been a matter that was arrived at exclusively by a small group of court officials. Those Moriscos languishing in the cells of the Inquisition for offenses against the Catholic faith were deported. The tragedy that had begun in 1492 with the expulsion of the Jews was played out in 1609 with the banishment of the Moriscos, creating a Spain that was now uniformly orthodox in religion, even if considerably poorer in culture.

Approximately 20,000 to 25,000 Moriscos remained behind, some of whom were the wealthy and assimilated elite who, by bribes and payments, obtained special permission to stay in Spain. A few others were slaves whose owners procured exemptions for them, and a few remained illegally. The Inquisition also allowed groups of Moriscos who had shown themselves to be good Christians to stay, although religious commitment to Christianity did not always save them. A community of six towns in the Ricote valley in Murcia whose 2,500 inhabitants were true Christians, according to a special report in their favor, were nevertheless expelled.

Those who survived and settled down in North Africa soon put their skills to good use cultivating the barren land and contributing to the commerce of the cities. Some became pirates in the Mediterranean and whenever possible avenged themselves on Spanish shipping. In 1610 the Morisco inhabitants of Hornachos in Extremadura moved out en masse and reestablished their community in Morocco, where they formed a pirate base at Salé on the Atlantic coast; but later, without success, they offered to exchange the base for the right to return to their Spanish homes. There were many accounts of Moriscos in exile yearning to return to the only home they had ever known. Moriscos were forbidden to settle in America.

Spain was at long last free of the Moors, but after nine centuries of occupation, their passing left a discernible whisper throughout much of the country. Hatred, religious bigotry, and exile generated by the crime of Muslims and Moriscos in not adopting Spanish Catholic ways failed to eradicate all their roots. The thousands of Arabic words in the Spanish language, certain culinary habits, architectural masterpieces, distinctive ceramics and colored tiles, and the physical features of many Andalucians continued to speak softly of their Moorish origins.

This final act in 1609 to expunge the second of the three great cultures of Spain was, according to many Spaniards and foreigners, a barbarous decision that was denounced for generations afterward. The Inquisition had also been deprived of easy victims and had to channel more effort into inquiries concerning Old Christians who deviated from doctrine. Nonetheless, between 1615 and 1700, 9 percent of those persecuted by the Inquisition were Moriscos who had managed to avoid the expulsions, and as late as 1728 a group of wealthy Morisco families were brought before the inquisitors in Granada.

MUSLIM WOMEN

Christian and Jewish society made provision for women's attendance in the house of worship. Muslim women (Moriscas) were expected to remain at home, where they were exhorted not to appear at windows. Unmarried women were never allowed out into the streets.

Moriscas were instrumental in the survival of Islam. Like Jewish women, they carried out religious rituals at home and taught them to their children. According to inquisitorial records the Moriscas were the ones who most faithfully observed the Muslim holy month of Ramadan, wore Muslim dress while their men adopted Christian garb, and performed daily prayers. They were often accused of hiding religious books and amulets, written in Arabic, in their houses and clothes. Muslim mothers failed to report births to the local priest, although required to do this, and midwives circumcised baby boys illegally. When convicted they were whipped, imprisoned (often in convents), and at times burned at the stake. In Zaragoza the Inquisition complained that the Muslim women were worse than the men who did not drink wine or eat bacon through fear of their wives.

The Inquisition allowed marriages between Christians and Muslims as long as the Muslim spouse converted. In 1548 the Spanish crown ordered converted Muslims to marry Old Christians. At the same time the purity of blood laws mitigated against this, and Muslim men who married

Christian women often assumed the surname of the wife to disguise their ancestry.

When a member of a household fell into the clutches of the Inquisition, the other members, including children, generally soon followed since it was assumed that acts of heresy were not in isolation. Moriscos were closely watched by the Old Christian community for any backsliding and lived in perpetual anxiety, never knowing when they would be taken away for the most trivial offenses. Nineteen-year-old María Páez of Almagro[7] was arrested in 1606 and, under torture, accused all her family and friends of Muslim practices. As a result, her father, who would not confess, was burned at the stake and her mother, who confessed, was imprisoned for life. In all, 25 Moriscos of Almagro appeared in an auto de fe in nearby Toledo, of which 4 were relaxed. From 1575 to 1610 in Toledo alone, 190 Moriscos—as against 174 Conversos and 47 Protestants—were brought before the tribunal.[8]

NOTES

1. Lea, *History*, 3: 332.
2. Read, 234.
3. Kamen, *The Spanish Inquisition*, 225.
4. Ibid., 220.
5. Roth, 152.
6. Lea, *Moriscos*, 129–130, for these examples.
7. Ibid., 109.
8. Lea, *History*, 3: 331.

8

The Court

The Spanish court and the Roman Catholic Church were intricately intertwined. Monarchs proudly bore the title of Catholic Kings, and their public appearances were generally connected with religious festivals or occasions such as an auto de fe or a Mass. Royal buildings also demonstrated this symbiosis with their private chapels and sometimes monasteries. Church, Inquisition, king, and court were considered the cohesive forces that insured the country's religious, political, and social stability. Most people believed that everything was ordained by God— that everyone had a role to play in the divine scheme, from the most humble peasant to the loftiest aristocrat. The king was God's appointee to rule over a worldly court not, perhaps, very different from the celestial realm over which God ruled.

ROYAL PALACES AND RESIDENCES

Isabella and Fernando lodged in various castles and grand houses as they traversed their realms but built no new residences. In 1527 Carlos I had a royal palace constructed on the hill above Granada, destroying part of the Moorish Alhambra in the process. Its two-tiered circular, colonnaded courtyard, reminiscent of the Coliseum in Rome, was unique, but the palace was little used.

From the latter part of the sixteenth century the court maintained its permanent home in Madrid, where the palace, or *alcázar* (a fortress constructed in the fourteenth century), had been restored and made into the royal residence. It was somewhat drab, made of stone and brick, but the marble balconies lent a certain elegance. Fixing the place of residence for the court gave a permanent location to the functions of government, diplomacy, and royal entertainment.

About 500 noblemen made up the royal councils whose offices and chambers were located in the palace courtyard inside the main gate. Here, opening onto patios were the offices of the Councils of Castilla, the Indies, and Finance, among others, where important decisions affecting an empire were made. Crowds of people milled about in the courtyards all day, where food and drink were sold in booths and hawkers walked among them, displaying their wares, tenaciously dogging anyone who showed the slightest interest in their goods. Great lords and the secretaries of the ministries came and went, followed by strings of pages. Unemployed army officers waited patiently to see someone, anyone, in the Ministry of Finance to ask for a pension, whereas others were looking for a new commission. Litigants waited beside their notaries who, holding a bundle of official papers tied up in red ribbon, hoped to catch the attention of some magistrate who could do them a favor or to plead with him to expedite a court case that had been pending for years.

Young lawyers scurried about in their lace frills and ruffles, clutching their university degrees, hoping to meet some grandee or minister who might look at their papers and offer the possibility of some employment in a government office. Other aspirants sat forlornly against a wall, as they had done every day for weeks, waiting to hear their name called by a receptionist to issue them the permit they applied for and needed to import goods or export their wares, to begin a new business, or just to beg in the streets.[1]

The first and second floors of the fortress-palace were occupied by the numerous rooms of the royal apartments connected by narrow corridors and staircases. The salons were draped with splendid Flemish tapestries depicting hunting or battle scenes or displayed religious paintings by Rubens, Titian, and Veronese. Thick carpets were spread on the cold stone floors, and the table in the great dining hall was permanently set with golden goblets and exquisite hand-painted plates. Heavily curtained bedchambers let in little light to illuminate the short, uncomfortable beds covered with a massive quilt and the richly carved wooden chairs, products of the finest craftsmen in the realm.[2]

In 1563, at great cost, Felipe II commissioned the construction of a new palace incorporating a royal residence, church, monastery, library, and royal mausoleum at San Lorenzo de Escorial in the cool foothills of the Guadarrama mountains, about thirty miles northwest of Madrid. Completed in 1584, it had a somber atmosphere, for the pious king preferred a simple life of work, devotion, and frugal meals. Felipe II resided much of the time in this huge, austere, rectangular granite structure where, surrounded by monks, he worked day and night personally scrutinizing and intervening in every facet of government.[3]

To the south of the city at Aranjuez, a palatial summer residence was used by Carlos I and later kings as a hunting lodge. Destroyed by fire, it was rebuilt in 1722 by Felipe V. Completed in 1723, another royal palace was built under the direction of Felipe V at San Ildefonso, north of Madrid seven miles from Segovia. Nearby was yet another royal hunting lodge, Valsaín, destroyed by fire at the end of the seventeenth century. Isabel Farnese, queen consort of Felipe V, had a palace built in 1751 at Ríofrío near Segovia.

Only about eight miles from Madrid, the palace El Pardo was constructed on the site of an earlier fifteenth-century royal hunting lodge. It was begun in 1547 for Carlos I and completed in 1558 by Felipe II. Burned in 1604, the present building dates from the reign of Felipe III but was enlarged by Carlos III, who spent winters there hunting. It included stables for 800 horses and 1,000 mules.

These retreats in the vicinity of Madrid allowed the royal family, the courtiers, and court officials to escape the blistering summer heat of the city and amuse themselves hunting, playing cards, or relaxing in the clean air of the countryside in peaceful gardens, elegant rooms, and colorful surroundings. The frescoes, tapestries, paintings, and candelabras were the best that money could buy and far from the noisy and tiresome rabble of the city.

For amusement closer to home, El Parque del Buen Retiro (park of the good retreat), laid out by Felipe IV, adjoining a convent on the periphery of Madrid, was a favorite place for the aristocracy to idle away their time. In this park of vast dimensions another palace was constructed comprising sumptuous salons adorned with paintings of Zurbarán and Velázquez, a theater, and beautiful gardens with numerous chapels. The nobility retired here behind iron gates for garden parties and picnics among statues, trees, flowers, and fountains. Plays by the best writers of the day, such as Lope de Vega and Calderón, were performed in the theater. The gardens were enlivened by more-or-less permanent festivals where the courtiers could wander around and amuse themselves. High officials of the court spent their time designing masquerades, balls, and mock battles in which court officials performed wearing extravagant costumes. The money spent on entertainment for the nobility was prodigious, and the nonstop festivities prompted critics at the time to compare the merrymaking with the days of Nero, who fiddled while Rome burned.[4]

The king was a figure both remote and yet the center of everything. These two factors preserved his nearly sacred image. If he had ridden a horse, no one else could ever ride it.[5] If he dismissed a mistress, no one else could ever possess her, and she was sent to a convent.[6]

Velázquez. *Felipe IV Praying*. (Madrid: Prado).

ORGANIZATION OF THE COURT

In the court of 1623 under Felipe IV there were three principal functionaries to see to the king's material needs: the *mayordomo mayor*, or lord high steward, who looked after feeding and housing the royal household; the *camarero mayor*, or grand chamberlain, who organized the king's personal requirements; and the master of the horse, or *caballerizo mayor*, who attended the stables and transportation. There was also a *capellán mayor* under the direction of an archbishop to administer to the king's spiritual needs. This included the royal confessor, ten royal preachers, a few lesser clerics, and a chapel master in charge of sixty-three musicians. Among the principal servants in the service of the king were a dozen *mayordomos*, eighteen gentlemen of the household, forty-seven gentlemen to wait on his table, and ten valets.

The lord high steward, like many others, received his salary in cash and kind. His job concerned every aspect of the palace including the preservation of the buildings, the forests, and the game animals. His privileges were many and included a seat in the royal chapel in front of the grandees. He had quarters in the palace, was the custodian of the keys, and was always near the monarch. The entire staff was under his orders.

There were some 140 different duties carried out in the royal palace that revolved around the household, the kitchen, chapel, stables, cellar, and the guard, each organized and headed by a nobleman. Felipe II spent about 400,000 ducats a year on the court in his secluded and frugal palace-monastery at El Escorial. Felipe III, with his new style of monarchy, which attracted numerous parasites to court, spent 1.3 million ducats according to complaints of the Cortes in the early years of the 1600s. About 1,700 posts existed in the royal household in 1623—a far cry from the 762 under Carlos I some years before.

The court employed a hierarchy of servants and staff that worked in the kitchens as cooks, their assistants, dishwashers, and pan scrubbers, in the laundry, in the gardens, and in the stables. Wood and charcoal carriers looked after the fires, candle lighters kept their thousands of little flames burning brightly, the clock maker wound up the royal timepieces each day and repaired those that malfunctioned, and a locksmith and his helpers looked after the security of the doors and cabinets. The royal commodes had to be emptied daily, and the carpets cleaned and floors polished. Maintenance personnel groomed and fed the horses and mules and cleaned the stalls and carriages. Servants sorted and stored the mountain of food, wine, and goods delivered to the palace every day and performed a host of other services. Three companies of guards, each with about 100 soldiers, protected the royal family, its property, and servants. Some 167 officials and servants tended to the king's sporting and hunting activities.

Of more exalted position were the courtiers and barber-surgeons who personally attended the king, dancing attendance on his every move, helping him rise in the morning, wash, dress, and shave. Physicians, clerics, and justices were always present and offered advice on all matters. Grandees of the court waited on the king's table, looked after the menu and wines, inspected carpets and tapestries, and organized the fireworks displays and other entertainment. Many of these great lords of the land performed the most menial tasks about the king to remain at court and vie for his attention. They even competed for the job of handing the king his shirt when he rose from bed.

Besides the king's household there were satellite households of the queen, the princesses, and other close members of the royal family. The queen's household included eight *mayordomos*, ten matrons of honor, eighteen ladies in waiting, twelve *meninas* (daughters of noblemen), and twenty ladies of the bedchamber, all which had numerous servants. No shadow of doubt could ever be cast on the queen's behavior. Restricted by a mode of comportment, she had to maintain her lofty dignity at all times.

While Felipe II was not overly fond of ceremony and formality but inclined toward a simple life, in the last dozen or so years of his reign, his court suffered from a lack of gaiety due to the king's declining health and his absences. Later kings cultivated an atmosphere of rigidity and excessive etiquette.[7]

On a lighter note, the court jesters in the royal entourage had only one role and that was to entertain. Their very appearance as dwarfs or with other pronounced physical deformities emphasized by their antics, dress, names, and incessant nonsensical chatter, but sharp wits, amused the royal household.

Elaborate balls and evening concerts and games were enjoyed by the courtiers and members of the royal family. Indoor games usually involved backgammon or cards, as gambling was a favorite pastime.

The enormous number of functionaries along with the strict etiquette made the Spanish court both the envy and brunt of jokes in other European capitals.

THE ROYAL REPAST

The king and queen often dined alone, although sometimes courtiers and others of distinction were invited to partake of a royal repast. The occasion was very formal.[8]

In the room in which the king was to dine, a large carpet was spread out and the royal table placed on it. Smaller tables were distributed near the king's chair on which were put items from the royal pantry such as wine, fruit, and sweets brought by the assistants of the royal quartermaster. When this was done, the usher assigned to the room would inform the gentleman of the pantry that everything was ready. A valet came with bread, knives, and serviettes while the chamberlain of the pantry finished laying tablecloths and arranged neighboring tables with toothpicks, chafing dishes, and other utensils.

The usher, accompanied by a squad of soldiers, proceeded to the kitchen for the food where it had been prepared. Meanwhile the bread was sliced, and the steward informed the king that the meal was ready. The king arrived and washed his hands with great ceremony while the steward knelt and waited for the king to approach the table. The senior prelate then said grace, and the king sat down. Then a swarm of servants reacted like robots with specific jobs to do.

Clutching his staff, the mark of his rank, the chief steward stood by the king's side. The carver, the wine steward, and the bread server (all nobles) began to serve. The monarch selected what he wanted to eat from about a dozen dishes. The food was ample: A plate of chicken would have no less than four birds on it, the platter of eggs would contain fifteen. When the king indicated he wished to have a drink, the cellar steward fetched a goblet from the cabinet nearby, handed it to the attending chief physician for inspection, then, accompanied by two mace bearers and a court footman, presented it to the king. When the king had drunk, the goblet was returned to the cabinet while the cellar steward brought the king a serviette to wipe his lips. A similar ceremony was repeated with the appearance of each dish.

When the meal was finished, a chaplain said a prayer of thanks, and the carver approached and brushed away any crumbs of food from the king's clothes. Again washing his hands, the king then retired to his apartments while the room was cleared and all signs of the elaborate meal disappeared.

The queen's repast underwent the same solemn procedure, sometimes with a jester in attendance who endeavored to amuse her. An account of one of her meals states that opposite the queen was a lady who placed each dish before her. On the right side of Her Majesty stood a woman who sampled the drink and, on the left, one who held a saucer and a napkin. Numerous dishes were served, and the queen ate what she wanted.

The queen was attended by ladies of the highest rank who themselves were the subject of attention of the courtiers seeking a wife or someone with whom to pass the time. These courtiers might be invited to the queen's dinner parties where they would attend to the needs of the ladies-in-waiting and could exchange surreptitious glances and limited conversation. A better opportunity to make acquaintances and banter, however, was outside the palace where the gallants would wait for the ladies to appear at their windows or balconies. Secret sign language previously agreed upon was often employed to communicate when under public scrutiny. The opportunity to flirt also arose when the queen took a coach ride with her attendants riding in several vehicles. This offered the men the chance to walk alongside the coach and pass the time of day with the women through the windows.[9]

CELEBRATIONS

The routine of court life was broken by celebrations to commemorate some special event. These occasions included a royal birth, the election of a pope, the reception of a prince or ambassador, the canonization of a Spanish saint, or a military victory. The entire population of the city could witness the festivities as spectators.

From March to September 1623, continuous celebrations were organized for the visit of Charles, prince of Wales (son of James I of England), who had come to ask for the hand in marriage of the daughter of Felipe IV. Processions, fireworks, banquets, and bullfights occurred on a daily basis. No expense was spared to impress and perhaps convert the young

Protestant prince. On this occasion, the duke of Medina Sidonia, proprietor of huge tracts of land in Andalucía, gave Felipe IV a gift of twenty-four horses sporting harnesses encrusted with gold and studded with pearls and accompanied by two dozen slaves dressed in blue and gold. Slaves and horses entered the city in line accompanied by the duke's chief seneschal and to the sound of a chorus of trumpeters, all in splendid uniforms. It served its purpose in drawing a record crowd.[10]

A favorite game of the courtiers during festivities was to throw eggshells filled with perfume at the ladies of the court. These might be dropped from balconies or hurled through the windows of a coach, causing no harm but fragrancing the ladies with an overdose of sweet-smelling essences.

EXPENSES AND INCOME

Money was always a major concern of the Spanish kings. There was never enough. The construction, improvements, and maintenance of royal palaces; the costs of the court; heavy interest on debts to foreign bankers; constant wars and revolts requiring weapons, ships, and men; royal patronage to favorites; travel; celebrations; banquets; the purchase of jewels, clothes, and works of art; and a host of other expenses—all left the royal treasury in a perpetual state of impoverishment. Income from taxes, from custom duties, from gold, silver, diamonds, and pearls from America, while they lasted, from sales of offices and titles, and from occasional income from the church granted by the pope from time to time to help pay for battles against infidel Turks or heretical Protestants was never enough.

By the time of Felipe III and Felipe IV the chronic shortage of money was compounded by the dwindling supply of silver from the Indies, and taxes were at the breaking point. Desperate attempts by Felipe IV's chief minister, the count of Olivares, to raise more money from all sectors of the empire ended in revolts in Cataluña and Portugal (the latter under Spanish domination), requiring still more expenditure to quell them.

By about 1652 the money ran out. The household budget was drained, and tradesmen, not paid in months, refused to deliver. Even bread became a scarce commodity in the palaces of the king. The queen, Mariana, complained that her favorite pastries were not being delivered. The pastry cook, who was owed a large amount of money, could no longer make them. The wages of the king's servants were paid in arrears, if at all. It was reported that the king ate more and more eggs since those in charge of the household had no money left to produce anything else. The royal painter, Diego de Velázquez, had not been paid in a year. There was not even sufficient funds to buy logs for the king's fire.[11]

LUXURY AND SUMPTUARY LAWS

Most high noblemen did not live on their estates but left them to managers, as they preferred to be at court where they hoped for favors from the king. To stand out it was necessary to establish status by eclipsing others with an elegant and extravagant way of life. Thus, for the grandee or nobleman of the first rank, appearances were of the utmost importance. From his humblest servant up to his wife and family, the most magnificent possible display of social rank was a matter of pride.

Much money was spent in this pursuit, and in 1611, the government of Felipe III decided to arrest this wasteful expenditure. A decree put a limit on the use of furniture, chafing dishes, gilded and silver-plated carriages, and the use of silver and gold in canopies and tapestries, vases, and other objects of ostentatious display that consumed so much wealth. The ban served little purpose and was not rigidly enforced.

The duke of Osuna, who had profited handsomely from his position as governor of Naples, appeared at a jousting tournament in the main square of Madrid during the reign of Felipe III with a hundred footmen attired in blue and gold uniforms and fifty officers wearing brilliant clothes studded with precious stones. In 1623 Felipe IV banned the wearing of ostentatious and expensive clothing. In order to free more hands for agricultural and other useful work, the king also limited the number of people the great lords could have in their trains. Grandees were now permitted eighteen and the king's councilors eight. In a decree of 1634 ladies were permitted only four squires to escort them. These measures seem to have had no great effect, as numerous grandees still had seneschals, squires, pages, footmen, and many other servants of their households to accompany them about. The king set a poor example by setting aside the decrees for grand occasions or court festivals.

NOBILITY AND THE COURT

Glittering costumes, ostentatious display of wealth and power, and romantic affairs were a common component of the high-living aristocracy. Courtiers, married or not, engaged in constant flirting, and a memorandum of 1658 denounced 143 married women of the court of Felipe IV, accusing them of loose living. The behavior of the king was far from exemplary.

A mistress, not necessarily of the court but sometimes an actress or prostitute, was often the ruin of a man's fortune. Not to buy her dresses, jewelry, a carriage, or furniture was dishonorable, and a man lost face if it became known that he could not, or would not, indulge her every whim. A wife and sometimes several mistresses could be very expensive. Courtiers of modest wealth turned to sycophantic fawning of the king to maintain their luxuriously indulgent lifestyle through his favors and subsidies.

In 1644 Felipe IV placed himself at the head of an army to reconquer Cataluña from the French. He had to threaten the nobility at court to accompany him, as few wished to exchange, even temporarily, courtly life for the hazards of the battlefield.

While at the top of the heap socially, the grandees were not necessarily well off financially. Many were in debt toward the end of the sixteenth century as the economy went into a tailspin. Their estates no longer brought in the income they were used to, and many mortgaged their lands to maintain their grand style of living and their many servants. Lawsuits over disputed land took their toll on the finances, interest payments on debt another big bite, and a dowry for daughters yet another hefty sum. Repairs and upkeep on their ducal palaces and grounds required still more money. Life at court was not cheap but exciting and preferable to tramping around their deteriorating country domains. They expected to make up costs by grants and favors from the king, who simply raided the royal treasury for money collected mostly from taxes on the peasants. Felipe III created three new dukes, thirty marquises, and thirty-three counts, which helped to insure that national wealth remained mostly in the hands of the few.

The Englishman Major William Dalrymple, traveling in Spain in 1774, was critical of the aristocracy who preferred to live like slaves at court while they squandered their wealth that should have been spent on improving their estates and the conditions of their vassals. He was also disparaging about their large number of redundant retainers, which even sometimes included a dwarfish buffoon such as the one who served the duke of Alba and who was obliged to greet the duke when the latter awoke in the morning with a funny story to put the duke in good humor for the day.[12]

The high nobility were not short of personal help, and the more they had, the higher their standing. The count of Olivares employed nearly 200 servants, the duke of Osma had 300, and the duke of Medinaceli later in the century had 700 on his various estates. Often the servants were underpaid, sometimes they were not paid at all, and many passed days and weeks hungry; but employment in a noble house was still better than no work at all.

Younger sons of the high nobility and impoverished hidalgos also flocked to Madrid in the wake of the grandees, hoping for a position in their service or even in the royal palace itself. Failing that, there were places to be found in the proliferating bureaucracy of the government.

The Spanish court was subject to changes from time to time as each of the monarchs and their queens had their own styles and standards of courtly comportment. The simple and austere court of Isabella and Fer-

Velázquez. *Count-Duke of Olivares on Horseback.* (Madrid: Prado).

nando became, under Carlos I, a complex and pompous institution in the Burgundian style, replete with attendants and staff. While Felipe II introduced a personal style of severity, his reign gave way to a new and more frivolous approach under Felipe III, who moved the court to Valladolid and left the running of the government mostly to others. Nearly everyone in Madrid directly or indirectly made their living from the court. As the long train of horses, wagons, and carriages departed and headed northward, the inhabitants left behind were in a state of shock. But five years later, in 1606, Felipe III came back to Madrid. He increased the number of servants in the royal palace and admitted many more grandees as gentlemen of the household.

French influences entered the Spanish court with Felipe V, a Bourbon, who acquired the throne upon the death of Carlos II in 1700, the last Spanish Habsburg. The princess des Ursins, lady-in-waiting to the young queen Marie Louise of Savoy (wife of Felipe V), controlled all court appointments. French ambassadors with direct access to the king helped form state policy. After the War of Succession, terminated in 1714, subsequent Bourbon kings and policies were thoroughly Spanish until the French invasion of the peninsula in 1808 when a Frenchman, Joseph Bonaparte, sat for a time on the throne of Spain.

NOTES

1. Doblado, 361ff.

2. This old, patched-up Moorish fortress was destroyed by fire in 1734 and replaced by the current, massive late Renaissance palace used for state functions.

3. The building ceased to be a royal residence about 1861.

4. Defourneaux, 54.

5. This custom was reported by Brunel, 213.

6. Aulnoy, in Ross and Power, 392.

7. According to François Bertaut, Felipe IV behaved like an animated statue, with never a change in his face or posture; nothing in the whole body moved except his lips and tongue. Bertaut, 35. Cited by Defourneaux, 49.

8. Defourneaux, 50, taken from an account by Brunel who attended a dinner of Anne of Austria, second wife of Felipe IV.

9. Aulnoy, in Ross and Power, 394.

10. Defourneaux, 58.

11. Ibid., 56.

12. Mitchell, 34.

9

Urban Life

Approaching Madrid did not inspire confidence. When the Mexican traveler Servando Teresa de Mier arrived there in 1803, he found the city surrounded on all sides by wretched inhabitants living in miserable, ruined villages with all the dwellings made of earth and not a tree to be seen on the barren landscape. The well-bred denizens of Madrid itself lived in the center of the city and shied away from the poorer quarters where life was lived on the streets. The upper classes often had to run a barrage of insults if they appeared there and, even worse, could be robbed of their belongings right down to their clothes.[1]

An anonymous Italian priest traveling with a papal delegation in the 1590s found the city unbelievably squalid and uncouth—houses of dried mud, often of only one story without chimney or privy. Men and women urinated in the street without regard to passersby. Their table manners were disgusting. Ignorant of the use of knives and forks, they dipped their fingers in a common dish.[2]

HOUSES

Houses in the capital were seldom aligned in rows along a street but were scattered helter-skelter. They were generally constructed of brick or adobe. A façade of stone might indicate the dwelling of a nobleman or a rich bourgeois. Small windows, many without glass, let in only a dim shaft of light through the paper or greased parchment that covered them, which was replaced by lattice screens in the summer. Windows

had grills to deter house-breakers. Gallants that came to serenade a se-
ñorita behind them pressed their faces against the bars to be nearer to
the girl of their dreams; the contemporary metaphor for courting, *comer
hierro*, "to eat iron," was derived from this act.[3]

The price of dwellings remained high as more people took up residence in the city during the seventeenth century. Most were single-story
residences to avoid an injunction by Felipe II in which he decreed that
owners of large houses, especially those of two stories, should consider
them in part the king's property to house his administrative staff and
government offices. While the owners of large houses had been allowed
to buy their way out of this decree after 1621, many still mistrusted the
government.

Around the *plaza mayor*, or large main square, built in the reign of
Felipe III, were the city's tallest buildings of five levels. The first floor
stood over porticos that sheltered shops and stalls. The upper floors, with
wrought-iron balconies, served as grandstands from which the king and
his entourage could gaze down on spectacles such as bullfighting, jousts,
or the equally popular autos de fe of the Inquisition that took place in
the square below.

If a house had more than one story, the warmest months of the year
would be spent on the ground floor in the cooler rooms. Ladies stayed
inside in the unbearable heat of summer in Madrid and other towns of
the high plateau, wearing only a short sleeveless shift covering them
from the neck down. Not until after sundown did the hot paving stones
of the city begin to cool down. In the winter the warmer upstairs rooms
were more comfortable.

The interior walls of the house would be decorated with tapestries and
mirrors, whereas the floors were flagged or tiled. In the houses of the
well-to-do, thick carpets were laid down in the winter months. If the
family were rich, there would be a room for receptions and ceremonies
where family treasures and beautiful furniture were displayed. Pictures,
mostly of religious themes, hung on the walls above ponderous carved
wooden chests inlaid with mother-of-pearl or ivory, standing next to
sideboards with shelves displaying silver plates.

Such a room might be partitioned, separating men and women, the
former sitting on chairs or stools, the latter on silk or velvet cushions or
squatting on the floor in Moorish style. Heat for the rooms was generated
by large metal braziers mounted on wooden stands. Olive stones were
often burned as fuel, as they gave off little odor; coal was more effective
but more expensive. In wealthy households a person was paid to maintain the braziers throughout the cold winter months. The fumes often
caused headaches and, on occasion, fatalities in the closed rooms. In poor
houses sulfurous dung was burned, emitting a bad stench.

Lighting came from oil lamps or candelabra. Ostentatious display, characteristic of the age, led to competition in home furnishings and decoration, sometimes reducing a modest family to penury trying to keep up with more affluent segments of society. The private sections of the house that visitors did not see were often uncomfortable and lacking light. There were no toilets, and the chamber pots were kept under the beds.

Social status could be easily determined by the number of servants in a household. The very wealthy rented suitable dwellings nearby for their staff, and slaves were often part of the entourage of a wealthy family. Most families of means, however, could afford but one or two servants.

STREETS OF MADRID

Madame d'Aulnoy, commenting on the streets of Madrid around 1680, stated that "there's no place worse paved; let one go as softly as 'tis possible, yet one is almost jumbled and shaked to pieces. There are more ditches and dirty places than in any city in the world."[4]

Goats, poultry, and even pigs wandered about, creating a traffic hazard for the coaches of the rich. Soot, fumes, and smoke from masons and brick factories, tinsmiths, potters, metalworkers, and a score of other sources heightened air and noise pollution. The streets of the poverty-stricken ghettos were little better than cesspools of sludge from rotten food and human excrement. Cleaners swept along the residue as best they could to keep it from overwhelming the narrow alleyways. An army of horses and mules adding to the squalor paraded through the streets, their owners delivering goods to various shops and ateliers.

Foreigners who visited Madrid were unanimous in their condemnation of the filth in the streets and squares.[5] The stench was at times intolerable. Chamber pots emptied out of the windows or doorways of the houses were the primary culprits.

Most of the new streets of the city were wide, which helped, but in the older section of narrow twisting lanes, paved with flint chips that cut the feet of the shoeless, the pedestrian walked in jeopardy of colliding with the contents of one of these vessels. The practice was eventually regulated so that they were emptied only at night when there were fewer people about. It was also customary for the dispenser of the contents of the receptacle to cry out, *Aqua va*! (water coming!), before releasing the contents. After enough suitors at the windows and balconies of their lady loves were "accidentally" enveloped in a malodorous essence, further measures were taken, and it became illegal to throw any substance from the house windows and balconies. Only the street door could be used for this purpose and only after ten o'clock at night in the winter, eleven o'clock in the summer. The penalty for infringement of this code was four years in exile for the house owner and six years for the servant who committed the atrocity. The servant would also receive a public whipping for good measure. The city bylaw, however, did nothing to lessen the sludge in the street, a sticky, smelly mass of ooze in winter converted to whirling clouds of noxious dust in summer. Down the center of some streets ran a ditch in which refuse was thrown for the pigs to eat. At night streets were lit by oil lamps that engendered clouds of acrid-smelling smoke.

Not until the early seventeenth century when King Carlos III insisted that the filth in the streets be cleaned up did dwellings begin to acquire a privy. This consisted of a hole in the kitchen into which the chamber pots were emptied as well as the remains of the meals. A holding tank below collected the refuse and was cleaned out every month or so and carted away. Many people of Madrid were initially against this new procedure because the corps of royal physicians felt that since the air of the city was thin (hence unhealthy) due to its altitude, it was better to impregnate it with the vapors from the filth. If little else, the dry air of Madrid, situated at about 2,150 feet above sea level, and the fresh water brought in through underground conduits from miles around were fresh and healthy.

A major street of the city, the Calle Mayor, leading to the royal palace, was daily thronged with the traffic of carriages and cavaliers and their escorts of squires and pages, often making it difficult to travel. Along its arcaded sidewalks, people strolled, stopping to talk with one another or to peer into the shops that sold expensive clothes, carpets, and jewelry or damascened and engraved swords and daggers. When a carriage carrying a lady stopped before one of the shops, the young men of means loitering around the street suddenly found more urgent business elsewhere. Gallantry required that a man deny a fair lady nothing, even if she were a stranger. If her fancy fell on a silver brooch, a gold necklace, or an amber comb, he would be obliged to buy it for her.

PROVISIONS AND THE ECONOMY

The position and growth of the capital posed problems in supply. Goods had to be transported overland on the backs of donkeys and mules, as few wagons were used due to the bad state of the roads, which were little more than rough trails. Long caravans of animals converged on the city from the vineyards of the river Duero in the north and the rolling wheat-growing hills of Salamanca. Fruits, vegetables, and olives from distant regions of the country found a place in Madrid markets. Congestion and long waits occurred at tax-collecting stations on the roads at the city's outskirts. The government struggled to keep necessities at an affordable level, but the threat of shortages and even famine was always a factor, and strict supervision was accorded the sale and price of wheat and bread.

Sheep, goats, and pigs were the principal source of meat and, along with cattle, could be grazed on the uncultivated lands near the city. On the many days of fasting, fish such as trout and carp from the local streams in the nearby mountains were in demand, but these could entail an all-day journey to market. On Fridays as the fish cart passed through certain residential districts to its place of sale, the residents complained to the authorities of the awful stench that forced them to close their doors.[6]

Most of the working inhabitants of Madrid found some way to make a living from the activity generated by the court. Some were employed there or in the chancellery, and many found work in the transport of goods provisioning the city or in distribution and resale. Others engaged in the production of bread and pastries or the manufacture and sale of lingerie.

The city produced no products for export. Besides dealings in food, the economy also revolved around trade in the arts and crafts. Occupations such as embroidery, tailoring, and gilding transformed imported materials into finished luxury products for the aristocratic society at court and government officials. An underground economy also existed among hawkers who sold crucifixes, perfumes, toilet accessories, trinkets, and tawdry finery such as bracelets and necklaces. This trade was often in the hands of foreigners, especially the French, who were well represented in Madrid and who smuggled in much of the merchandise. Laws prohibiting the sale of objects originating in other countries had little effect on the trade.

THE *MENTIDERO*, "PLACE OF LIES"

Courtiers or beggars—anyone with time on their hands—frequently congregated at specific places to discuss recent events, the latest court scandal, or the merits of some play or to complain about the government. These so-called *mentideros*, or centers for gossip, often referred to in the chronicles of the times, operated in the palace itself as well as in the city. Participants were generally of similar backgrounds. Actors and actresses had their *mentidero* in which they were joined by playwrights and poets and discussed the latest literary pieces or theatrical performances, tearing to shreds the work of their rivals. Others gathered to discuss the gossip of the court, the latest romantic fling of the king, the gallant escapades of a noble lord with an actress or lady-in-waiting, or the magical conjugations of a grandee to enhance his prospects of an heir.

On the steps of the church of San Felipe el Real, the local inhabitants gathered to listen to and talk about the latest news. Military or ex-military men assembled here to disseminate what they had heard or fabricated concerning the state of affairs in Italy, sea battles in the Indies against English or French pirates, outbreaks of violence in the Netherlands, or the latest moves of the Turks in the Balkans.

The *mentideros* were the basis of public opinion. Rumor, gossip, or the truth mattered little. People made up their minds on issues set forth by the participants, and expressions of anger or dissatisfaction with the establishment often found their way into political cartoons and satirical verses in pamphlets circulated in the city.

THE PROMENADE

People appeared in the early evenings to saunter along the major avenues, both to see others and to be seen. The streets became crowded with strollers free of the confines of their shops, offices, and dwellings. For young upper-class, heavily chaperoned girls it was an opportunity to at least see young men and cast a flirtatious glance, even if talking was out of the question.

A little out of the city center the Prado, a long, wide avenue endowed with cool fountains and shady poplar trees and cafes, was a favorite haunt of the aristocracy in the stifling summer heat. They lingered here often well into the night under a canopy of bright stars. The ladies arrived by carriage, and the gentlemen came mounted on their fine steeds. If a woman was not already escorted by a mounted attendant, she could be engaged in conversation through the window of her carriage. As darkness fell, further obscuring the woman already hidden behind her mantilla, intrigues easily developed. She might then lift a corner of her veil to expose a quick glimpse of a bit of her face as a further enticement for the moonstruck swain. The anonymity could and did favor professional ladies who came to haunt the lanes and dark groves of the Prado, looking for business.

THE RIVER MANZANARES

For the less affluent, the banks of the little Manzanares River provided a popular place to amble along in the evening. Here they could greet their friends and meet new ones. The sometime river that ran alongside the city was not much more than a large stream and was often dry in the summer. Nevertheless, the sparse shade trees and a few patches of dried-up grass gave some relief to the common people, allowing them to escape the crowded city. When the river flowed, the lower-class women of Madrid bathed naked in its brown waters, and maids from the city came to do their laundry and gossip about the habits and conduct of the occupants of the noble or bourgeois houses in which they worked. Families also came to picnic by the river, where the children could play along its sandy bank.

On the first of May every year a festival and procession took place beside the river that brought all classes together. It was nicknamed *el Sotillo* from the area in the city where the procession began. This was a chance for the women to show off their latest fashions and the dandies their elegant attire. The commoners came to watch. The grandees in the parade hitched their carriages to four or, if extremely rich, to six horses or mules. The ladies rode in the carriages, the modest ones with the curtains drawn, others with them fully open to display their beauty and finery. As usual, if the lady was accompanied by a man, she could not be spoken to, but those unaccompanied were fair game within the bounds of decorum. The ladies asked whom they pleased to purchase for them biscuits, limes, and sweetmeats, all on sale along the parade route. They directed the seller to their admirers who, by the prevailing code of conduct, would be extremely discourteous and ill-bred if they refused to pay what was often an exorbitant price.

The highly decorated beribboned horses with braided tails and manes, with fine saddles and bridles, put on a show for the shopkeepers, artisans, and other commoners who came to watch and to eat their frugal lunch on the stretch of grass by the river. The king, normally residing at his summer palace at Aranjuez, just south of Madrid, at this time of year, would make the journey to be present for a short period at the scene of the festivities. In a rather curious ritual, all the curtains of the carriages were pulled closed when the king passed. This sign of respect was another manifestation of the rigorous etiquette of the times.

THE URBAN POOR

The largest concentration of the poor was to be found in the southern sector of the city. Here life was lived in the narrow passageways, and loud squabbles between neighbors as well as tavern brawls were common. Street names stemmed from the occupations of the people living there, such as *Plateria*, or Goldsmith Street, and *Lenceria*, Linen Street. There were streets of mostly halter makers and those of hatters, and here also was a street with the largest number of wet nurses in the city called *Comadre*, or Street of the Midwife. Their husbands and others of the poorer classes of society had occupations that included constables, masons, tanners, halter makers and shoemakers, coachmen, muleteers, bakers, soldiers, textile workers and leather workers, blacksmiths, tailors, barbers, wigmakers, bookbinders and sellers, servants, street porters, stall vendors and agricultural day laborers and other unskilled workers, lowly members of the staff in the royal palace, and beggars.[7] These families barely scraped out a living, and the wives were often concerned

Murillo. *Urchins Playing Dice.* (Munich: Bayerische Staatsgemäldesammlungen).

about their children, who generally attended the free school with no shoes and in rags. Sometimes their frustration reached the boiling point.

The religious procession of Easter 1766 was turned into a political statement by the poor women of the city who diverted its course to the royal palace, where they hoped to complain to the king. For their pains they were shot down by the palace guards while the king fled the capital to avoid the disturbances. These women who engaged in occupations that brought in a pittance, such as wet nurses and orange, flower, and chestnut venders, seem to have presented a threat to the established order—a burning fuse in an explosive atmosphere.

The large unemployed population mingled with the crowds of strollers in the public squares and found refuge from the summer sun in the shade of awnings or in the clear sunshine on cold winter days. While a homeless man or woman might freeze to death on a Madrid street on a cold winter night when the temperature dropped below freezing and the north wind blew, most of the time the climate made it possible for people to spend their time out of doors in the open.

The working poor lived so close to the edge that the loss of an employed member of a household, another mouth to feed, a prolonged illness, old age, or a rise in prices and no concomitant rise in pay could spell disaster. (During the second half of the eighteenth century there was a 100 percent rise in commodity prices and over a doubling of food prices, accompanied by a rise of only 20 percent in income for the Madrid worker.)

Some other jobs not always associated with the poorer people were clerks, custom officials, teachers, barber-surgeons, and a few shopkeepers and innkeepers. The large number of unskilled in the workforce of the major municipalities can be in part explained by the many rural agricultural workers who came to the cities to seek employment or charity.

The poor dominated public places and could be seen on most streets slouching, squatting, and often begging. They would lie in wait outside the churches for the faithful to go in or come out and plead for a few pennies. They harassed servant girls buying goods at the market and housewives at the entrance to shops when they emerged with their parcels. Any conspicuous foreigner in town would be followed about by a gaggle of poor, hoping for a small handout.

Along with the genuinely unemployed cluttering the streets of the city was a rabble of beggars, purse-snatchers, smugglers, confidence men, house breakers, military deserters, paid assassins, and an assortment of other disenchanted people. Many spent their days playing cards, waiting for the monasteries' soup kitchens to disgorge their watery broth, or making plans to ransack a promising house. The quartered remains of criminals displayed in various parts of the city and police efforts to patrol the town made little difference. Crimes increased with the growth of the city. Nighttime in many sections was particularly dangerous for the citizen out on some urgent errand, unless well guarded.

SEVILLA

Sevilla reached its heyday near the end of the sixteenth and beginning of the seventeenth century. The city was at the time the sole depot for all commerce with the West Indies. The inspectors of the *Casa de Contratación*, or "House of Trade," had assumed for Castilla the monopoly of all trade with the Americas since the time of the Catholic monarchs. They organized the merchant fleets that sailed to the New World, trained the captains and navigators, and formed a tribunal to handle all problems arising from commerce.

The city of Sevilla sustained a dynamic commercial and opulent social life among those able to profit from the American trade. The great Hall of Merchants was contracted in 1598 to accommodate the business community whose associations had previously been conducted on the steps of the cathedral and, in bad weather, in the cathedral itself. The streets of the city were replete with shopkeepers from Italy, France, England, Portugal, Greece, and nearly every other country in Europe. In one quarter of the city were the workshops of silversmiths, jewelers, wood-carvers, and silk and linen merchants. Here gold, silver, pearls, crystals, enamels, coral, brocades, and costly materials were to be found. Due to the influx of large numbers of merchants and traders, the population of the city doubled in the second half of the sixteenth century to become for a time larger than Madrid.

Trade with the Indies was a gamble, an adventure. It could bring a 100 percent return on the value of merchandise going both to and from America, making millionaires in quick order, or it could bring sudden and shattering losses when ships were captured or sunk, resulting in immediate bankruptcy for those merchants who had pledged their capital to the enterprise. A desire to enjoy the pleasures of life that wealth could buy as disaster lurked just around the corner led to conspicuous spending. Unlike before when the interior of houses was all that mattered, the merchants and aristocracy of Sevilla constructed splendid façades on their houses, an indication of who was winning in the game of commerce. The result was a more attractive city, with neighbors vying with each other to make it even more so. The houses were generally two stories, with a central patio with a corridor running around it both up- and downstairs, onto which all rooms had access. Walls were whitewashed throughout.

About the middle of October every house in the city was in turmoil as all the furniture was moved upstairs for winter habitation. About the end of May the entire household moved downstairs again for the hot summer months. An awning was stretched over the patio to ward off the rays of the sun, and the window shutters were tightly closed to keep out the heat, creating a dark interior. The tiled floors were washed every morning and sprinkled with water throughout the day. The evaporation helped disperse the hot air. The patios were ornamented with grapevines and flowerpots, situated around a central fountain. During the hot season the ladies sat and received their friends on the patio, which was illuminated by lanterns. The doors remained open until about eleven o'clock at night, and the gatherings were visible from the street, giving the city a lively scene. The poor spent a good deal of the night sitting and talking in the doorways of their houses to escape the heat inside. In the winter the routine changed: Doors were closed and the nighttime streets became dangerous. At this time of year, to enter the house of a friend, one knock on the door was customary. And in response to the question, "Who is there?" the answer was, "Peaceful people." Beggars called out at the door, "¡*Ave María purisima*!" (Hail! pure Mary), and the answer from within was always, "*Sin pecado concebida*" (Conceived without sin).[8]

The inhabitants of Sevilla who could afford it dressed in an ostentatious manner. Clothes were made of fine silk, satin, or velvet. Women also made use of muslin, embroidery, and soft flannel. All cloth was of the finest weave. Travelers' reports confirm the grace and elegance of the Sevillian ladies, who were very upright and walked with small steps, giving the appearance of noble bearing.

Festivities in the city during Holy Week or on other religious holidays, or when the fleet came home, were unrivaled. Sumptuous feasts, merrymaking, and processions were legendary. Each quarter of the city and each guild had its own confraternity and bedecked their virgin or patron saint in vivid colors, precious stones, gold, and jewelry and carried them, decorated with rich tapestries, swaying through the streets on platforms supported by a dozen strong men.

CORRUPTION

The flashy, brilliant life of Sevilla had its darker side. Magistrates and the Municipal Council were generally in league with the rich speculators who controlled monopolies on certain goods. By the time food reached the common people of the city, for example, it had been through the hands of these speculators, resulting in high prices. The Municipal Council that controlled prices turned a blind eye to the higher costs since they received presents and kickbacks from the great merchants. If litigation arose, the magistrates protected the merchants for the same reasons.

Grievances concerning these grave matters were brought before Felipe IV in 1621 by representatives of the people and also included the neglect for public welfare shown by the twenty-four municipal councilors. The streets were in poor condition and seldom improved and were full of refuse that could give rise to an epidemic. Documents denouncing the filth are abundant and contrast the embellishment of the city through new public and private buildings with its dire foul and unhealthy condition.

When the Englishman Henry Swinburne visited the city in 1776, he found the streets crooked, dirty, and so narrow that in most of them two coaches found it difficult to pass abreast.[9]

There were many people who were not directly involved in trade and its concomitant wealth but who were compelled to snatch at whatever scraps might fall from the city's prosperity. Among the poorly paid were the police who were sometimes the accomplices of criminals. Thieves and murderers also had recourse to unhindered activity through the use of bribes to court clerks, attorneys, and judges. Those who lacked a full purse, however, were punished and often sent to the galleys.

Swarms of beggars, ruffians, robbers, swindlers, and hired assassins roamed Sevilla. Some plucked tidbits from the merchandise piled high along the river banks; some specialized in purse snatching or pickpocketing; the most formidable were hired to kill an adversary. The

Court of the Elms and the Court of the Oranges, located on each side of the cathedral but within the chains that marked ecclesiastical jurisdiction, served as sanctuaries for the criminals. Secular power was forbidden jurisdiction in these hallowed spots, which also housed several taverns. Here the mavericks gambled, fought, and entertained the women of the streets.[10]

PRISONS

Despite contrary evidence, some police were doing their duty, as is clear from the 2,000 or so inmates that were incarcerated in the Carmona Civil Prison of Sevilla at the beginning of the seventeenth century.[11] (Cervantes was once locked up here.) Most were common thieves. No sunlight reached the prisoners with the exception of two of the yards, and the only ventilation in the dungeons was by a hole in their doors. The floors were damp, and rats, cockroaches, and fleas infested the cells. In the exercise yard, food was cooked in one corner and clothes washed in another. Typhoid fever often claimed the lives of inmates. In the absence of strict discipline, escapes were common with or without the connivance of the guards and prison officials who often accepted handsome bribes to look the other way.

When an inmate entered the confines of the cells, he was put to the torture by other inmates to see how stout a man he was. If he turned out to be a "musician" (one likely to sing—that is, inform on his accomplices), he was banished to a spot by himself, and no one would speak to him.[12] The brave ones were admitted to the prisoner society to the sound of drums and guitars. A steady stream of people came and went from the prison gate, which closed at ten o'clock at night, bringing provisions to the inmates, for their food was not always provided by the local government, and if it was, it was far too little or confiscated by the guards and sold to the prisoners.

Prisons throughout the country were usually established in whatever buildings were available, such as disused monasteries and palaces, castles, fortresses, and even private houses rented by the authorities for the purpose. It was not unusual for the jail to be in the center of the town and for prisoners to beg for alms with outstretched hands through the bars of a window facing the street.[13]

When George Borrow was confined to prison in Madrid for selling bibles, he was treated well with the British embassy looking out for him, but he described aspects of the prison that were far less comfortable. With regard to the three large vaulted dungeons, he states that one was large enough to hold 100 men, another one 150. They were

horribly filthy and disgusting places; . . . Of the two dungeons one was, if possible, yet more horrible than the other; it was called the *gallinería*, or chicken coop, and within it every night were pent up the young fry of the prison, wretched boys from seven to fifteen years of age, the greater part almost in a state of nudity. The common bed of all the inmates of these dungeons was the ground . . . other dungeons in various parts of the prison; some of them quite dark, intended for the reception of those whom it might be deemed expedient to treat with peculiar severity. There was likewise a ward set aside for females . . . many small apartments where resided prisoners confined for debt or for political offenses. And, lastly, there was a small *capilla* or chapel, in which prisoners cast for death passed the last three days of their existence.[14]

GUILDS

In the cities and towns the workers organized into guilds that arose when a group of artisans who had similar interests such as shoe menders or carpenters united for mutual aid and protection. The members of a craft guild were divided into three classes: masters, apprentices, and journeymen. The master, who was a small-scale proprietor, owned the raw material and the tools and sold the goods manufactured in his shop for his own profit. The apprentices and journeymen often lived in the master's house. The apprentices, who were beginners in the trade and learned it under the direction of the master, usually received only their board in return for their work. After an apprentice had completed his training, he became a journeyman and was paid a fixed wage for his labor. In time a journeyman might become a master. Funds collected by the guilds from new memberships or dues often went to help widows or orphans of deceased members or charities.

Guilds had regulations concerning access to their trades: for example, technical expertise and social acceptability. The carpenters, for example, wanted their members to be married or at best have a house of their own. This was no doubt partly due to the fact that the guilds felt responsible for their members and helped them through hard times such as sickness or accident. But money that could have been better spent, some members complained, was wasted on festive events celebrating the patron saint of the trade and other fiestas, instead of on charity and pensions. Many guilds ostracized minorities such as Jews and Muslims and insisted on purity of blood.

NOTES

1. Aulnoy, in Ross and Power, 365; Mier, 116–117.
2. Mitchell, 14.
3. Crow, 176.
4. Aulnoy, in Ross and Power, 191.
5. For example, Major William Dalrymple, the Venetian Giacomo Casanova, and Joseph Baretti, all of whom visited Madrid in the eighteenth century.

6. Defourneaux, 65.

7. For a discussion of the urban poor, see Sherwood.

8. Doblado, 22–23.

9. Swinburne, 264.

10. Defourneaux, 223.

11. Ibid., 89.

12. Ibid.

13. Griffiths, 124ff.

14. Borrow, 275.

10

Rural Life

In the sixteenth century, about 90 percent of the population of the country lived in rural villages and hamlets. Most were peasants who worked on the land. But whether they lived on the wind-swept plateau of Castilla, among the stony hills of Aragón, in the green valleys of Asturias and Galicia, or amid the olive groves of Andalucía, they often existed in wretched conditions. Depending on crops and animals for their livelihood, peasants were often the victims of perverse natural events—droughts, floods, or outbreaks of plague—and of heavy taxation by the crown and landowners. Economic stagnation accompanied by epidemics and crop failures in the late sixteenth century drove many young men to find a new life in the New World. Others enlisted in the military and perished by the scores in European wars. As the villages were abandoned, only old people were left behind, with nowhere to go.

In 1647, Andalucía had its worst harvest in a century, and in the same year, about one-fifth of the population of Aragón, Valencia, and Andalucía died of a plague epidemic. In some cities half the inhabitants perished over its five-year duration. Between 1676 and 1682, floods followed by drought, successive crop failures producing large-scale famine, and a major plague immediately followed by an epidemic of typhus engulfed most of Castilla. No rain fell in 1683 until the end of November, and the earth dried up in most of Andalucía. Famine again in 1684 gave rise to very high grain prices. In 1687, locusts devastated Cataluña, and lack of food precipitated a peasant rebellion. About half a million people died as a result of these disasters. But the worst was over, and by the mid-eighteenth century, the country regained its previous level of population and the economy gradually began to show signs of improvement.

Disease was always present, but those who survived its ravages grew old rapidly, and people died young. The heavy work plowing the fields all day under a broiling sun, the women carrying loads of water and washing clothes in the rivers and streams, the icy winter wind, the family huddled around a charcoal fire in cramped cold rooms filled with toxic fumes—all took their toll. Poor-quality food led to malnutrition, making people more prone to disease and less able to produce. Country peasants who migrated to the cities looking for work often lacked a roof over their heads, sold their clothes for a morsel of food, and then begged. According to the census of 1787, about 36 percent of the population were under sixteen. Only about 14 percent outlived their fiftieth birthday.[1]

DAILY WORK

The landless day laborers (*jornaleros*) were the most unfortunate of the rural inhabitants and in some regions made up as much as half the population. They owned little or nothing and supported themselves by working for wages in other people's fields. They were often on the move in search of work, and lacking the means to save any money, they could never better their social condition. If there were seasonal labor shortages, they could demand higher wages, but often such boldness was quickly squashed. Laws were sometimes passed by local authorities that fixed the wages a *jornalero* could earn based on the price of food; the authorities were also the landowners who sold the food and paid the wages. Rural workers who became too vociferous in their demands were arrested and put in the pillory to be exposed to public ridicule.

Somewhat better off than the *jornaleros* were the independent peasant farmers who owned land. The *labradores*, who farmed their own fields, often possessed a pair of oxen and were self-employed. The oxen could be used to till the peasant's field, and they could also be rented out to neighbors.

Even the fairly well-to-do peasant lived on the edge of indigence, however, and could sink into the abyss of abject poverty at any time. The death of his beasts or a bad harvest could reduce him to the level of the day-wage laborer. But with good fortune such as a number of bountiful years, he could also acquire more wealth. He might buy more land to lease out to others and animals such as sheep and goats for meat, milk, and cheese and graze them on common land. He could then live in a fine house and hire a few servants.

There were few, if any, jobs in the villages other than those related to agriculture. The *labradores* and *jornaleros* generally toiled all day in fields

A country peasant at work on a loom.

sometimes far removed from the village, entailing wasted time getting from one field to another.

Wheat was the principal crop on the central plateau of Castilla, and plowing the fields with oxen or mules, or hoeing the smaller patches of land in preparation for planting, was time-consuming and backbreaking work. Similarly, seeding the ground and tending the fields during the growing period, if vegetables or vines were involved, kept the farmer busy. The time of year and the phases of the moon dictated when planting and harvesting would take place. With the harvest finished in October, the peasant family worked in and around the house during the winter months doing the odd jobs that required attention. Wine vats and irrigation ducts might need cleaning, the adobe walls of the house or the thatched roof repairing, farm implements and harnesses mended, cleaned, or sharpened, and animal manure collected to fertilize the fields. Besides cooking and sewing and tending the young children, the women usually looked after the domestic chickens or ducks, feeding them and gathering the eggs, and milking the goat or cow and making butter and cheese. They might also tend a vegetable patch near the house and sell some of the produce locally. Peasants' wives often spent the slack winter months engaged in artisan work such as spinning wool and making clothes, some of which might be sold at market.

Extreme poverty of the peasant class was recorded in the early seventeenth century by, among others, the Benedectine Benito de Peñalosa y Mondragón.[2] He described their simple coarse meals of garlic and onions and bread made of barley and rye; their rough clothes of hemp sandals, burlap shirts, ragged sheepskin coats preserved with resin; their miserable dwellings, cottages, and huts with mud walls crumbling or fallen in; pitiful possessions; poorly cultivated fields with emaciated cattle. The very idea of peasant had a terrible connotation. They were considered by the upper echelons of society as low-class taxpayers (indicating their lack of prestige), boors, and scoundrels who wore ridiculous hats and lived in crude hovels beside ill-tended fields.

RURAL HOUSES

The type of construction of peasant houses depended on the region: Stone and wood were used where available, but often the soil itself was all there was to erect a dwelling. Village and farmhouses on the plateau north of Madrid were made of sun-dried mud bricks or blocks of clay about three feet square, studded with pebbles. The one-story farm buildings were easy to build but disintegrated in heavy rain or under a hot sun. In La Mancha, south of Madrid, village houses were similarly constructed but had tiled roofs. A roughly hewn table and a few wooden benches made up the furniture, whereas the beds, in the small dark rooms leading off the central living space, were often a single plank or a woolen mattress on the floor. The ample fireplace in a corner of the main room served to cook food (usually stew) and sometimes contained a brushfire when the temperature dipped low. In the poverty-stricken far north of the country the entire house was a single round room shared by humans, pigs, and cattle. If there was an upper story, then the lower floor was used for the livestock.

The villages of Extremadura and Andalucía contrasted sharply between the widely separated large manorial houses, sometimes displaying a coat of arms, and the lowly mud-brick quarters of the laborers clustered around them. In some hilly regions such as the town of Quadix in Granada where the porous tufa rock was soft and eroded, peasants hollowed out their homes in the sides of the cliffs, creating comfortable rooms that were cool in summer and easily heated in winter, with chimneys protruding from the tops of the hills and the gullies between the dwellings serving as streets. In the more prosperous regions of Cataluña, peasant estates flourished around the *masía*, a solidly built farmhouse of stone with a wooden-beamed roof. A peasant farmer here might have a number of workers on his land living in comfortable conditions.

THE PEASANT COMMUNITY

The peasant community was regulated by ordinances set out by the Council of Castilla and by the landowners. Such matters as election to the local village council, daily wages, the use of common or crown property, and mercantile activity were all controlled.

Along with numerous peasant farmers, the village might consist of a priest, mayor, councilmen, a constable or two, a tailor, barber, innkeeper, a notary who kept the town records, and perhaps a sacristan. In the larger villages there might be a doctor or at least an amateur or charlatan who knew something about herbs and astrology and maybe a teacher who guided the young children, both of whom would be paid through the municipal office.

The most important officials of the community were the mayor and the councilmen, who decided on the use of common land. In villages of less than 500 inhabitants, they were generally elected each year, which was an important event in the lives of the local people. In the larger towns the aristocratic or church landowner often designated the mayor and his councilors from among those inhabitants proposed by the community. Their terms in office might be perpetual. In other cases the landowner appointed them himself and expected them to do his bidding. Conflicts between peasants and landowners were not uncommon, as were squabbles between the crop farmer and those raising livestock over common land.

Often living at the subsistence level in the countryside were the shepherds who owned a few sheep or looked after the animals of a more affluent neighbor. Woodcutters and charcoal makers lived in the vast hinterland often well away from civilization and only came into towns to sell their products. Charcoal was always in demand in the winter months when families sat around the glowing brazier. Some peasants managed a living by hunting game in the forest or open table lands to sell at market.

There was no real concept of nation nor a spirit of nationalism in the countryside, but within the local communities, social ties and loyalties were strong. Communal working of the land was often practiced, and the *patria chica*, the little fatherland—that is, the local district—commanded the peasants' allegiance. Anything beyond was a foreign territory.

OWNERSHIP OF LAND

Land was the single-most important ingredient in the economy, and its ownership was the only means to a better life for most people; but few were able to possess it and exploit its potential. Even as some peasants became prosperous and began to form a rural middle class, the grip on the agrarian economy and the extraction of its wealth remained solidly in the hands of the aristocracy and the church.

An inquiry based on a questionnaire ordered by Felipe II into the conditions of towns and villages in Castilla revealed that the peasants seldom owned the land they farmed. Nearly all were tenants of the local nobility or of bourgeois landlords residing in neighboring towns or of the church or great monasteries. Only in isolated mountain villages did nearly everybody own some land, but all shared a common denominator: They were all poor.[3]

Conditions and details of landownership were far from uniform throughout the different regions of the peninsula or even within the same region, but some basic features were widespread: Besides the landowning institutions or individuals, some was held under common public usage by the community. This municipally owned property was reserved for the benefit of the inhabitants, although there was often land that was not allowed to be cultivated except by special permission and other property that might be rented out by the town council for income to offset municipal expenses, thereby taking it out of common usage.

Communal ownership of property encompassed not only pastures and fields on the outskirts of town but the village green and sometimes the public threshing and winnowing floor, the rubbish pile, and slaughter pen. The town may also have had ownership (or shared with other towns) of nearby streams, lakes, and woodlands. There was also the community-owned enclosed pasture for work animals such as oxen and mules.

Drinking water for residents and animals was considered public property and was generally controlled by the public officials. Another custom was the right of public gleaning for the benefit of the masses of rural poor. This allowed collecting apples, grapes, olives, and other fruit or vegetables that were overlooked during the harvest or permitted gathering of leftover grain when the regular harvest was finished. The old, the infirm, children, and women who could not support themselves from regular wages were entitled to participate in this practice. In regions where chestnuts and acorns grew, they were considered a common resource along with uncultivated berries, fruits, or vegetables such as wild asparagus, figs, and mushrooms. These could be harvested even on private lands if not cultivated by the owner. In general, anything supplied by nature without being the product of man was common heritage. Such rights might include hunting and fishing and gathering firewood.

While cultivated land occupied a perimeter around the living areas, between villages lay large sections of heath or common land. Here, even the poorest peasant could graze a cow, goat, or sheep. Customary rights governed the use of this land, but peasant communities always were forced to defend these rights against the encroachments of large landowners who, if given the chance, would fence them off for their own use.

Intercommunal common ground was also not unusual, and councilmen from various towns met every year to reaffirm their commitment to uphold these lands. Villages participating in these enterprises might be only 5 or 6 in number or as many as 300. For some hamlets with no common ground of their own, the intercommunal public lands were of supreme importance.

The practice of communal property existed also among villages on seignorial and royal lands. The lords who had jurisdiction in the towns were obliged to respect the rights of the inhabitants mostly through fear of losing them through emigration to places with more amenable common privileges.

Throughout much of Andalucía, massive tracts of land planted with olive trees extended over the rolling hills for many miles on end. The huge estates that belonged to a few privileged families who preferred to live in the cities such as Sevilla and left an overseer to manage the property were cultivated by agricultural laborers who lived in broken-down hamlets dotted here and there among the olive trees. Entire families picked the fruit and were hired seasonally by the estate managers a few months a year for a pittance. Hunger always dogged their footsteps, especially when their work was no longer required for a number of off-season months. In the north, such as in Galicia, about one in five peasants owned property, but even then the patch of ground was often barely large enough to sustain a family.

A peasant's ownership of land, unless he was one of the rare wealthy ones, did not necessarily mean he was better off than others who rented or leased the land as tenant farmers. If a plot was small and the soil poor, he would be among those with a very low standard of living. Tenant farmers, on the other hand, might work rich, fertile soil and be more prosperous. The peasant owner's payment on debt might be higher than the tenant farmer's payment of rent to his landlord.

BOURGEOIS AND ARISTOCRATIC LANDOWNERS

Since most people maintained the conviction that land was the only source of real wealth, merchants, bureaucrats, and artisans who could get a little money together invested in rural property that they considered more secure than investments in trade. These owners generally lived in the cities near their investment where they would have a say in the management of the property, enjoy its fresh produce, and bathe in the prestige of ownership. Madrid, Toledo, and Valladolid generated a number of these urban owners of rural land, but smaller towns had their share of them.

Bourgeois ownership of land was something recent at this time, and many of the new landowners, often Conversos, formed a budding class outside the traditional distinction of nobility and commoner. This class became more important than local (often impoverished) hidalgos, sought titles for itself, and began to monopolize the municipal offices of the villages for its own purposes. It grew wealthier by snapping up the properties of bankrupt peasants and was resented by the local inhabitants.

Small peasant holdings, where they existed, were often encumbered with a kind of mortgage. In order to improve cultivation or buy seed in a bad year, the landholder took a loan from the local bourgeois in the nearby town with the property as collateral. If for some reason, such as drought leading to a bad harvest, he could not meet the yearly payment, his creditor could seize the property.

A little over half the land of Spain consisted of manor property. (Much of the rest was subject to the direct control of the king.) The lord of the manor held nearly absolute power of life and death over his subject workers through his control of local justice and unrestricted authority over their possessions. He demanded and received allegiance from everyone, including the sheriff and the councilors of the towns in his jurisdiction. All knelt before him, swearing to pay the tributes and taxes he required in return for the safeguarding of the customs and usage that they enjoyed such as the right, upon death, to be buried and the use of the oxen to plow the fields and the mill to grind their wheat.

The peasant had to pay dues to the landlord (not unlike tithes to the church that he also paid), which consisted of a portion of his agricultural production in wheat, wine, oil, wool, cattle, or poultry, the amount of which was fixed by custom. Conditions of the peasant varied from region to region. In Galicia where many peasant families occupied monastic lands, the abbot claimed the right, when a tenant died, to the best animal in his herd. In default of an animal, any four-legged piece of furniture such as a table or chest sufficed.

With the advent of the Habsburg dynasty in the early sixteenth century, about half of the towns in Castilla were under seignorial jurisdiction. The large towns were generally under the authority of the crown or the crown-controlled military orders. The cash-starved Carlos I and his son Felipe II sold towns to prestige-oriented nobles to enhance the royal treasury. Ownership gave the nobles the right to appoint the town council and issue decrees and hold court. They could place restrictions on cultivation, hunting, wood gathering, and pasturing or any other activities that pleased them. Noble landlords tended to be liberal in their ordinances, however, so as not to scare off settlers. Arrangements between lord and peasant differed from town to town. In one place in the province of Toledo, for example, the lords allowed the peasant settlers full ownership of the lands they cleared and plowed in exchange for a tribute of one-twelfth of the produce. However, the peasants were not allowed to sell the land to anyone of noble or ecclesiastical status since such a person would be exempt from the one-twelfth tax. In other places, peasants acquired land but were obliged to plow at least half of it every year, or it would revert back to the lord.

To maintain property intact, Castillian nobles adhered to the system in which the eldest son inherited his father's entire estate, thus preventing its breakup among the rest of the children, who had to find some other means of livelihood such as government service, the military, or the priesthood.

The system of land tenure in Valencia exercised over Moriscos was grim. The subjects handed over about a third of the harvest and were obliged to transport it to the lord's dwelling. After the expulsion of the Moriscos, Christian vassals were installed on the land, but they proved less amenable to the conditions, and conflicts ensued for generations. About the only redeeming grace for the peasants was the fact that custom prevented the owner or overseer from evicting them arbitrarily from land on which they toiled, giving them a certain amount of security.

ECCLESIASTICAL OWNERSHIP OF LAND

Not unlike the nobility, the church owed much of its influence to wealth acquired in the pursuit of property. Like the nobility, it came to possess land as a result of the Reconquest from the Moors and royal grants from the crown for services rendered. The church given land and jurisdiction in the newly acquired territories did what it could to construct towns and attract settlers. The monarchy gave the archbishop of Toledo the town of Alcalá de Henares, a little east of Madrid. This grew into a thriving agricultural center on the road to Zaragoza; a new university was founded there in 1508, contributing to rapid growth. Many acres under ecclesiastical jurisdiction belonged to monasteries under the control of an abbot or parish churches and bishoprics.

The church acquired vast properties including entire villages from bequests made by devout aristocratic individuals who died without heirs, from royal grants, and from outright purchase. In the sixteenth century a large increase in convents was often accompanied by land grants given in exchange for the care of a daughter of a noble family.

Cash donations from the wealthy contributed further to the growth of ecclesiastical property by enabling the church to purchase more land. It was not uncommon for it to own all the grounds of a village as well as the best property in most regions. As the church, like the nobles, was exempt from many forms of taxation, its wealth accumulated quickly. Like the aristocracy, the church promoted fairs and markets on its estates to promote economic advancement.

By the sixteenth century as free peasant labor through work levies on landlords' properties was becoming a thing of the past, the church turned to leasing out parcels of land, which provided an income to peasants and replaced the uncertainties for the church of drought, flood, and crop losses.

In addition to church property, it was not unusual for the parish priest to own a parcel of land comprising a vineyard, orchard, or vegetable patch, some of which was rented out to the locals. Some priests also kept a few sheep or goats. These extraecclesiastical activities that brought in income over and above the priests' benefices were not necessarily appreciated by the parish peasants, who were always in dire need of more agricultural land.

The lordship of bishops over major towns began to slip away in the sixteenth century as the towns became stronger and more independent and constantly contested ecclesiastical authority. Rural villages, on the other hand, remained in the clutches of the prelates and monasteries. In Galicia ecclesiastical control was strongest while the region remained the poorest. Of the nearly 4,000 towns and villages in Cataluña, only 660 belonged to the monarch, the nobility held some 1,200, and the rest fell under the jurisdiction of the church, mostly Benedictine abbeys.

SHEEP AND SOLDIERS

A source of aggravation for the peasant of Castilla was the destructive practice of the *Mesta*. This powerful corporation moved 2 to 3 million sheep to the south of the country for pasture in winter and back north again in summer.[4] Guided by shepherds and protected by large, powerful dogs, the advancing flocks moved along the roads and through the fields, devouring everything in their path and raising vast dust clouds in their wake. Strings of mules and donkeys accompanied the flocks, carrying essential supplies, cooking pots, and firewood, food for both shepherds and dogs, salt for the sheep, and even the lambs that were still too young to keep up. While crossing cultivated fields, certain marked-out paths (*cañadas*) were supposed to be followed, but the sheer number of animals made this difficult and village crops would sometimes be devastated. The peasant had no recourse or compensation.[5]

The *Mesta* had the backing of the kings of Castilla who, anxious to increase the wool industry, its exports, and the taxes gained from it, granted many privileges to the wealthy owners of the sheep that were harmful to the interests of the peasants. The latter were forbidden to cultivate the commons or fence their fields and were compelled to permit the sheep to forage on their fallow land, to the detriment of their own livestock. Quarrels that arose from these conflicts were generally settled in favor of the *Mesta*, which had its own sheriffs with wide-ranging judicial authority and the power to summon uncooperative peasants to its own tribunals. The benefits were great for the owners, for the sheep produced large quantities of wool as well as milk, butter, cheese, and meat.

Worse than the *Mesta* was the obligation of the peasants to provide food and lodging for the army when it was on the move to ports of embarkation or the frontiers of the country. When the king's troops descended on a village, the inhabitants were in for an expensive and frustrating time. Notoriously unruly and dishonest, the soldiers when passing through a village stole livestock, abused the women, and threatened the men. The supposed compensation for the peasants, if given at all, was well below the costs they incurred. What the entire peasant family ate in a week, a couple of soldiers consumed in two days. Unpleasant incidents between surly soldiers and hostile locals were not uncommon. The army requisitioned what it needed in grain, farm animals, and even people to help it along its way. As a result, peasants often remained indoors and out of sight while the army was in the area. Along routes commonly used by the military, villages were either nonexistent for that very reason or greatly reduced in population as people did their best to move away.

PEASANT OBLIGATIONS

Peasants paid about one-third to one-half of their harvests in rent if they did not own the land, and another tenth or so to the lord of the manor for use of plowing oxen, and still more for the use of the threshing floor if it was not communally owned. They would then need enough of the harvest to feed the family and some to sell for cash to buy needed items, with still some left over for seed. Along with ecclesiastical and seignorial taxes, and sometimes merchants' fees, it often happened that nothing was left over.

The peasants paid out the majority of the money required to support the vast Habsburg empire. Taxes were raised by the crown to the limit and sometimes beyond endurance. Near the end of the reign of Felipe II, many of the peasants could no longer pay the taxes imposed upon them, and a long period of rural decline began to set in.

If in a bad year the peasant could not pay his royal dues, tax collectors came around to the village and confiscated his possessions right down to the miserable bed in which the family slept. These were then sold and the money used to pay not only the taxes but the tax collectors' wages. If no buyer could be found for a confiscated peasant house, the tiles and wood were ripped from the roofs and sold piecemeal, while the poor man and his family were set on the road toward a life of begging. The crushing burden of taxes sometimes led to the abandonment of entire areas.[6]

The councils of all cities, towns, and villages were endowed with the power to fix prices for agricultural products such as wine, oil, fruit, vegetables, grain, meat, and cheese. They granted monopoly rights to tavern keepers, butchers, and other dispensers of food and drink for the region. The official prices even applied to markets and were fixed to benefit the consumer, not the producer. Low prices drove some farmers out of business, for the councils attempted to regulate everything including working hours, milling procedures, and salaries. There were also prices fixed on the national level, where the crown dictated maximum legal prices, the *tasa*, for grain to insure the poor could buy bread. The fact that there were no ceilings on the costs of farm tools, draft animals, seed, and other means of production often drove the producer to cheat on the system, in spite of high penalties if caught, and sell at black-market prices higher than those set by the government in order to make ends meet.

The tithe paid to the church was seen as God's right to one-tenth of everything: wine, grain, fruit, animals and all their byproducts, and even salaries of hired hands. Nothing, neither costs of seed, planting, nor of tools, could be deducted, and the tax was collected in kind or money.

WINE PRODUCTION

With the economy geared to local self-sufficiency, vineyards were particularly important, and in most areas of the country, they were in the hands of small peasant owners. The careful labor-intensive cultivation of the vine did not interest absentee owners, but for the peasant it represented a minimal amount of financial outlay. While tending the grapes was often not his only occupation, the peasant farmer had the time from grain farming to supply his own household with wine, with a little surplus to sell for cash. The typical vineyard was small and often shared the patch of ground with olives and fruit trees, but in the major wine-producing areas such as Ciudad Real, about 20 percent of the land was given over to the vine. In many villages even the day laborers with no substantial land of their own had a few grapevines in a small melon or vegetable patch.

NOTES

1. Casey, 32.
2. Domínguez Ortiz, 153.
3. Casey, 48.
4. Ibid., 49; see also Defourneaux, 101.
5. Kamen, *Spain 1469–1714*, 52. The flocks of sheep were theoretically prohibited from encroaching on cornfields, vineyards, fruit crops, hayfields, and livestock pastures.
6. Defourneaux, 99.

11

Family Life

The day-to-day running of the household was usually the joint concern of the husband and wife: The former looked after outside matters, and the latter domestic affairs. The basic family was, in the main, nuclear, consisting of the parents and the children, but by the late sixteenth century, it was not uncommon in many regions to find the extended family under the same roof. For farmers in need of additional help, this arrangement proved useful. Even when members of the family lived apart, however, the cooperation between them remained close and loyal. The elderly were taken care of if the means were available, and the children were raised to meet their responsibilities.

CHILDHOOD AND UPBRINGING

The attitude of the church toward the family was that it was better to abandon an unwanted child to a foundling home than to interfere with pregnancy; and as far as feeding another mouth was concerned, such matters must be left in the hands of Divine Providence.

The average size of the family was, in spite of the prohibition of contraception and abortion, not large. This was in part due to the high infant mortality rate and the interruption of marriage through early death of one of the spouses. Family size varied depending on urban or rural locations and regions but was generally between four and five: two adults and two or three children.[1] In the countryside mortality rates among infants were around 40 to 50 percent.

Children were born at home, and a doctor was normally not present. Female friends and relatives helped out, and often a midwife was in attendance. Professional midwives were available in the cities for people with money; otherwise, they were a friend or neighbor who had learned the trade through years of experience. A doctor might be summoned if complications arose, and a father might help out if capable hands were in short supply. Cesarean extraction was sometimes needed to save the life of the child if the mother died, but midwives were capable of performing this operation. It was far from rare for women to die during childbirth, especially in the country villages.

The birth of a child was generally an occasion of great ceremony. When a woman was in labor, friends, relatives, and neighbors gathered around to offer encouragement and assistance, and the new baby was the center of attention for everyone. Baptism followed as soon as possible after birth to insure the child its place in heaven if it should not survive. During the baptismal ceremony a Christian name was given, often that of a favorite saint or the name of the saint on whose day the child was born. Names of relatives or of godparents might also be used. In the more affluent families it was common to have a little party after the baptismal event, at which time the parents and baby usually received a few small gifts.

The upbringing of the infant fell to the mother and other females in the household such as sisters or aunts, and until the child was about six years old, it was seldom outside the circle of the women. Breast feeding the baby was considered the only safe means of insuring a healthy child since animal milk was thought to be potentially hazardous for a delicate digestive system. If the mother was not capable of this method of nourishment or preferred not to perform it for whatever reason, the baby was given over to a wet nurse if the family could afford it. She either lived in, or the infant was sent to her domicile. Generally, she would be a woman who had lost her own infant. With the high rate of mortality among babies, there were always more women in a position to nurse a child than there were children to be nursed.

After a few months the infant's swaddling clothes were exchanged for a more sanitary shirt and gown, and as it learned to walk, a protective padded bonnet cushioned the head from the inevitable falls.

For amusement, the baby was given a rattle to play with, which gave way, as it grew, to an assortment of toys such as dolls, whistles, tops, blocks, and hobbyhorses, plus the usual natural items of sand, wood, and stones from which the child built miniature castles, churches, and houses as well as dams, boats, and mills if water were close at hand.

Until the age of six or seven, the daily life of the child revolved around sleep, food, and play. Then the sacrament of confirmation marking the child's official admission to the church was given, and around this age girls and boys began to be steered by parents and society into their own differentiated spheres.

In the country it was customary for the sons of peasant farmers at a young age to be moved away from the guidance of female members of the household into male company. In the vast majority of cases, this meant into an orbit of farmwork where they learned the tasks of herding animals, plowing as they grew stronger, planting and harvesting, milking and sheering sheep, and snaring rabbits and birds for the table.

Most children never had the opportunity to go to school and remained illiterate. A little instruction from the parish priest was about all they received. For the majority, reading and writing were unobtainable goals, and instead they might learn to memorize the *Ave Maria*, the Creed, and the Lord's Prayer, all in rather meaningless Latin. Responsibility for a child's education lay with the parent, as did the actions of the child, who was considered too young to know the difference between good and bad behavior.

The father exercised full authority; the rest of the family were subject to and obeyed his wishes. The husband was responsible for the administration of his property along with that of his wife, including the dowry that he acquired at marriage. A wife could not enter into private contracts without the authority of her husband. The only condition was that he keep an accounting of her property in case the marriage was dissolved. In exchange for these property rights the husband was obliged to care for the needs of his wife; feed, clothe, and educate the legitimate children to the best of his ability; and establish a dowry for his daughters. It was also the father's responsibility to discipline the children if necessary and to authorize their marriage up to, in some places, twenty-five years of age. Actions contrary to the father's wishes could result in loss of inheritance.

City boys from reasonably well-off families of the bourgeoisie generally received two or three years of schooling learning to read and write and some arithmetic. Then it was common for them to learn a trade. Sometimes this happened at home, with the boy following in his father's footsteps; otherwise, he was sent to learn and not uncommonly to live in the home of someone else skilled in a trade. An apprenticeship was a desirable option, and room and board were provided even if little or no pay was forthcoming. Sometimes the father had to pay the master to take on his son. The master had the right to treat the boy as his own, even to punish him if he was not always up to standard. Conflicts naturally arose between them, and often enough the apprentice ran away from the job.

Although these apprentices were mostly boys, it was also possible for girls to gain acceptance into one of the trades that admitted them such as lace and veil makers or producers of silk ribbons. Alternatively, domestic service was one of the few respectable options.

The urban poor, both boys and girls, received little or no schooling nor vocational training and worked as unskilled laborers or servants, going to work as soon as they had the physical stamina for the job. Aware that girls reached physical maturity earlier than boys, the church set the age of girls at twelve and boys at fourteen for the first confession. Teenagers were considered to be adults with corresponding responsibilities. At fourteen or fifteen, they were considered eligible to labor in the fields and serve in the militia.

DOMESTIC CONFINEMENT

Urban girls, between the ages of twelve and twenty from well-off, socially oriented families, referred to as *doncellas* (maidens or virgins), were expected to be chaste, obedient, modest, and retiring and to maintain a serene countenance, downcast eyes, and a serious demeanor. Enclosed behind the bricks and mortar of the house and locked doors, they were protected from all possible dangers that might impugn family honor. Some of these girls spent their young lives indoors, even hidden from view when visitors called at the house, but others were allowed to attend church, their faces covered with a *mantilla*, where socializing with the opposite sex might afford a small opportunity under the watchful eye of their escort, sometimes rented for the occasion. A note might be surreptitiously passed between admiring couples and coquettish glances exchanged.

Processions, religious festivals, and pilgrimages afforded other opportunities to escape the house, and girls with lenient fathers were sometimes allowed to visit the homes of girlfriends, where they could chat, eat fruit, and drink chocolate. Moral critics and the church frowned upon even this activity, which gave females too much freedom, claiming it was offensive to God.

MARRIAGE, DOWRY, AND WIDOWS

Girls generally married at about age twenty-three and men at about twenty-five. The number of women who never married at all also varied with the region, but overall the rate was about 10 percent during the Early Modern period.[2] In Cataluña the son was expected to bring the bride into the parental home, whereas elsewhere it was the other way around, the young man entering the bride's home to take part in the family business.

Marriage negotiations were often a delicate affair conducted by intermediaries. The economic aspects were settled beforehand between the partners, stipulating the assets to be brought by the wife into the marriage and the property contributed by the groom. Marriages were often arranged within a circle of friends or business associates with the view to committing the family networks to continuing cooperation and prosperity.

When a girl was old enough to marry, she went from the confinement by her parents to that of her husband. Most houses had windows that overlooked a patio or garden and not the street, so women of this elite group had little contact with the outside world except, perhaps, through the servants.

With few exceptions, marriage was for life. The couple were required to cohabit, and neither was permitted to enter a monastery or convent or become celibate without the consent of the other. Divorce was not sanctioned. On occasion marriage could be annulled if it had been invalid in the first place—for example, on the basis of bigamy or close kinship—or if it was never consummated. An official separation, releasing the couple from the requirement of cohabitation, was also allowed in matters of cruelty or adultery. Remarriage was permitted on the death of one of the partners. The purpose of marriage in the view of the church was procreation; abortion, contraception, or sexual acts that would not lead to conception were, therefore, prohibited.

In practice the woman in the marriage was a subordinate member. The husband could use corporal punishment to discipline her, just as he might do to a servant, with no fear of communal or ecclesiastical disapproval. The wife's relatives, however, might not be so tolerant.

Women remained at home looking after the children, tending to the requirements of the house, sewing or embroidering, or sometimes, if they were sufficiently educated, reading some romantic or devout book. The tiresome existence would at times be lightened by female neighbors calling in for a visit and a chat about the newest fashions or scandal. Kneeling on the carpet or pillows, they could exchange the latest news while sipping chocolate or chewing pieces of *búcaro*, a kind of clay imported from the Indies for making pots but with an aromatic flavor and medicinal attributes. *Búcaro* was so popular among Spanish women that their confessors sometimes imposed upon them the penance of abstinence from it for a day or two.[3] A man's social life, for the most part, was spent outside the family circle and the home with male companions and acquaintances, gossiping in the open air or playing cards in the taverns.

Too often in the rural communities marriages were related to economic conditions. In good times, with substantial employment, young people married without due consideration or an eye on the future, had offspring early, and then found their lives in shambles and poverty when bad harvests, plague, or other calamities engulfed their regions.

Marriage fell under the legal jurisdiction of the church, and the match

had to be announced in the parish church of both parties. The announce-
ments, or banns, gave members of the community the opportunity to set
forth any objections to the union. The ceremony was celebrated in the
church, followed by a nuptial Mass and then festivities.

A woman of the upper classes was not likely to contribute in any
significant way to household finances, and it was important that she
bring to the marriage a substantial dowry of money or land. This involved the transfer of property from the parents of the girl to the future
husband to be kept as financial protection for the wife. It helped provide
a material foundation for the new family.

Dowries were often a hardship for many families and became increasingly so as they grew ever larger. They might consist of land, or liquid
assets such as cash or jewels, and in many cases, parents left the rest of
the children with nothing in order to marry a daughter off into a wealthy
family. Sisters who were left with no promise of a dowry were often sent
to live out their days in a convent.

The Sumptuary Laws of Felipe IV in 1623 attempted to include restrictions on the size of dowries, but a good marriage for the daughter of an
elite family brought valuable connections and influence, and the parents
were willing to pay dearly for this, even depriving their sons of their
inheritance. Sometimes the amount of the dowry was settled by annuity
to make it easier to pay.

Among the peasants, dowry was also significant and could enhance
the economic prospects of a family if the man were to marry a girl who
was in line to inherit some property such as a field or house in the
village. But dowry or not, in the country villages it was expedient to
marry one of the local girls, most of whom had learned a handicraft at
a young age and could help support a family. Among commoners a
healthy, industrious woman was a significant asset in family finances.

When the husband died, a widow could count at least on the return
of her dowry (if it had not been squandered), along with whatever else
had been promised her in the original contract or the will. Widows made
up about 10 percent of the population in any given community[4] and were
the most disadvantaged of all the poor, especially those with small children. There were many and their options were few.

In rural hamlets and villages widows whose husbands had been killed
in war, in accidents, or by disease were numerous and their options were
few, and those left with little assets apart from the cottage they lived in
often subsisted on charity from the parish church and neighbors or from
grown-up sons and daughters. They collected what leftover food they
could after the harvest and gathered wild fruit. They had the option to
remarry if the opportunity arose, but like most country women, they
often appeared old and haggard from heavy toil by age thirty. A last
resort was to move to the large cities and join the ranks of urban widows
begging on the street corners.

INHERITANCE AND ILLEGITIMACY

In some ways the system of inheritance helped shape the society. Medieval practice in Castilla was to divide the property up equally between heirs upon the death of the father. If a farm was involved, for example, each received a small parcel of land, which, often unable to sustain a family, then led to poverty. In much of Aragón and Cataluña the eldest child often received the inheritance, maintaining a continuity of property and with it supporting the other members of the family. As a rule these practices continued into Early Modern Spain. Particular regulations in the matter of inheritance differed from place to place. For example, in a village in the region of Guadalajara, east of Madrid, a possessor of common land could transfer his plot to his offspring, but if he died before this was done, it reverted to common status and could be occupied by the first person to claim it. In Belinchón, Cuenca, the children could inherit the father's plot of land if they plowed it within twelve days of his death. In this way the land could pass from generation to generation without reverting to common property.

The birth of many illegitimate offspring among the upper class was always a significant problem. If the father's legal spouse objected to them living in her house, they would be reared away from home. With a proud name but few resources, these children fell easily into a life of poverty and begging.

Among the average citizenry, illegitimate children could expect almost no help. Often they were simply unclaimed and taken from the village to a neighboring large town and left on the doorstep of a church. If an unmarried village girl was discovered to be pregnant, she might be driven from the village. If she could not find work as a maid in an affluent city household, she was often forced into prostitution in order to survive, and the baby more often than not ended up as a foundling.

Possibilities for a somewhat better life for illegitimate children as they grew up were either to embrace the church and seek admittance to a nunnery, monastery, or the priesthood or to try to obtain passage on a ship to the New World where opportunities for employment or a career were better than in Spain. These solutions to evade a miserable life at home, apart from a convent, were not viable options for girls.

EMIGRATION

Since its discovery, America irresistibly attracted many Spaniards to its distant shores, seeking fame, fortune, or land and escape from the class-bound restrictions at home. Stories circulated, often much exaggerated, about the wealth and opportunities of the New World, but there were abundant examples of men who had returned home rich after an exciting life of adventure. Cases of the many who died of disease or shipwreck deterred few. Families were often split up as many individuals saved their money or sold their property to purchase passage to the new land. Young people saw in the prospect of emigration a future far from the drudgery, hunger, and toil of everyday life in the villages or cities of Spain.

Migrations arising from desperation to other regions of the country occurred from time to time. Drought and famine were major causes, but sometimes opportunities arose to acquire more land. When the Muslims were expelled from Granada, Christian families moved into the void. Complaints at the time blamed these migrations of nearly entire villages in some districts for the ruination of agriculture and of the landowning nobility itself. As the vassals left, there was no one to work the land and pay the rent.

OLD AGE, DEATH, AND BURIAL

If a person was fortunate enough to reach the age of about twenty-five or thirty with no major disabilities from disease or accidents, he or she was well on the way to eventually reaching old age. At the time this was about sixty, and retirement, at least for those with family backing or wealth, became a possibility. Society made no provisions for a man or woman's golden age, and individuals either provided it themselves or continued working until they dropped dead. Aristocrats with land and rentals, well-heeled bourgeois, and some members of guilds had little problem securing a pension for their declining years. Wealthy peasants or even those not so wealthy might exchange property holdings for financial support and a house to live in. Even a faithful steward or cook on a baronial estate might be looked after in old age by his employer. Similarly, monasteries sometimes took in the aged and gave them a room and meals in exchange for property, cash, or something else of value.

The many hundreds of thousands without and with negligible family connections—itinerant workers, lowly paid clerks or municipal employees, service staff, small entrepreneurs, landless peasants, poor writers, soldiers and sailors—were all vulnerable to an unmemorable old age of begging on the streets and dying in the gutter or in a charity hospital. Uneducated peasant women, who at the time of marriage were generally younger than their husbands, could often expect to spend long years in lonely widowhood and extreme poverty.

The Grim Reaper was always present in the form of disease, accident, war, and childbirth with complications, as well as in numerous other guises. Pending the final event in one's life, the priest was called to administer the last rite of Extreme Unction.

At all levels of society, on the death of someone, friends and neighbors immediately rallied to the side of the bereaved. Dramatic funerals were common, characterized by an emotional gathering of friends and family with women weeping and wailing. They were affairs with large congregations of people parading through the streets of the city. Gatherings of the clan would take place to show solidarity and support long after the corpse was buried. The rallies were so large that the church and the state tried to curb them by stipulating the number of people who could hold candles in the funerary procession, restricting mourning dress to only members of the household, and ordering that no food be served at the gatherings. With these limitations fewer people would be involved, lessening the threat of vendettas and civil disobedience that might come with a large crowd. These restrictions were not very successful, did not apply uniformly to all areas, and applied not at all to the region of Aragón.

Lineage and class were nowhere more evident than in the burial site. Commoners were interred in the churchyard with neither coffin nor commemorative marker. For people of noble background, or those wealthy enough to afford a substantial donation to the church and a stone coffin, a niche inside the church would be found.

Members of the same noble family tended to be interred in a communal vault, but each time a particular branch of the family came to an end, or when one branch superseded the others in wealth and power, a new vault would be constructed. Sometimes this took the form of a new chapel in the church where the bones of the deceased would rest. The burial site was then to remain as a testimony to the family that established it. Burial chambers were not cheap, nor were carved stone figures and marble sarcophagi, so their use was restricted to the wealthy. The practice generally gave way to a simple inscribed slab of marble over the grave site.

Each year thereafter, on All Souls Day at the beginning of November, quantities of candles were lit to commemorate the deceased. The church made no effort to curb the sometimes extraordinary number of Masses for which the dead man or woman had paid in order to redeem their souls. The cult of the dead occupied much of individual energies and reinforced common ancestral ties.

NOTES

1. Alcalá-Zamora, 53.
2. Casey, 27ff.
3. Aulnoy, in Ross and Power, 212; Defourneaux, 153.
4. Alcalá-Zamora, 54.

12

Clothes and Fashions

In the decades following the voyages of Columbus, when Spain began to consolidate a global empire and Carlos V, as Holy Roman Emperor, dominated the politics of Europe, the country acquired great prestige.

Along with this political ascendancy came enormous wealth from the continuous stream of precious metals from the Americas, which translated into sumptuous luxury for the upper classes. The spread of Spanish influence from the end of the fifteenth century reflected the wealth and power of the nation.

By the middle of the sixteenth century, Spain was a leader of European fashion, the dress of the nobility in the court being adopted by many of the countries of western Europe.[1] Later, when her international power began to decline, so did Spain's influence on European costume. By the beginning of the eighteenth century, when a Bourbon mounted the Spanish throne, France had taken over in the fashion world, and everyone, except the country people, had adopted the French style of dress. At their zenith, however, Spaniards were famous for the cut of their clothes, the austere elegance, flawless fit, and the precise distinction of line that piqued the interest and envy of meticulous dressers all over Europe.

Courtly fashions revolved around the colors red, yellow, and green, whereas blues were seldom used due to their excessive costs, coming, as they did, from the tropical Asian indigo plant. Black became the symbol of Spanish elegance, however, perhaps due in large part to the lengthy periods of mourning of Felipe II when the entire court was plunged into funeral trappings. Materials were rich, but after this time, colors tended

Velázquez. *The Infanta Margarita* (from *Las Meninas*). (Madrid: Prado). She is wearing the ultimate farthingale. Note the hair extended to complement the skirt.

to be in dark tones, and the predilection for black spread particularly through Italy and France.

WOMEN

Fashion tended to mirror society as a whole, and the more limitations placed on behavior by matters of etiquette and by the Inquisition, the more restrictive became the clothes. From head to toe, women's dress was rigid so as to express the moral preoccupations of the Spanish clergy.

The most characteristic of garments in high society among aristocratic women who sat for court painters, an idle minority with little to do but think about their appearance, was the *guardinfante*, an offshoot of the European sixteenth-century farthingale, an inflexible hooped support worn under the skirt to blossom it out at the hip line. This was a padded framework of whale bone or cane hoops under the petticoat and skirt that became progressively larger as they went from waist to hem. The upper skirts, which were not gathered at the waist, were flared and distended over the hoops in a cone shape. In these exaggerated garments a woman walked gracefully as if floating over the ground; but trying to enter the narrow portal of the church or even sitting down presented a major undertaking.

When the hoop skirt first appeared in the middle of the sixteenth century, only women of the court wore it. During most of the next hundred years, it was used on formal occasions by all women aspiring to elegance.

In Spain the farthingale continued to be used until the middle of the seventeenth century, long after it had ceased to be worn in other parts of Europe. Its use was aided and abetted by Felipe IV's second wife Mariana of Austria, thirty years his junior. She set the example by wearing a larger and more voluminous farthingale than had ever been seen before. Only in the following reign of Carlos II did the fashion disappear.

One description of a wealthy woman's clothes given by Madame d'Aulnoy states:

This lady soon came in in a dress used by the Spaniards this hundred years; she had a kind of pattens on, or rather stilts, which made her look prodigious tall, so that she was fain to lean on two persons' shoulders when she moved. . . . The singular dress of the Countess de Lemos appeared to me so extraordinary that I could hardly get mine eyes off it. She wore a kind of black satin gold-embroidered bodice, and buttoned with great rubies of considerable value. This bodice came down from her neck just like a doublet; her sleeves were strait, with large wings about her shoulders and other sleeves hanging as low as her gown, which was fastened on each side with roses of diamonds. She had a dreadful farthingale which hindered her from sitting otherwise than on the ground. She wore a ruff and several chains of great pearls and diamonds.[2]

Along with hooped skirts, fashion decreed that the torso be rigidly confined, and under the tight-fitting bodice, a boned corset was worn to emphasize a long, fragile waist, almost giving the effect of cutting the body into two halves and eliminating any suggestion of breasts. In some cases lead was employed to clamp them down and retard their growth.[3]

The stiff, high bodice ended with a point at the waist and was lined with canvas edged with wire. Voluminous ballooned sleeves terminating in decorated and embroidered cuffs were popular for some time. These were often removable and attached separately by laces to the armholes of the bodice.

By about 1590 the neck ruff had come into fashion. It was originally a frilled narrow neck band worn to finish the high collar of the bodice. As it became larger, so also did the farthingale to offset it. In the mid-sixteenth century, ruffs with high collars began to be used. The collar, when not worn straight, was turned up, and when the ruffs became more and more voluminous, wire and pasteboard frames (*rebatos*) were used to support them. After 1590 ruffs grew to monstrous proportions and were very costly to purchase and maintain. Numerous servants, often of a young age, were employed in ironing and fluting these extravagant pieces, and it was thought by many that these people might be more usefully employed in the service of the state or in agriculture.

Ruffs were banned by the Sumptuary Laws of Felipe IV in 1623 along with the silver and gold embroidering of clothes, but in fact, modest ruffs continued to be used in Spain long after they were abandoned in the rest of Europe.

The Pragmatic Sanction (royal decree) of 1639 vainly attempted to prevent feminine décolletage, which, since the beginning of that century when the bodice had been tight and fitted closely to the throat, had gradually developed into lower and lower necklines revealing first the shoulders, then part of the back, and eventually the part where neck and bosom met. The dimensions of the dress were often the butt of jokes of satirists and moralists. A satirist of the time thought that women who dressed à la mode would be more decent if they went around naked.[4] This was the preferred style of prostitutes and courtesans (who were still permitted to wear it), and the decree was meant to dispel confusion between the women of the street and those of the court. As with so many other laws, however, once the matter had settled down, women reverted to doing as they pleased.

It was considered immodest in high society to reveal the feet, which were hidden under the full-length gown of heavy material such as taffeta or brocade over the farthingale. In fact, while walking, women mastered the art of making their skirts sway from side to side so that it appeared as if they were moving along gracefully on casters. A pleat insert above the hem of the skirt permitted women to be seated without exposing their feet. Outside, clogs (*chopines*) with cork heels were worn. These gave the short Spanish ladies a little more height and could be covered with leather or velvet. They also were useful to avoid the dusty or muddy streets of the town.

Eventually, Queen María of Savoy, wife of Felipe V, rejected the uncomfortable *tontillo* worn over the skirt to keep it down to avoid exposing the feet and legs when seated. Madame d'Aulnoy commented that the highest kindness a woman can pay to her suitor is to show him her foot, adding that

their [Spanish ladies'] feet are so small that their shoes look like those of our [French] babies. They are made of black Spanish leather, cut upon coloured taffeta, without heels, and as strait as a glove. When they go, you would think they flew; we should not in a hundred years learn their way of walking. They keep their elbows close to their sides, and go without raising their feet, just as one slides.[5]

Aeneas Vico. *Habitus Nostrae Aetatis. 1556.* (London: Victoria and Albert Museum). A middle-class woman wearing a wimple. Her skirt falls in natural folds. The *chopines* (clogs), to avoid the dirt and dust of the ground, were usually made of cork.

Gloves were required for all formal occasions, and popular among the rich were plumes, lace handkerchiefs, jewelry, and crucifixes. Perfumes were in demand among all classes, especially, perhaps, since bathing was not particularly frequent in this society, and embroidered handbags were used to carry around aromatic pastilles.

Of special importance was the fan. Although a luxury at first, it grew to become an indispensable item in the fine art of flirting. Every movement of the fan generated a message of its own: All depended on the way of opening and closing or raising and lowering it. It was useful to giggle and whisper behind or to hide a blushing face when a gentleman made overtures. Leucadio Doblado in his *Letters from Spain* describes the use of the showy and indispensable fan employed in all seasons both in and out of doors as having an advantage over the natural organ of speech (the tongue) as it conveys thought at a greater distance. He says:

A dear friend at the farthest end of the public walk, is greeted and cheered up by a quick, tremulous motion of the fan, accompanied with several significant nods. An object of indifference is dismissed with a slow, formal inclination of the fan, which makes his blood run cold. The fan . . . now condenses a smile into the dark sparkling eyes, which take their aim just above it. A gentle tap of the

Sanchez Coello. *Woman with the Fan.*
(Madrid: Prado).

fan commands the attention of the careless; a waving motion calls the distant. A
certain twirl between the fingers betrays doubt or anxiety—a quick closing and
displaying the folds, indicates eagerness or joy.... The fan is a magic wand
whose power is more easily felt than described.[6]

The fan was changed for every occasion, and husbands began to complain at the expense of so many of them and the requirements of their
wives to wear new clothes for every event, only to discard them afterward. Women of the wealthiest families purchased multitudes of extravagant bracelets, earrings, and necklaces for every conceivable eventuality
and frequently provided a great source of stress on the family finances.

At the beginning of the seventeenth century spectacles (known as *quev-
edos*) came into fashion among both sexes. Young and old, laymen and
clerics, all wore them though they served no verifiable purpose. Shapes
varied with social standing. Aristocrats wore large ones hooked over the
ears. A young woman appeared her most elegant with her face half hidden behind them. Among some, they were only removed at bedtime.[7]

Madrid set the styles, and women visiting the capital from the provinces often felt out of their element and were even subject to ridicule

until they had determined what to buy and wear to fit in with the luxurious attire of their city cousins.

The black *mantilla* was the national headdress worn by all classes of women, both indoors and out. Often made of tulle or transparent silk, it varied in length according to the wearer. The widow's *mantilla* reached to the ground, enveloping her from head to foot. For matrons or young virgin girls they were shorter. A young unmarried girl out of doors, accompanied by her chaperone, held her *mantilla* from the inside in such a way as to cover her face completely, allowing only one eye free to see where she was going. For both the single woman and the widow these stringent customs were more prevalent in the south of the country than in the north, where (particularly in the Basque region) the women were not required to cover their heads since they were considered to be on equal status with the men.

Over the shoulders a loose outer cloak (*ropa*) was often worn, sometimes covering the body completely and preserving a woman's anonymity when necessary. Outings were not taken for granted among women of high caste; a cogent excuse to escape the house was needed, and such opportunities were afforded by the observance of religious duties at the parish church. A lady of quality would normally go out into the streets accompanied by a married female chaperone or by her squire who, when necessary, took her hand, which was well wrapped in the folds of her cloak, thus avoiding skin contact.[8] Especially in Madrid, those not wealthy enough to maintain a permanent squire could rent one for the day at various locations in the public squares. Pages could also be obtained in this manner, and they would follow along behind, carrying velvet cushions for the mistress to kneel on when praying.

The veil (*tapado*) was also often worn by respectable women in the streets, providing complete anonymity and imagined charms to unattractive women who otherwise might be unable to catch men's interest. Other difficulties caused by this were that veiled courtesans could pass themselves off as high-born ladies, and all could engage in coquettish behavior without risk. Fathers could not recognize their daughters nor wives, nor brothers their sisters, and hence not know what they were about. As all women could wear them, men, according to the complaints of the day, might accost the wives or daughters of gentlefolk as if they were common people and fair game. During the reign of Felipe II the Castillian Cortes protested this custom that gave women too much freedom. By a decree issued in 1590, Felipe II forbade the use of the veil, but it was mostly ignored. In 1639 Felipe IV announced a fine of 1,000 maravedís for those caught wearing it, except inside the church, where it was permitted.[9]

Women still went out of doors enveloped in an enormous sleeveless cape that covered them from head to foot, the face hidden if not by a

Woman dressed for the street.

veil by the cape itself. Married or single, they could thus mix with the people on the street and enjoy a little liberty. In spite of royal edicts, the style persisted throughout the seventeenth century and beyond.

While visiting the south of the country as late as 1801, Doblado stated:

Some of the ladies wore their *mantillas* crossed upon the chin so as to conceal their features. A women in this garb is called *tapada*; and the practice of that disguise, which was very common under the Austrian [Habsburg] dynasty, is still preserved by a few females in some of our country-towns. I have seen them at Osuna and El Arahal, covered from head to foot with a black woollen veil falling on both sides of the face, and crossed so closely before it that nothing could be perceived but the gleaming of the right eye placed just behind the aperature.[10]

Women also wore black or dark purple capes, but near the end of the eighteenth century, some noblewomen appeared on the streets of Madrid wearing them in bright colors. Such attire invited grimaces, hissing, and booing by the male population. The matter reached its crescendo on a Good Friday when a few women came out in even more lively colors including rich red capes. Their pages were forced to draw their swords to protect the ladies from the threatening mob gathered around them. A law was passed in 1799 proscribing the wearing of anything except black, a somber color that reflected constraint, sobriety, conservatism, and tradition.

HAIRSTYLES AND HATS

Hairstyles were different in Spain from other European countries of the period. In the middle of the sixteenth century the tendency was to draw the hair tightly back from the face and coil it at the back. Later, a pad was placed on the forehead and the hair drawn over it, piled up, and coiled on top of the head in a diadem, sometimes reaching a point. This changed by the early seventeenth century when hair was still piled high on top of the head but left thick at the sides and coiled at the back. By about 1650 long hair came into favor, and Spanish women let it fall down and spill over their now-bare shoulders. In the eighteenth century wealthy women found it necessary to employ private hairdressers to do their coiffure in accordance with new styles introduced from France. The hair was carefully powdered and braided along the neck, with curls held in place by ornaments.

Hats were sometimes worn over the *mantilla*, and those with a wide brim were generally placed forward to shield the face a little and protect it from the sun. There were also stiff bonnets worn over the *mantilla* as well as softer ones with feathers on them. Some might be trimmed with lace. Various regions had their own distinctive styles of headgear: For instance, in Cáceres stiff bonnets covered with little mirrors showed a girl to be unmarried. In Vizcaya the feminine hat was the shape of a pot with a necklace. Poor women of the Basque region often wore felt hats kept in shape by wooden or copper bands around the inside. In Toledo a felt Egyptian-style hat was worn. There were also various kinds of high felt or velvet soft hats worn with a wimple (a cloth covering for the neck and sides of the face, attached to the hat).

COSMETICS

The use of cosmetics, like other aspects of daily life, has been described by travelers and contemporary playwrights and depicted in portraits. The application of beauty aids was often a matter of a box of paints applied to shoulders, neck, face, and even the ears. The foundation creme was ceruse (a cosmetic containing white lead).

The lips were covered with a thin layer of wax to make them gleam, or they were painted red. When ruffs went out of style, heavy rouge began to be used extensively, along with other kinds of makeup, applied without discretion to draw attention to the face. For hand care an ointment made from bacon fat and almond paste was used. Rose water and ambergris served as perfumes.[11] It often took hours before the bedroom mirror with the help of a servant for women to make themselves look their very best before they could be seen by others.

HORSES AND CARRIAGES

The highest distinction for a woman was to have her own horses and carriage. They were expensive, but more and more carriages came to replace the sedan chair and litter as a mode of transportation around town. During the seventeenth century it increased to the extent that in the late afternoon when people came out of their houses to see and be seen, traffic in the main street of Madrid often resulted in bottlenecks that immobilized the vehicles for long periods. The craze for carriages became so acute that some cities such as Barcelona, Valencia, and Sevilla restricted their usage to a minority of the very rich by prohibiting those drawn by less than four mules, an expensive proposition.

The demand for carriages often bankrupted families as the most penurious hidalgo or nobleman would not allow his wife to ride in one less grand than that of his neighbor, although it might cost him his entire inheritance. The preoccupation with secret amorous liaisons and the protection of girls' virtues, coupled with carriages whose leather blinds could be let down, converting the interior into a sanctuary of illicit activity, prompted edicts in the time of Felipe III that blinds remain open and women travel with the face hidden from view. Such regulations in the use of carriages soon faded away, for, as usual, women ignored the impositions.

For a woman living well away in the country, in the hamlets and villages, the trappings of cosmetics, fashion, carriages, and other pretensions to the grand life were simply another world utterly foreign to her own.

MEN

During the sixteenth century men tended to wear clothing that magnified their masculine attributes at the same time as it imitated armor—a style that symbolically yielded both a protective and hostile significance in a warlike country where almost everyone carried a weapon. Tightly fitting stuffed or quilted doublets, a row of buttons in the front, reached to a point below the waistline whose slimness was accentuated. Thighs were emphasized, and parts of the body were often lightly padded to increase the volume of certain sections of their outline. Short pantaloons and stockings were also inflated, especially in the later sixteenth century. In the same period, the peasecod doublets and jackets represented the extreme of armor mimicry. Sometimes enormous, prominent codpieces were worn to call attention to the virile attributes of the wearer.

Sanchez Coello. *Don Juan of Austria.* (Madrid: Prado). Note the frilled neckband and breastplate that, together with the shape of the trunks, accentuate the smallness of the waist.

Jerkins were commonly worn over doublets after the mid-sixteenth century, but especially typical of Spain was the height of the collar, which, after first being a kind of neck support, turned into a ruff having the same effect as it did with the women of making the head seem as if it were completely detached from the torso. With the head held at such an angle, a man was forced to remain straight and alert. By the beginning of the seventeenth century Dutch lace had made its appearance in Spain and was comfortably used in place of the stiff ruff.

At the end of the century, square-cut jackets and trunks that went almost down to the knees came into vogue and remained until knee breeches of all types, from tight to baggy, took precedence.

For gentlemen at court, shoes generally fitted closely at the ankles and had narrow soles and often square toes and a flower design on top. At first they were made of satin, but after the beginning of the seventeenth century, leather was almost always used. The long, soft riding boots, looped from below the knees to the bottoms of the trunks, seem to have been exclusively Spanish. Among the lower classes, feet were often protected by wooden soles strapped on by cords. Otherwise they went barefoot.

Men kept their hair reasonably short until toward the end of the six-

Rodrigo de Villandrando. *Felipe IV as a Boy with the Dwarf Soplillo.* (Madrid: Prado). The voluminous trunks are stiffened in the style of the farthingale. The ruffs have triangular pleats; the cape, a high collar; and the shoes have square toes with rosettes.

teenth century, when long hair in the front brushed straight back over the ears became the fashion. It was the style worn by Don Juan of Austria, the hero of the victory over the Turks at Lepanto in 1571. Mustaches, which came and went in vogue all over Europe, were popular among Spaniards, but only in Spain did one see the waxed mustache as worn by Felipe IV.[12]

Like the women, men of rank wore stiffened bonnets sometimes studded with gems (usually placed on the left side). During the reign of Felipe III, many styles of headgear appeared, including hats with tall crowns and broad brims. These continued in use until the middle of the seventeenth century when they were replaced in much of Europe and Spain by the wide-brimmed, soft slouch hat with or without feathers. Spaniards tended to turn up the brim on the right side, and the hats were worn straight and not at rakish angles, as was the case elsewhere.

Laborers and artisans in northern Spain had their own style of hats: Peaked leather caps with buttons appeared in Navarra and Viscaya, Basque regions, and to some extent, perhaps coincidentally, among the Moors of the south.

Full-length woolen cloaks, which had been worn by Spaniards since the Middle Ages, gave way after 1550 to shorter capes, which proved to be more manageable, especially on horseback and with the long swords of the time. Cloaks appeared in varying lengths and styles—some cowled, some with high collars, some with fine materials and fur lining for formal wear. Others were made of a circle of material with armholes and a hood. Horsemen sometimes wore a double cape of felt (*fieltro*) that was of shorter length, with a hood and high collar. None of the styles that were imported to Spain featured hoods, but they proved to be the main distinguishing feature of the Spanish mode. After about 1620, three-quarter-length capes seem to have become popular. They were often held in place by cords attached to the back of the jacket and hung in straight folds off the shoulders, with the arms left free.

In 1766 long capes under which ill-gotten goods could be concealed were forbidden by the government. This led to riots in Madrid, especially when the police came out with measuring rods and shears, backed offenders wearing long capes up against a wall, and cut the offending garment in half![13]

Cloaks in Europe now began to go out of style as coats came in, but the Spaniard, with plumes in his hat and sword at his side, still cut a fine figure in his cape. By the eighteenth century, the cape was worn by nearly everyone in the country; it was a national symbol and occasionally even used to bury the dead.

LOWER-CLASS ATTIRE

Lower-class women who needed and were used to freedom of movement in the fields or marketplaces did not wear the farthingales, even on formal occasions such as weddings. Instead, they wore skirts that fell in folds, or they used padding on the hips that permitted the skirt material to fall naturally.

Artisans, laborers, and peasants generally wore brown shirts and knee-length trousers made from sheep's wool or linen from the flax plant, and woolen hose, whereas the women dressed in a simple slip-on garment or tunic made with or without sleeves and with attached hood.

There was a variety of regional dress; for example, in Valencia the lowland peasants wore canvas breeches, whereas those who inhabited the highlands usually wore wool from merino sheep raised near Segovia. When in town it would not be unusual to see the peasant dressed with a canvas jacket over his shirt—a kind of cloak or pancho with sleeves and a hood at the back—large, wide, and ill-made trousers (breeches) with a rope or cord belt, leggings, hemp sandals, and a wide-brimmed hat.

According to one traveler during Napoleonic times the clothes of the Andalucian peasant consisted generally of a light jacket with three close rows of oval buttons and two rows of loops and tassels. Buttons were hung on silver chains down to each knee of the breeches. The men braided their hair in a neat manner and fastened it at the end with a black ribbon, tied in a bow, which hung halfway down the back.[14]

Children of the lower classes, as well as those of the upper levels of society, wore clothing reminiscent of adult attire.

Wealthy merchants imitated the dress of high society, while the clothing of the lower nobility was determined by their occupation and income.

NOTES

1. Reade, 5.
2. Aulnoy, in Ross and Power, 122–123.
3. Reade, 8.
4. Defourneaux, 157.
5. Aulnoy, in Ross and Power, 200.
6. Doblado, 55–56.
7. Aulnoy, in Ross and Power, 209; Defourneaux, 155.
8. Defourneaux, 158.
9. Alcalá-Zamora, 175.
10. Doblado, 187.
11. Defourneaux, 155.
12. Reade, 13.
13. Casey, 249.
14. Blayney, 194.

13

Food

BREAKFAST

Spaniards rose early in the morning, and breakfast, if eaten at all, was very light—usually a little bread or biscuits, perhaps a mouthful of sheep cheese, a drink or two of wine or a cup of chocolate.[1] A rasher of bacon, roasted not fried, was served in every eating house for breakfast and was inexpensive. Only a little dish of liver cost less.

By six (seven in winter), the vendors in the markets already displayed meat and fish and baskets of fruit, and stalls in the plazas were ready to dispense their products, including brandy. For many, a swallow of brandy was breakfast, especially on cold winter mornings. It was often taken with a little thick jam, honey, or marmalade. A drink in the morning to fend off the cold was not looked upon by the authorities as a good thing, and many attempts were made to prohibit it, but the tradition persisted. After breakfast, gentlemen went off to their occupations, and in the larger towns, ladies went to listen to a sermon and music at the church.

DINNER

Around noon, the women were generally at home doing needlework or looking after the children and expecting the morning calls of their friends. For most people, the midday meal, the main repast of the day, coincided with the high point of the sun, about one o'clock, although

Stirring the pot.

some put it off until the meat markets reopened. Butchers generally did their business between six and ten in the morning, opening again at two in the winter and three in the summer. With the exception of a few grandees who had a larder, no one kept food in the house, and for every meal, people went out and bought the necessary ingredients. With the lack of refrigeration, food, especially meat and seafood, did not last long, especially in the sweltering summer months, although keeping it chilled or even frozen through the use of ice was known. Spices and herbs played an important role in preservation, as did pickling, but items so treated constituted a luxury ill afforded by most and were not part of the diet of the average family.

Invitations to dine were rare. Only on certain occasions, such as a young priest having performed his first Mass or a daughter taking the veil, might a dinner party be held. If there was to be a celebration at the house with invited guests, the food would be prepared at the local inn and delivered.[2]

Venders were not permitted to sell their products at any price they chose. The municipal authority was always on the lookout for elevated prices or fraud in weighing the merchandise, and its agents circulated among the stalls of the markets, taverns, and eating houses, always vigilant for unfair practices. Both buyer and seller knew that once a sale was completed, one of these agents might take the item in question and remeasure it or reweigh it to check the accuracy of the transaction. If fault were found, a loud argument ensued, people crowded around to watch, and if the vendor could not defend his deceitful behavior, a large fine would be imposed.

Rich and powerful people of the court tended to eat their big meal of the day later than most, sitting down to a sumptuous table of many and varied dishes. A siesta or nap was usually taken after the midday meal.

Velázquez. *Kitchen Scene*. (London: National Gallery).

In contrast, the peasants working in the fields all day long reserved the most substantial meal for the evening.

MEALS OF THE AFFLUENT

Food was prepared in wealthy houses by professional cooks and servants who also did the shopping. A great deal of animal flesh was consumed, and several different kinds were devoured at one meal. Meat was often served as a stew (*cocido*) or marinated. Spices and condiments usually consisted of pepper, garlic, and saffron. Certain dishes were common, including *olla podrida*, a pork-based stew, and blancmange—the latter, a kind of hash incorporating a base of thin slices of chicken simmered in a milk sauce with rice flour and sugar.

In general, pork and mutton, widespread and easily obtainable, were the principal ingredients in most meals, but also consumed were a broad variety of other meats including ox, goat, and beef. Poultry and game such as partridge and pigeon were also popular except during Lent or on Fridays or other days of fasting when eggs and fish made up the menu. Trout, carp, cod, sole, sea-bream, anchovies, and sardines, when available, rapidly disappeared from the vendors' stalls. Fish clearly defined one's social and economic position. The wealthy elite had fresh fish from the streams and rivers or even from the sea in winter, brought to them by relays of horse teams. When the fresh item was not available, then pickled, salted, or dried fish would do, which allowed its transportation to cities far from the sea such as Madrid.

Ordinary food could be much enhanced by sauces of which there were many different varieties. For example, with peacock, a sauce might be composed of bacon and onion, chicken broth, minced almonds, lemon juice, bitter oranges (or pomegranates), sugar and honey, walnuts, cinnamon, cloves, and ginger, all mixed with the fat from the roasted bird.

Another sauce, which was piquant and which usually went with poultry, was prepared with almond milk mixed with chicken broth, chopped chicken livers, grenadine, red vinegar, cinnamon, and a lot of ginger, along with walnuts, sugar, and again, the fat from the roasted bird.

A typical sauce to serve with game was composed of toasted bread soaked in vinegar, pepper, cloves, and ginger mixed with beef broth, saffron, almond milk, and some minced meat of the bird or animal being cooked. This sauce was introduced in a much earlier time by the Romans, who served it with roast boar.

To conclude the meal there were desserts that usually consisted of fruit in season, olives, and cheese in winter. The fresh fruit, even according to travelers accustomed to deprecating the cuisine of the country, was the best they had ever tasted. It was inexpensive and came in a wide variety. Only strawberries, often taken with sugar and wine, commanded a high price, one that was often the subject of municipal attention. Other fruits were lemons and oranges from Valencia and Murcia; a variety of apples and pears from Aragón; cherries, limes, and pomegranates from Granada; plums, figs, dates, apricots, and peaches from the south, and of course, grapes. In addition, berries, melons, and a wide variety of nuts were often added to dessert dishes.

Fruit pies, egg yolks preserved in sugar, and a variety of almond cakes (inherited from the Moors) were favored desserts, as were anise bonbons and sugared almonds. Delicacies made with honey or sugar were eaten along with a large variety of sweet pastries, confectionery of fruit and nuts made with milk, eggs, and spices. There was also an assortment of *turrones* (nougat) especially popular around Christmas, the most expensive and best being produced in Alicante. Confectionery was generally reserved for picnics and receptions, as it was too expensive for most people to consume on a regular basis.

Meals were usually served on small tables in the living room, as most private houses did not have a dining room. In many homes, especially where the Moorish culture was influential, only men sat on chairs to eat, whereas the women and children occupied cushions beside the table. While the wealthy ate to excess, the poor often lived on the verge of starvation.

Members of monasteries and convents were seldom lacking wholesome nourishment, much of the produce raised in their own gardens and orchards. Some conceived unusual recipes such as spinach cooked with tender garlic and almond milk, or spinach and leeks in a sauce of pine and hazel nuts. Squash soup garnished with cinnamon and milk, produced at one convent, was shared at the gates with the poor.

MEALS OF THE LOWER CLASSES

Among the lower classes, meat was consumed in small quantities, and middle-class people in general would have just a slice of goat or lamb for a meal. About 50 grams a day per person for those who could afford meat at all constituted a rather small quantity compared to the aristocracy, whose intake was in the neighborhood of 350 grams per person each day.[3]

Among poor people the wife, assisted by her daughter, prepared the food, and families ate mostly vegetables, which included artichokes and beans, garlic, onions, and olives and perhaps a bit of goat or sheep cheese. The diet depended somewhat on the location, but bread was a universal staple of all households. A rise in the cost of bread sometimes led to riots. In the seventeenth century a three-pound loaf of bread, just enough to feed an average family, cost about half the daily wage of a working man.[4]

As long as the supply of bread for the communities was adequate, the populace remained tranquil. When the rains were too abundant or insufficient and the harvest failed and the supply dried up, civil strife was just around the corner. The *tasa*, the fixed maximum price for grain, was, like many other regulations, only sporadically enforced. In good times the price of grain was below the fixed price, but when disaster struck and prices climbed due to shortages, the *tasa* was disregarded even by the government.

Food riots occurred in Andalucía when the price of bread tripled in 1648. Crowds gathered in the city of Granada, the *corregidor* left town, and the mob advanced on the High Court, shouting, "Down with bad government." The ringleaders forced the president of the court to closely examine a loaf of bread whose wheat was mixed with millet and ashes. A fresh supply of grain soon arrived in the city, and coupled with a general pardon for the rioters and the promise from the authorities of lower prices, the situation cooled down.

Since wheat was generally the basic ingredient of bread throughout the Spanish realms, cities tried to maintain control over surrounding areas for the purchase of wheat and bread to feed the populace; for example, the villages within a radius of about sixty miles around Madrid were required to supply quotas of grain for baking bread, although the system was abolished in 1758 as unworkable.

There was a good deal of speculation in sales of wheat and bread, and marketplaces in the cities were policed to see that food supplies reached the consumer directly and did not fall into the clutches of hoarders and speculators who could withhold stocks for prices higher than the *tasa*.

Except for some convents that baked their own bread, average households and even the nobility relied on the public ovens, which were crucial in the network of supply, and many were owned by the church or the aristocracy. Nevertheless, the size and price of a loaf was fixed by the magistrates.

Varieties of bread included the *empanada* or small pie made up of wheat flour and of rye and filled with tidbits of meat, fish, or vegetables. In some areas in the south of the country, rice was a staple. The potato plant, native to the Peruvian Andes, was brought to Europe in the sixteenth century by Spanish explorers but did not become an item of regular consumption in Spain (as it did in more northern countries) until the eighteenth century, then primarily in Galicia and Asturias. Corn (maize), also a native grain from the New World, became part of the Spanish diet relatively late when it began to be cultivated in the northwest in the seventeenth century.

On meatless days, the lower classes resorted to dried hake or cod, which were the least expensive. Some bourgeois pickled their own fish at home in large jars. On warm days it smelled so bad that laws were enacted against throwing the brine into the streets. A very popular dish when in season was fresh peas cooked with pork sausage or bacon. Beans, lentils, chickpeas, and noodles, the latter seasoned with grated cheese, accounted for much of the diet.

At the base of the culinary pyramid, the poor peasants' diet consisted almost exclusively of turnip stew, a few vegetables, rye bread, onions, and cheese and, in the south, olives. Those of the central provinces were reliant on a kind of porridge or gruel instead of bread, as they boiled their rye, millet, or barley instead of baking it; but some form of grain provided the main part of the rural diet. Shepherds, for example, would eat bread crumbs fried in milk or simply bread and water, whereas the peasant villager ate his with a little stewed vegetables and bacon. In times of fast, the bacon would be replaced by chickpeas. Although wheat was the basic ingredient throughout the country, other components were frequently mixed with it to make the bread cheaper to produce. In the northwest, chestnuts were sometimes added, giving it a savory flavor, whereas on the Mediterranean coast carobs were used as an additive. Bran was sometimes mixed with wheat, and around Córdoba, barley was baked into it in bad years.

Chicken was not an important ingredient in the peasant diet unless peasants were well off. It was a luxury and often sufficed as part payment of the rent on their lands. Eggs, on the other hand, were devoured in great quantities. Olives from Sevilla and Córdoba were the best and most expensive. Ordinary olives cost about 10 to 12 maravedís a pound, those from Sevilla about 55 maravedís. Sheep cheese was also more expensive than goat cheese—and still more so when it had been aged. Dessert delicacies, especially those made with sugar, were never cheap and always beyond the means of the poor.

FAST FOOD

Stalls were to be found in the plazas of the cities where a person in a hurry could eat or drink at the counter or standing up, but the food appears not to have been particularly appetizing. Some people crossed themselves before consuming the little meat pies (*empanadillas*), for example, which had the reputation of being made from the minced-up bodies of people who had been hanged on the gallows outside the city. Others maintained that the pies were made from ground-up cats. True or not, it gives a picture of dismal quality.

WINE AND OIL

Wines of good quality were produced all over the country, although they were not appreciated by foreign travelers who found them too much flavored by resin and the pig- or goatskin containers in which they were stored. There are reports that women seldom drank it and that the average man consumed it sparingly. While it was drunk at every meal including the first one, about a quarter of a liter was sufficient for the day. Beer was not popular.[5]

It was socially unacceptable to show any effects from drinking, and to actually get drunk was considered in the worst taste. The accusation of drunkenness was an outrageous insult, and few men or women would allow themselves to reach that stage.

Wines were classified as good and expensive and ordinary and cheap. Both kinds could not be sold in the taverns at the same time. Presumably, the tavern keepers could not be trusted to give the clients what they paid for. Clever men knew how to adulterate and disguise poor young wine so that it seemed older and tasted like the more expensive kind and could be sold as such. Often, even the poor wine was watered down so much that the ingenious vender had to reconstitute it so it tasted less insipid. This might be done with chemicals dangerous to the clients' health or even by the addition of animal blood to red wine. City officials did their best to keep watch over the enormous wine trade, but it was an impossible task.

It was also difficult to obtain a license to sell the good wine because the grandees and others in high places sold that produced on their own estates at prices higher than the taverns. To discourage loitering in the taverns and drinking too much, benches and chairs were not provided.

Olive oil was consumed in great quantities, especially in the south and east. It has been reckoned that around 1650 a household in Toledo, for example, might use about one liter of oil a week for both lamps and cooking.[6] In the north of the country, butter and lard were generally employed for cooking rather than oil from the olive.

REFRESHING DRINKS

Cold drinks in the form of orange or strawberry juice and almond-flavored syrup were popular. To cool drinks in the sweltering Madrid summer and make sherbets, which were much appreciated at the time, large quantities of snow and ice were transported in wagons drawn by mules from the mountains some forty miles way throughout the winter months and deposited in snow pits especially dug in the city. It was sold from six in the morning to eleven at night so it could be added to drinks and food for the chilling effect.

The municipality maintained a monopoly over this important trade and fixed both the wholesale and retail prices. In 1607 the price was 8 maravedís a pound; in 1694 it cost 10 maravedís for the same amount. (In that year a strike of the snow workers occurred, one of the first strikes of any kind recorded in Spain.) The process began early in the seventeenth century, and the country had a virtual love affair with snow. About this time, Tomé Pinheiro da Veiga, a Portuguese visitor to Valladolid where the court happened to be at the time, alluded enthusiastically to the abundance of snow "even in summer." Others were just as appreciative in describing Madrid where the highest officials or the lowest servant could find cold drinks in special long, narrow jars that allowed faster cooling when they were buried in large, wide-necked, snow-filled copper containers.

The preservation of food with ice from the mountains led to the consumption of fresh fish, meat, and chicken pies, blancmange, and other things that could be preserved longer, which allowed ordinary citizens to eat on a grander scale, a matter resented naturally by the upper classes, but to little avail. Similarly, thick cream, once reserved for royalty in the reign of Felipe II, became, fifty years later, the delight of all members of the public.

By the middle of the century everyone needed their snow in summer and winter. In 1642, with war on two fronts against Portugal in the west and the insurrection in Cataluña in the east, the government decided to requisition all available horses and mules for the war effort. The officials in charge of snow appealed to the Court of Justice, making clear that no snow could be transported to the Royal Court. As a result, the decision was reversed; the king and court had to have their chilled drinks.

While the inhabitants of Madrid were pleased to drink cold water and wine at the beginning of the seventeenth century, they soon expanded their repertoire. The temptation to cool or freeze other liquids was compelling. A popular drink called *aloja*, a kind of mead made of water, honey, and spices, was next to be attempted. The town authorities objected, however, claiming that the frozen drink could be injurious to health. The producers of the drink called in three doctors who claimed the opposite—that it was good for everyone—so City Hall relented, opening the door for many more products to be committed to cold storage. When there was not enough variety to satisfy the thirsty public, other mixtures were invented. In 1630 an old soldier applied for a license to sell a concoction of water, cinnamon, viper's grass, and anise. The number of new creations multiplied, and soon sweet cherry water (an expensive item), jasmine water (much cheaper), orange-flower water, and carnation water appeared on the market. Milk of the almond (*horchata*) and seeds from melons, squash, and grapes were distilled to provide even more choice, while large quantities of iced, fruit drinks such as orange or strawberry juice were drunk throughout. *Aloja* began to go out of fashion, but since it was inexpensive, it continued to be sold. Sherbets also made an appearance and, in spite of high prices, became popular. Queen Mariana was greatly addicted to most of the drinks and sherbets and ordered vast quantities to be sent to the royal palace.

The popular hot drink *hipocrás*, which developed in the early seventeenth century, consisted of heated wine with sugar and spices, but it also succumbed to the insatiable demand for cold beverages and, in spite of the City Council's objections, soon became a cold drink.

The beverage most favored by rich and poor alike, however, was chocolate made from the seed of the cacao plant. It was brought to Europe by the Spaniards, who learned its use from the Aztecs at the time of the conquest of Mexico. Introduced into Spain about 1521, it had been warmly welcomed and became one of the most sought-after drinks in the country. Drunk at breakfast and on many occasions throughout the day in a very viscous or gluey state, often helped down with a glass of water, it was enjoyed by all classes due to its reasonable cost and delightful taste. The duke of Olivares tried to turn the lucrative sale of chocolate into a state monopoly in 1628, but he was forced to back down when confronted by an angry citizenry. The beverage soon joined the list of others for the cooler, however, and began to be drunk cold and eaten frozen, the latter becoming most popular in the hot summer months.

Cooking took strides forward, perhaps due to French influence and to the use of new ingredients that became available by improvements in transport and the use of snow. Sugar had been known since Muslim times, but its consumption had been confined to the rich. With shipments of sugar from the Americas, it became more common, and confectioners could employ their creative talents and produce exquisite pastries that once were only dreamed about by the commoners.

INFLUENCE OF THE INQUISITION ON DIET

Certain dishes became famous such as the heavy meat stew known as *cocido* or *olla podrida* (literally "rotten pot"), which itself was inherited from an old Jewish recipe called *adafina*. Whereas the Jewish dish was based on chicken and beef, vegetables, and hard-boiled eggs, the *olla podrida* consisted of pork, beef or mutton, chicken, bone marrow, sausage, blood sausage, and a ham joint along with chickpeas. Cooked with the meat were vegetables such as cabbage, carrots, and squash, and for additional flavor, garlic, pepper, olive oil, vinegar, and bacon were added. This was all simmered together in an earthen pot until it had a thick consistency. One reason for its popularity was that most of the ingredients could be put together during the morning and left to cook on their own without further attention. Perhaps the most famous *olla podrida* was (and still is) the *cocido madrileño* typical of the central provinces. Due to the pressure exerted by the Inquisition against Moriscos and Conversos, it was important for Spaniards to demonstrate their religious beliefs openly so that the eggs of the *adafina* were replaced by pork, and pork fat was used in the making.

Moors and Jews, forbidden to eat pork for religious reasons, once converted were obliged to show they were true Christians by eating pork at least once a day in the public taverns or city stalls. They could never afford to be caught off guard even at home; so when someone came to visit or share the food, that person had to be clearly able to see the pork in the pot as well as hams and sausages hanging from the ceiling, as was the custom. Hence the *olla podrida* became the most commonly employed dish whereby a person could prove he was of the true faith. Similarly, even those who were not Conversos or Moriscos but Old Christians demonstrated their pure Christian bloodlines through conspicuous consumption of bacon and ham. The less one knew about one's ancestry, the more pork products were eaten, just to be on the safe side.

MORISCO DIET

While Christians were fond of meat and ate it at every opportunity, along with wheaten bread and wine, Moriscos, on the other hand, consumed little meat and wine but ate quantities of rice, fruit, vegetables, and greens. Their dietary habits earned them derision from their Christian neighbors in spite of the fact that Moriscos enjoyed a healthier and longer life than their detractors. For Christian doctors this longevity was a mystery.

A cold tomato and garlic–based soup, *gazpacho*, was popular among the Moriscos and was, to Andalucía, what the *olla podrida* was to the center of the country. The name *gazpacho* is derived from the Arabic, meaning "soaked bread"; its purpose was to be light, to quench the thirst, and to replace salt lost in the heat. Each town had its own version, the most well known being the one served in Sevilla.

For sweetmeats, there were a variety of small cakes made with ground almond and egg yoke.[7]

More substantially, the Moriscos relied heavily on wheat in their diet in the form of pastas, gruel, pancakes, unleavened bread, and couscous. The breadlike flat round cakes were often made at home, baked on ceramic dishes heated in the oven.[8] Moriscos used rice, beans, and various other vegetables along with meats such as lamb, chicken, or pigeon to make imaginative dishes spiced and seasoned with saffron, cumin pepper, vinegar, oil, honey, and mustard, among others. Fruits and nuts also made up no small part of the diet.

HUNGER

The specters of drought and famine were omnipresent, and it was the peasantry who suffered the greatest hardship in such times, especially on the high plateau of the peninsula where wheat was the principal and sometimes the only crop. The preoccupation with food found in the picaresque novels of the time was a reflection of the concern of much of the populace. The best guarantee against hunger pangs for the poor male was service in the church or the king's arms, but not everyone could aspire to these occupations. Impoverished women, widows, and children had fewer options: beg or starve.

When famine struck, as it did on many occasions throughout the period, entire villages packed up and headed for the larger cities. The hungry trekked from town to town, begging as they tried to reach Madrid or Toledo, where there might be food and work. The adults covered in filthy rags, the children naked and exhausted, eating roots and grass, died in droves along the roads. Such was the famine of 1585, and such was the hunger in Galicia in 1609.

The first Spanish cookbook, translated from Catalán, came on the market early in the sixteenth century. By the 1650s there were many others. Following is one of the variations of *cocido* and of *gazpacho*.

Cocido Madrileño

1 cup chickpeas, washed and soaked at least 2 hours in plenty of water

1 stewing chicken

2 lbs. beef brisket

1 lb. ham

½ lb. salt pork, rind removed

2 carrots, 1 onion, 2 leeks—all chopped

bay leaf

2 cloves garlic, chopped

5 garlic-seasoned smoked pork sausages

1 cabbage, cut into wedges and the core removed

5 small potatoes, peeled and chopped

parsley, black pepper

Preparation:

After the chickpeas have soaked for the required amount of time, drain and add 5 quarts cold water, chicken, and beef and bring to a boil over high heat. Skim off any foam that comes to the surface. Reduce heat and simmer 1 ½ hours. Add ham, pork, and vegetables, along with garlic, bay leaf, some chopped parsley, and pepper to taste. Cook about 30 minutes, partially covered.

In the meantime, with a fork, prick the sausages in several places and put in a pan with enough water to cover them. Bring to a boil, then lower heat and simmer, uncovered, about 6 minutes. Drain and transfer the sausages to the pot with the meat and vegetables. Add cabbage and potatoes and simmer again 30 minutes or until everything is tender.

To Serve:

Cocido madrileño is traditionally served in three courses: soup, vegetables, meats. The broth, with fine, cooked noodles in it, should be served first. Next, take the drained vegetables and arrange them on a large platter with the chickpeas in the center. Finally, the meats should be placed on another serving dish and presented separately.

Serves 6.

Gazpacho

4 large tomatoes

1 cucumber, peeled and chopped

1 medium green pepper, seeded and chopped

2 garlic cloves, finely chopped or mashed

2 cups bread, crumbled

2 cups cold water

4 tbsp. wine vinegar

4 tbsp. olive oil

1 ½ cups tomato juice

Preparation:

Dip the tomatoes in boiling water and remove the skin. Then take out the seeds. Chop.

Take the tomatoes, cucumber, pepper, garlic, and bread and puree with a mortar and pestle, by grinding the mixture with a food mill, or by rubbing the mixture through a sieve with the back of a large spoon. Add water, vinegar, olive oil, and tomato juice and mix. Cover and chill for several hours (ice cubes can be added if desired).

To Serve:

Stir the soup to recombine the ingredients and put into bowls.

For garnish place the following finely chopped ingredients into separate dishes for each person to add as desired:

cucumber

green and/or red peppers

hard-boiled egg

ripe olives

green onions

Serves 6.

NOTES

1. Doblado, 45.
2. Ibid., 49.
3. Casey, 36.
4. Ibid., 135.
5. Defourneaux, 152; Alcalá-Zamora, 327.
6. Casey, 35.
7. Read, 235.
8. Bernard Rosenberger, "Dietética y cocina en el mundo Musulmán occidental," in Garrido Aranda, 25.

14

Arts and Entertainment

The last few decades of the sixteenth and most of the seventeenth century are known as Spain's Golden Age (*Siglo de Oro*), a time of the greatest flowering of literary genius the nation has ever known. Playwrights and poets, novelists, and satirists were at their prolific best, filling the world of letters with new styles and genres. Essays, stories, plays, and poetry depicted customs and traditions, but the personal struggles of the artists to successfully practice their craft, fairly well documented if they became famous, tell us as much about the life and the times as do their works. It was also the era of the great masters in painting whose portraits of the nobility and of religious scenes are unsurpassed. The lives of writers and artists were often precarious. To have time for their work, they had to find a wealthy sponsor to supply meals and lodging and other necessities of life.

PLAYRIGHTS, POETS, AND WRITERS

Miguel de Cervantes Saavedra, whose satiric novel *Don Quijote* is one of the masterpieces of world literature, was born into a large family in Alcalá de Henares on 29 September 1547. His father was a barber-surgeon of little means. In 1568, when Cervantes was a student, a number of his poems appeared in a volume published in Madrid to commemorate the death of Queen Isabel de Valois, wife of Felipe II.

To become a successful dramatist, his ambition, he needed to find a patron in Madrid, but the city teemed with other young men seeking sponsors. Restless and frustrated in his literary pretensions, he opted for one of three alternative paths open to youths with few ties and poor prospects: the king's service, emigration to the New World, or a career in the church. He chose the king's service and enlisted in the army. He was sent to Italy and in 1571 was engaged in the naval battle of Lepanto.

Back in Madrid at the age of thirty-three, he turned out poems and plays at a prodigious rate between 1582 and 1585. But, still without a benefactor, he was always short of money and in search of employment. Some of his plays were accepted for the theater, but they fared poorly. At any rate, the paltry income from stage plays did not pay the bills.

With a crippled hand as a result of the war, options were limited. Through a petition to the king he secured a job as a messenger delivering dispatches and later took a post in Sevilla as commissary to the Armada, which was undergoing provisioning for the grand enterprise that, it was thought, would reduce England to the status of a Spanish province. Cervantes spent his time on the dusty dirt tracks of Castilla, requisitioning supplies for the ships from the country towns and farms.

After the failure of the Armada, Cervantes continued with his job for the Council of War, collecting supplies for the Spanish forces in North Africa and Italy. Tired of the unrewarding and difficult work and with no pay coming his way, he tried to find employment in America for the government but was rejected. He gave up the unpleasant work after seven years and returned to Madrid.

Still impoverished, he landed a government job as a collector of overdue tax debts in Andalucía. With much of it collected, but reluctant to travel the dangerous road back to Madrid with so much money in his pocket, he turned the cash over to a merchant friend in Sevilla in exchange for a money order, to be cashed on his return to the capital. When time came in Madrid to cash the money order, the money was not there. The merchant had gone bankrupt and absconded, whereabouts unknown; but Cervantes was responsible to the royal treasury for the money. Cash raised from the departed merchant's estate by order of Felipe II appeared eighteen months later, and the royal treasury was satisfied, but money that Cervantes' sister Magdalena had borrowed to pay some of her brother's debt to the royal treasury before the merchant's estate was settled was never returned by the government, nor was Cervantes's salary for his tax-collecting work ever paid to him. He gave up the ruinous job and joined the ranks of the unemployed.

Returning to Sevilla he continued to write, but in 1597 he received notice from the royal treasury that he was being held responsible for the taxes due in 1594 in Andalucía. There he had been able to collect only about half of the amount owed in back taxes, and the government now wanted the rest out of his own pocket. A subpoena was issued compelling Cervantes to come to Madrid with the money. He could not raise it, and a high court judge in Sevilla had him arrested and sent to the royal prison to languish for seven months in the filthy cells. Here, it is thought, he began to write *Don Quijote*, which soon became a best-seller. Spain's most celebrated writer died on 23 April 1616, the same day of the same year as William Shakespeare.

The most prolific writer of Spain's Golden Age, Lope de Vega Carpio, born on 25 November 1562 in Madrid, was the son of the proprietor of an embroidery shop. While attending the Jesuit school in Madrid, his talents came to the notice of church officials, who helped young Lope achieve a place at the university of Alcalá, where it was assumed he would take holy orders. He left the university without graduating, however, and after a stretch in the royal navy, he returned to Madrid and set to work supplying Jerome Velázquez, the manager of a theatrical company, with a number of plays that soon established him as a playwright. As his reputation grew, Lope invented credentials of noble birth based on descent from Bernardo de Carpio, a seemingly fictitious eighth-century Spanish aristocrat.

He also had his eye on Velázquez's daughter, Elena. With the aid of Elena's mother, Lope seduced her, but while he was away in Sevilla, Elena found another more wealthy suitor. Bent on revenge, Lope shifted his allegiance to another producer of plays and wrote mean, satirical verses about Elena and her family. Charged with libel, he was arrested, found guilty, and given eight years' banishment from Madrid and two years' exile from the kingdom.

Meanwhile, Lope had already consoled his injured feelings by courting Isabella de Urbina, but her middle-class parents were against any liaison between her and the impecunious poet. Lope persuaded a constable friend to go to the girl's house and, using the dreaded name of the Inquisition, tell her she had been summoned. No one dared refuse such an injunction, and once she was out of the house, Lope ran off with her to Valencia. He still had to leave the kingdom and sent the tearful and pregnant girl back to Madrid, but in a gallant gesture he arranged to marry her by proxy.

Caught up in patriotic fervor surrounding the great Armada gathering in Lisbon, Lope joined the expedition. After that fiasco, he made his way back to Valencia, where he was joined by Isabella. Here, he wrote plays for the theater and was widely acclaimed, but he was anxious to return to Madrid. His term of exile from the kingdom had expired but not his banishment from the capital. Settling for nearby Toledo, he obtained the patronage of the powerful duke of Alba, and they departed for the duke's estates in Alba de Tormes, a small town near Salamanca. Lope was soon involved in the hectic activity of student life in the university city, engaging in frequent amorous affairs. Isabella died and a quarrel with the duke prompted him to leave the palace and return to Toledo.

The death in 1597 of Princess Catalina, daughter of Felipe II, led to the closure of all theaters for the period of bereavement. This was an opportunity for the pious theologians to convince the king to ban theatrical productions completely held by them to be sinful schools of immorality. Since directors of theater companies were no longer buying plays, Lope was out of work. The duke of Sarria took him on as private secretary with the special job of writing the duke's love letters.

At the time, Lope began paying court to Juana de Guarda, a daughter of a wealthy wholesale grocer who supplied food to Madrid. Juana lacked charm, but the size of the expected dowry made up for any of her defects. The girl's father, not impressed by poets or playwrights, was against the match, so Lope seduced her, which hurried along the nuptials. His new father-in-law, however, refused to give his daughter a dowry.

Shortly after this marriage, Lope begin courting an actress called Micaela de Lujun. Like everyone else in the profession, she was out of work and already married to an actor, the father of her three children. Pretty and witty Micaela, about twenty-eight years old, succumbed to Lope's charms. The conquest was completed just in time, for the duke of Sarria ordered Lope to accompany him to Valencia to attend the celebrations in honor of the marriage of Felipe III to Margaret of Austria. Lope delivered a poem and a eulogy to the king but found time for a brief affair with a Valencian woman that resulted in a son. When the duke's entourage returned to Toledo, Lope again resumed his liaison with Micaela, whose husband had departed for America. This relationship also resulted in children. The reopening of the theaters in the year 1600 by decree of Felipe III prompted Micaela to go on tour and gave Lope the opportunity to sell his plays again. He left the service of the duke of Sarria to become secretary to the duke of Sessa, a young man of twenty-three, who charged Lope with writing letters to women of his fancy. Lope meanwhile broke off contact with Micaela and in 1610 moved to Madrid (since his term of exile had expired), where he bought a little house. His reputation as dramatist and poet was now at its peak. From 1608 he had added the title Familiar of the Holy Office to his name.

In 1613, shortly after the death of unhappy Juana de Guarda, his legal wife, Lope, at age fifty-two, took holy orders in Toledo and became a priest. On the same day as his ordination he went to live with a new mistress, the actress Jerónima de Burgos, whom he had come to know a few days before the death of Juana. The new priest also continued to conduct the love affairs of the duke of Sessa and at times joined him in romantic escapades.

Jerónima was shortly superseded by another actress, Lucía de Salceda, whom Lope mentions in his letters as the crazy one (*la loca*), but in 1617, he met Marte de Nevares, a beautiful married woman of twenty-six with several children. A cultured poetess in her spare time and until then faithful to her aging husband, she succumbed to Lope's advances after he, in his priestly robes and dignified manner, wormed his way into her household as a spiritual guide. He soon made her pregnant. Marte's husband died a short time later, and she went to live with Lope in his Madrid house, where she gave birth to two daughters, registered as father unknown. Their father, the priest, regularly said Mass at the Convent of the Magdalena. After receiving more prizes for poetry, he was honored by Pope Urban VIII with the title doctor of theology, among other awards.

In spite of his renown and production of several thousand plays and other works, Lope remained insolvent and unable to support his children. While he sold his work at the highest price, other factors worked against artists of the times. Managers of theatrical groups engaged in an uncertain and erratic business, often bankrupt before the authors of their plays were paid, and the lack of copyright laws left the original writer open to the plagiarist. On one occasion Lope took a man to court who had reproduced some of his work and sold it. The individual, who had prodigious mental retention, had attended three or four plays, memorized them, and written them down later. He was found not guilty since recording spoken lines in one's memory was not considered theft.

Returning to the duke of Sessa, Lope asked for handouts—clothes for the children, the loan of a horse and carriage, money—and offered to say Mass for the duke every day as his private chaplain, for a fee. Marte de Nevares died in 1632, and a few years later, in August 1635, Lope de Vega Carpio was carried to his final resting place in a procession of Familiars of the Holy Office, of Knights of Saint John, and of all the priests in Madrid.[1] His most distinguished disciple, Tirso de Molino, produced the famous Don Juan, a character in Spanish drama of international stature.

Meanwhile, poetry tournaments, a regular feature of cities and towns, became so popular that nearly every literate person took part. People of all classes wrote, recited, or became devotees. Literary debates and poetry found expression in academies under the patronage of the wealthy, and the king himself presided over the Palace Academy. Prizes offered to the contestants included articles of clothing such as gloves, belts, purses, and even garters. Cervantes, for example, in a poetic joust put on by the Dominican Order to celebrate the canonization of Saint Hyacinth, won three silver spoons.

Francisco Gómez de Quevedo y Villagas exemplifies another aspect of the struggling writer. Born in Madrid in 1580 of a noble but impoverished family, he was orphaned at an early age but obtained an education at the universities of Alcalá and Valladolid. While in Madrid in 1611 he defended a lady who had been insulted, challenged the malefactor to a duel, and killed him. The victim was an aristocrat, and Quevedo was forced to flee. Arriving in Italy he took up service with the duke of Osuna and held important posts, one of which required him to travel to Venice in 1618 on a secret mission involving a plot to annex Venice to the Spanish crown. The plot was given away, and Quevedo barely escaped the city, disguised as a beggar.

When Osuna fell out of favor, Quevedo was exiled to his ancestral estates but was later returned to service and made a secretary to the king. One morning the king found a poetic note on his napkin sharply criticizing the king's favorite minister, the count of Olivares. An informer revealed to Olivares that Quevedo had written the piece in question, and that night he was hustled off to prison in remote León. There he spent two years in solitary confinement without ever being brought to trial and was only released in 1643 when Olivares fell from power. By now a broken man, Quevedo died two years later.

Quevedo reveals in his numerous written works his sentiments toward contemporary society. No one was spared his biting wit, including judges, aristocrats, chemists, dentists, doctors, and many others. About the only organization that escaped his censure was the church. This may have been due to Quevedo's strong Catholic beliefs or to the ever watchful eye of the Inquisition.

Born in Madrid in 1600, Calderón de la Barca began his education at the Jesuit Imperial College and continued on to university, where he studied canon and civil law and won prizes for his poetry. During a brawl in which he participated at the University of Salamanca, a man was killed, and Calderón's parents paid out 600 ducats in order to secure his pardon.

Upon the death of Lope de Vega in 1635, Calderón succeeded in the master's footsteps, becoming the toast of Madrid for his plays, and was appointed court poet by Felipe IV. His one love affair seemed to suffice, and he never married. His son Pedro passed as his nephew. Calderón produced 120 plays and a variety of other works. Like the plays of Lope de Vega, his dramatic pieces, a string of popular cape and sword plays, revolved around love, honor, and revenge for the ever-hungry theater of which he, for a time, was king. Ordained in the priesthood in 1651, Calderón withdrew from society but continued to write *autos sacramentales* (religious plays) for the municipality of Madrid and some mythological sketches for the royal court, which were performed at the Retiro Palace. The last thirty years of his life were solitary, contemplative, and alone with his books.

BOOKS AND THE INQUISITION

The first ban on Lutheran books in Spain occurred in 1521. The Inquisition attempted to prevent heretical literature from entering the country at the French frontier and sea ports, where it stationed its agents. By 1550 the Inquisition assumed the role of censor of all written material. An Index of banned books was made up in 1551 by Inquisitor General Fernando de Valdés, and the regional tribunals distributed copies of it to book vendors. The Index included works in Hebrew or Arabic, by Protestants or heretics, bibles not in accordance with orthodox theology, books written by anyone once condemned by the Inquisition, all written material with an anti-Catholic bias as determined by the censors, books on magic, all verse using quotations from the scriptures in a profane way, and all pictures and illustrations disrespectful of the Catholic faith. The Spanish Index was controlled by the authorities and had little connection with the Index put out in Rome. One might list books not found in the other.

The Inquisition was not working alone to ban books. In 1558 the monarchy prohibited by decree the introduction into Castilla of books in Spanish printed in other realms, obliged local printers to seek licenses from the Council of Castilla, and formulated strict procedures for state censorship. Manuscripts were to be checked for heretical material both before and after publication, and booksellers were to keep close at hand the Index of prohibited books.

Some Spanish literary pieces also found discredit with the censors. The well-known *Lazarillo de Tormes* written by an anonymous author was included. Lazarillo, a street urchin, lived by his wits and served many masters in his quest for survival. The miserly characteristics of a hypocritical clergyman portrayed in the book, and the unflattering remarks about an indulgence seller and of the pope, offended the church officials. Further editions of this highly popular picaresque (roguish) novel were prohibited. The book remained in demand, however, and pirated copies were plentiful. Felipe II then ordered the novel purged of objectionable features since its sale was impossible to stop. The unreal world of heroes, chivalry, good deeds, saints, and miracles was the image the church and monarchy wished to convey, not the hunger, poverty, and struggle for survival of a good segment of the population.

The Inquisition also condemned the works of prominent churchmen if its suspicions were aroused. Luis de Granada's *Book of Prayer*, published in 1559, went through twenty-three editions before it was placed on the Index. Fray Luis appealed to the Council of Trent and the pope to have the ban lifted. Both approved the work, but the Inquisitors demanded and got corrections in the text before it was allowed to circulate freely. The duke of Gandía, Francisco Borja, a distinguished Jesuit, found his *Works of a Christian* on the Index. This threatened to bring disrepute to himself and the Society of Jesus. Fearing arrest, the future saint (canonized in 1671) fled to Rome and never returned to Spain. Even the *Spiritual Exercises* of Ignatius Loyola, founder of the Society of Jesus, which were used in manuscript form to train novices, were proscribed.

Burning of nonconformist books was always practiced by the Christian church. The medieval Inquisition burned them, and Torquemada made a bonfire of books in Salamanca. At Toledo in 1490 Jewish books were the victims of the flames. Arabic books were consigned to the fires in Granada in 1501, and from March 1552 the Inquisition ordered heretical books burned publicly. Many precious manuscripts were lost, even some on medicine. A Jesuit in the employ of the Holy Office reported from Barcelona in 1559 that on seven or eight occasions mountains of books had been burned in the Jesuit college.

An Index of banned material published in 1583 appeared in two volumes: one of prohibited books, the other, of those from which offending material had been removed. To strip books of certain content, church officials ripped out pages or carelessly defaced them by inking out passages and pictures. The process of censorship relied on so-called expert theologians to make the changes. What was to be changed, however, was not always agreed upon. If censors could not agree, or as sometimes happened they could not be bothered to read the work in question, the book was simply banned. Nearly all the works of the great thinkers of Europe were prohibited or defaced.

While visiting churches in Sevilla in 1775, Henry Swinburne came across a list of books condemned by the Inquisition. Among them were the famous *Fray Gerundio* by the Jesuit Father Isla (a satire on bombastic pulpit oratory banned in 1760); some French books dealing with geography; some of Voltaire's publications; and the political history of European settlements by Diderot and Raynal for passages derogatory to the glory of Spain (because of attacks on the clergy for their conduct and policies toward the natives in the Indies).[2]

FOREIGN IMPORTS

Charged with the book import trade at the frontiers, the Inquisition was inadequate in both staff and funds, and many Spaniards ignored the laws in spite of possible dire penalties. Authors published without permission or had it done in France or Italy and secretly imported their books into Castilla. Informers for the Inquisition were active in foreign countries and sent information to Madrid about the activity of printers and traders. In 1556 Felipe II's regent in the Netherlands, Margaret de Parma, advised the Castillian Council of State that heretics intended to send some 30,000 Protestant books to Sevilla, the majority of which were destined for the colonists in America. One recipient of the illegal books, a heretic, was caught and relaxed in the auto de fe in Sevilla in December 1560.[3] In seaports such as Sevilla, under close scrutiny, even foreign sailors were subject to arrest if caught with incriminating Protestant material. The Inquisition demanded the right to be the first to visit foreign ships as they entered Spanish waters and to search sailors' bunks and gear for contraband books. Local authorities sometimes objected but were ordered by the crown to give precedence to the inquisitors. Some merchants, nevertheless, made a successful business of smuggling Protestant works into Spain from Geneva and Antwerp, hidden in bales of merchandise.[4]

Attention was also paid to the northern rugged Basque coast, ideal for smuggling operations. Among the victims of all this surveillance were booksellers who were often deprived of their legal goods for years while the authorities confined the merchandise to warehouses and took their time examining the contents. When the Inquisition ordered its agents in Bilbao and San Sebastián in 1564 to send on to the booksellers in Medina del Campo a cleared shipment of 245 bales of books imported from Lyon, the books were still on the docks three years later.[5]

Since there were never enough financial or human resources in the employ of the Inquisition to check all the books in transit from diverse sources, libraries and bookshops became targets of inquisitorial investigations. Bishops and their staff were encouraged to visit those in their dioceses and weed out any suspicious material. Familiars also made raids on bookshops, sometimes in coordinated attacks throughout the city so the sellers could not warn each other and hide the merchandise. For the majority of people, the restrictions on books and other written material had little direct influence on their everyday lives. Professionals, intellectuals, and students, on the other hand, were deprived of new concepts and viewpoints emanating from other countries and from within Spain itself. To what degree the restrictions inhibited social progress and even scientific development in Spain is still debatable.

PAINTERS, SCULPTORS, AND ARCHITECTS

Painters and sculptors fought for recognition in a society that thought of them as mere artisans, and they were subject to rules laid down by their guilds and by clients who were particular to the detail about what they wanted. While great painters of the period were only names to the common people, the grandees and the wealthy merchants, along with the church, who employed their services were often on intimate terms with them. The Roman Catholic Church was a highly influential patron, and its Counter Reformation to combat the spread of Protestantism demanded emotional, realistic, and dramatic art as a means of preserving the faith. Intense spirituality was often present in works of Spanish baroque art, the artistic style employed in the seventeenth century, which included scenes of ecstasies, martyrdom, or miraculous apparitions. In 1586, El Greco (the Greek), born on the island of Crete, whose real name was Domenikos Theotokopoulos, painted his masterpiece *The Burial of*

Count Orgaz for the Church of Santo Tomé in Toledo. The painting portrays a fourteenth-century nobleman laid in his grave by Saints Stephen and Augustine. Above, the count's soul rises to a heaven densely populated with angels, saints, and contemporary political figures.

Considered Spain's greatest baroque painter, Diego Rodríguez de Silva y Velázquez moved from Sevilla to Madrid in 1623, at the age of twenty-three, to serve as portraitist to Felipe IV, a post he retained throughout his life. His series of royal portraits culminated in *Las Meninas* (The Maids of Honor) in 1656, representing the royal family, court functionaries, and the artist himself.

Two other important artists of Velázquez's generation were also from Andalucía—Alonso Cano and Bartolomé Esteban Murillo. Cano, also a sculptor and architect, was well known for his painting *Descent into Limbo*, one of the few Spanish treatments of the nude. Murillo, the son of a Sevillian workman, specialized in sentimental genre paintings and renderings of the Immaculate Conception.

Born in 1746, near Zaragoza, Francisco José de Goya was Spain's first modern artist and the first artist of stature to have to defend one of his paintings, *La Maja Desnuda* (The Naked Maja), before a tribunal of the Inquisition.

Spanish baroque sculpture was an outgrowth of the medieval wood-carving tradition. Among the most important works are numerous carved wood altar pieces, many of prodigious size and richness. Spanish wood sculpture was usually polychrome, and at times, human figures were provided with glass eyes, hair, and garments. Seventeenth-century palaces and churches in major cities were also constructed in an exuberant, richly adorned baroque style.

MUSIC

The wealthy aristocracy of Castilla and Aragón had their own resident musicians who performed at festive events. When soft music was required at weddings, string players often performed. In contrast, bagpipes were commonly used to vigorously celebrate the birth of a child. Other instruments included drums, trumpets, tambourines, and woodwind.

Members of the royal family were often trained in music. The *vihuela* (Spanish guitar) was a favorite instrument of Isabella and her son Juan. The *vihuela* was considered indispensable as an accompaniment to songs and dances and was employed as much by the general populace as it was by the nobility. This practical instrument was easily portable and used inside or outdoors. There were several different kinds in use throughout the period with a varying number of strings usually plucked with the fingers, although a plectrum was sometimes used. Sevilla was the first center of instrument making, as it was for the publication of printed music.

One of the most distinguished of the poet–musicians during the reign of the Catholic Kings was the priest Juan del Encina, who composed some of the best poetry and music of the fifteenth century.[6] During the closing decades of the fifteenth century and the beginning of the sixteenth, the *cancioneros* (songs) were written. Their themes concerned chivalry, politics, history, religion, love, and humor and were composed for three or four voices. Those concerning rustic life were known as *villancicos* in which the music followed closely the form of the verse, enhancing and emphasizing the meaning of the words. They were usually accompanied by a dance. The *villancico* was to Spain what the madrigal was to the rest of Europe.

Plays set to music (operas) first appeared in 1629 when Felipe IV was presented with a performance of *La Selva sin Amor* (Forest without Love), a one-act play by Lope de Vega, the musical score of which has since been lost. The musicians performed behind a curtain.

But it was Calderón who was responsible for uniting music and poetry into an indigenous form, writing operas or *fiestas cantadas*, with the score written by Juan Hidalgo, one of the more famous Spanish musicians of his time. After experimenting with this type of entertainment, Calderón turned his attention in the mid-seventeenth century to the *zarzuela*.[7] The name of this characteristic Spanish-type opera was taken from the royal hunting lodge outside Madrid (which derived its name from the *zarza*, or brambles, in the area) where performances of the *zarzuela* were held. The opera consisted of two acts with alternating dialogue, song, and dances. The first performance, entitled *El Golfo de las Sirenas* (Gulf of the Sirens, or Mermaids), was held in 1657. The following year a *zarzuela* by Calderón was commissioned by the king to celebrate the birth of his heir. The musical score has been lost, but the program consisted of the following:

1. Chorus of shepherds and shepherdesses
2. Apollo and Cupid musical dialogue
3. Solo of Apollo with chorus of nymphs
4. Rustic song and dance
5. Double chorus accompanying solo of Iris
6. Dialogue between Daphne and Apollo, sung and spoken
7. Chorus of shepherds, and a solo shepherdess
8. Final chorus[8]

Strumming the guitar.

The instruments used were a combination of strings, wind, and per-cussion—usually harps, violins, guitars, bassoons, trumpets, a kind of clarinet, and kettle drums.

By the end of the seventeenth century many composers were writing for the theater. The priest Jose Marín, born in 1619 and who was tenor at the royal convent of the Encarnación in Madrid in 1644, found another way to make a living apart from the church. In 1656 he was involved in robbery and murder for which he was defrocked, tortured, and sent to prison. Then exiled for ten years he went on a pilgrimage, repented, and was welcomed back into the church. Until his death in 1699 he was respected internationally for his *zarzuelas*.

Ballads Next to the *villancico* the ballad was the most widely used song form of the time. It was originally derived from earlier versified epic tales of chivalry. Ballads recounted the adventures of all manner of people and were enormously popular with all classes of so-ciety. The short epico-lyric poetry represented the traditional spirit of Spain and was originally intended to be sung to the accompaniment of a single instrument such as the guitar. Simple, direct, and highly con-densed, the ballads dealt with the Reconquest, the heroic deeds of the Cid, treachery and heroism, and the attributes of beautiful women. Bal-lads of seventeenth-century Castilla showed a certain compassion for outlaws, but usually after they were caught and hanged.

A ballad concerning the *Mesta* was:

Ya se van los pastores
Ya se van marchando
Más de quatro Zagales
Quedan llorando

Ya se van los pastores
a la Extremadura;
ya se queda la sierra
triste y oscura

Now the shepherds are going
Now they are going away
More than four women
Remain weeping

Now the shepherds are going
to Extremadura
the hills remain
sad and dark.

POPULAR ENTERTAINMENT

Once the court moved permanently to Madrid, its presence provided many pretexts for celebrations at which the people could participate, at least as spectators. The provincial capitals did not lag far behind in festivities for which almost anything was an excuse. Rural villages also organized their own, less extravagant events. Festivals were often a mix of the religious and profane in which colorful religious pageantry and Te Deums coexisted alongside poetry contests, plays, jousting, bullfights, dancing, and masquerades.

An occasion for revelry might be the birth of a child, the marriage of a noble son or daughter, a visit by the king or queen to one of the towns, or the anniversary of an important historical event. Religious festivals were also very popular forms of entertainment. Besides the usual Christmas and Easter or the arrival of one of the many Christian holidays, there were also the special occasions such as the founding or consecration of a new shrine, church, or monastery, the appointment of a bishop or cardinal, or the canonization of a Spanish saint. When Saint Ignatius Loyola, Santa Teresa, and Saint Francis Xavier were canonized, Madrid remained in a festive mode for the entire month of June 1622. No sooner was this over when another fiesta began in honor of Saint Pedro of Alcántara. Church celebrations included colorful processions and ceremonies and were replete with pomp and solemnity. The formidable auto de fe of the Inquisition, another popular event, of course attracted large crowds.

In the remote countryside, for example, in Galicia or Asturias, where theaters and other forms of entertainment were scarce, peasants went on pilgrimages in the summer months, which lasted for days. Near the shrine in question they set up their tents, built bonfires, set out their barrels of cider and wine, and engaged in feasting and dancing. Courting couples took advantage of the situation to see each other on a more intimate basis, while the elders took the opportunity to do business. The site became a fairground where cattle were sold and clothes and jewelry were exchanged or put up for sale. These pilgrimages accounted for most of the local trade. In 1769 the church tried to curb what it considered the licentiousness of these outings.

DANCE

Dancing amounted to a national passion. The aristocrats enjoyed the *paván*, a sixteenth-century court dance of Italian origin, which consisted of a majestic procession performed by a column of couples in ceremonial dress accompanied by woodwind instruments. It went out of fashion near the end of the century.

The sixteenth- and seventeenth-century courtly dance the *allemande*, of German origin, made up of gliding steps, also involved a line of couples in moderate 2/4 or 4/4 time. In certain processions, professional dancers performed various kinds of allegorical ballet and sometimes went into the churches and performed before the high altar.

Popular dancing among the lower classes was very different from the measured and formal steps of the aristocracy. In villages and city streets, dancing was vigorous and even frenzied, executed to the strumming of guitars, to the sound of tambourines and the snapping of fingers. (Castanets began to make their appearance in Spain in the seventeenth century.) The notorious but popular *saraband* was banned in 1583 for its suggestive movements and obscene lyrics sung to its rhythms. Another dance, the *chacona*, emerged about 1600. This, too, along with other popular dances, was condemned by the clergy, but not even fire and brimstone hurled from the pulpit, where the dances were alluded to as inventions of the devil, could dampen the enthusiasm of the participants. In Cervantes's play *The Illustrious Kitchen Maid*, muleteers and Galician girls danced to the refrain

> El baile de la chacona
> encierra la vida bona[9]
>
> The dance of the chacona
> embraces the good life

Lamented by the church, the lascivious movements of the *chacona* purported to offend the virtue, chastity, and decency of women. A Jesuit priest complained that even nuns in the convents were doing it.[10]

The national dance of Spain, introduced in the late eighteenth century, the *bolero* involved abrupt turns and stamping feet in syncopated rhythm. The dancers, solo or in couples, were accompanied by a guitar, and the performers sometimes sang and used castanets.

The intense and emotional Gypsy song and dance known as *flamenco* was just beginning to make an appearance at the end of the eighteenth century.

MASQUERADE

Fondness of the masquerade involved all levels of society. During the reign of Felipe IV, the king and nobles of the court rode through the streets of Madrid at night in extravagant cavalcades, their ornate dress of silver and gold glittering in the light of the torches. The Corpus Christi festival, honoring the presence of Christ in the sacrament of the Eucharist, was the most popular of all the religious festivals due to the masquerades that accompanied it. The feast was characterized by solemn outdoor processions in which guilds, merchants, magistrates, nobility, and clergy participated. Afterward, mystery and miracle plays were performed in the public square.

In Madrid, the king and members of the various councils escorted the coffer containing the Host. They were preceded by dancers and acrobats and followed by the *gigantes*, paper-mâché figures ten feet tall with enormous and grotesque heads, clumsily dancing down the street, energized by men concealed inside.

An observer of one such event described a long-tailed, scaled pasteboard serpent of enormous proportions and horrifying eyes, three protruding tongues, and wicked-looking teeth being wheeled along the street. This provided a good laugh for the town's people who, instead of looking at the dragon, watched the open-mouthed country bumpkins who had come to the city for the event and stared at the dragon with apprehension bordering on terror.[11]

Most towns had seasonal carnivals during which masques were popular. Oftentimes the people dressed as animals, and groups of them wended their way through the narrow streets, singing and dancing. Pranks were not uncommon, such as stringing a rope across the street to trip passersby in the night or pelting them with rotten eggs. In Valencia, oranges were used as projectiles.

BULLFIGHTS

The spectacle of the bullfight was attended by all classes, even the clergy who had been forbidden to witness it by Pius V in 1572. The king, guilds, local authorities, and aristocracy all organized bullfighting events, and they were performed on all festive days, whether religious or secular. The spectacle, an exercise in which the nobility could show off their prowess and skill to the public, took place in the public square of the towns. In the Plaza Mayor in Madrid the commoners crowded onto grandstands, while the high nobility, often including the king, watched from the surrounding colorful, richly draped balconies.

The event began with an introduction of the noble champions armed with a sword and daggers and clad in short capes and multiplumed hats and attended by their squires. This was followed by a salute to the king, if present, and the local dignitaries. Eventually the bulls were released from their pens, and the toreadors or noble horsemen rode in for the attack, which consisted of planting a wooden iron-tipped spear in the side of the animal. The shaft then was designed to break off, leaving it in the hands of the horseman while the tip remained in the flesh of the animal. The winner was the one who would up with the largest number of broken spears. Numerous horses were fatally injured on each occasion, gored by the engaged and desperate bull.

When the bull was seen to be exhausted from the struggle, trumpets sounded the final stage of the performance. The toreadors left the ring, leaving the peons, whose role up to then had been to tire the bull by harassing it with their capes and banderillas, to finish off the wretched animal. It was then hamstrung and, once immobilized, slashed to pieces.

In the villages where the ritual slaughter of the bull was organized by local authority, nobles were generally not involved, and local amateurs or professional matadors (bull-killers) hired for the event fought on foot and were the prototypes of the modern bull-slayer of the corrida (bull-fight) who finishes the wounded and exhausted animal off after it has undergone teasing, torture, and futile charges at an elusive cape.

THEATER

The Spanish theater appealed to everyone from nobleman to peasant. The only subjects that were prohibited on the stage were criticism of the monarchy, the church, and the Inquisition. The two theaters in Madrid, the Correl del Príncipe and the Correl de la Cruz, were rectangular areas with the stage at one end and a wooden balcony at the other reserved for women. In this section, the *cazuela* (stewing pot), men were not allowed. Here the women talked incessantly, argued, fought, ate snacks, and watched the play. In front of them was the pit, a kind of promenade where people remained standing during the performance and often moved about. Between the pit and the stage were benches for the merchants and artisans who could afford the better position. Lateral balconies along the sides of the theater were reserved for gentry. Only the *cazuela* and the gentry sections had a wooden roof, while a canopy stretched overhead protected the audience in the pit and on the benches from the sun; but the show stopped if heavy rain began.

The performances generally played to a full house, and a given drama rarely ran for more than a few days. Only the expensive boxes could be reserved in advance of the play, which commenced between two and four o'clock in the afternoon, depending on the season. The doors nevertheless opened at noon as crowds milled around, hoping to get in early. Since there were no tickets, and seats were for first come, first served, there were frequent quarrels over who sat where. On occasion a serious fight erupted, knives were drawn, and one of the patrons would lose his seat and perhaps his life.

Attendants tried to collect the price of admission as the crowd rushed in. Many would attempt to enter without paying, claiming they were officials who paid nothing or playwrights themselves, who had the privilege of attending free of charge the works of their colleagues. Some claimed to be friends of the actor or actress and demanded free seats. A free seat was a status symbol, and those who got them often brought in their friends to occupy more free space. In 1621 the government adopted regulations that forced police and officials to pay admission to the theater, as the situation was getting out of hand. Another official ordinance allowed ushers to wear leather doublets such as those worn by soldiers, to protect themselves from angry patrons when trying to collect the admission fee.

When the crowd finally settled down to only a mild commotion, the spectators passed the time before the show purchasing food and drinks from vendors carrying trays of assortments. This was the time for those in the pit to direct loud comments toward the women who occupied the balcony above and who in turn shouted to the men below, made rude gestures, and threw candies, limes extracted from their drinks, small cakes, orange peelings, and nuts and shells or other missiles that came to hand on the milling mob below.

The three-act plays were generally accompanied by dances and short skits during the intermissions, and by the beginning of the seventeenth century musicians were employed to provide background and interval music. The instruments were generally tambourines and guitars. In some theaters a chorus with guitar and harp accompaniment signaled the beginning of the play.

All kinds of people went to the theater, including cobblers, grocers, shop assistants, and workmen who went truant from their jobs to attend. The men arrived with cape, sword, and dagger and called each other by the title *caballero*. It was not uncommon for the audience to throw turnips, tomatoes, or rotten fruit at the actors if the play did not suit its fancy. The most troublesome were the *mosqueteros* who stood in the promenade section of the pit, like the soldiers from whom they took their name, and maintained a constant applause or noises of disdain throughout the performance. Most carried concealed vegetables. Many claimed to be great critics of the theater; their applause, jeers, or whistling could make or break a play on opening day.

It was not unknown that during a particularly bad play or poor performance the audience rioted and tore the theater to pieces, breaking up the benches and tearing the curtains and decorations to shreds.

The *doctos*, or learned and cultured people, who sat in the boxes along the sides of the theater were the most feared by the playwright, for, less disturbing than the *mosqueteros*, their sarcastic pronouncements on the play would be the talk of the town the following day. Playwrights sometimes tried to assure support in advance of the performance by bribing the most notorious of the critics.[12]

The theater gave to the people in popular form the things they were proud of and never grew tired of hearing about: the virtues of their kings and of the church, patriotism, honor and the privilege of having been born in a country of *caballeros*, heros and saints—a country superior to all others.

While large cities supported professional theatrical companies and smaller towns had their own theater in which amateurs organized the performances, villages relied on strolling players to give their inhabitants the opportunity to enjoy plays. Traveling from one town to the next over bumpy and dusty roads in uncomfortable wagons loaded with stage sets, costumes, musical instruments, and makeup boxes, along with paraphernalia for cooking and sleeping, itinerant performers generally led a hard life.

Having entertained in one place the actors and actresses moved on to the next, but when villages were only a few miles apart, they might do the journey in full costume and stage makeup in order not to lose time changing clothes. It was one of these troops in full regalia that the knight Don Quijote encountered on one of his outings. As described by Cervantes, the coachman was a vile demon, and in the open cart sat Death himself with a human face. At his side stood an angel with huge painted wings and an emperor wearing a gold-colored crown. At the feet of Death sat Cupid with his bow, quiver, and arrows. There was also a knight in armor, but instead of a helmet, he wore a hat adorned with multicolored plumes. There were also other people in various kinds of dress. Sensing a situation of high adventure, Don Quijote demanded to know who they were and was told they were a troop on its way to the next engagement. Being Corpus Christi week, they were performing a play called *The Parliament of Death*.[13]

Not all rambling theatrical troops possessed ample costumes and stage props. Some traveled with only the bare rudiments of stage scenery, a few clothes, false beards, and wigs. A well-worn blanket with cords at-

Street theater.

tached served as the stage curtain. They set up their performances in the town square or in a closed street, where the stage consisted of a few planks laid out on top of some benches. A colored canvas behind the makeshift stage served as the backdrop. The windows and balconies of surrounding houses became the theater boxes. The actresses, when not on stage, were often besieged by men in the audience but tried to maintain some decorum, lest the more obnoxious males booed or heckled and ruined the performance. For a small town audience the stage became for a little while their entire universe, taking their minds off the daily drudgery of village life.

While staying the night in an inn in Andalucía the traveler Leucadio Doblado described a performance of players who appeared and set up stage in the courtyard using a cow shed open on one side for the stage. "A horrible screaming fiddle, a grumbling violoncello, and a deafening French horn, composed the band." The play, called *El Diablo Predicador* (The Devil Preacher), relates the struggle of the devil with the Franciscan Order, which threatened to overwhelm his evil empire. Satan, who appeared in a black velvet suit and scarlet stockings, mounted on a griffin, got the upper hand for a time, but the Franciscans were saved by divine intervention.[14]

Members of the clergy were apt to be critical of the theater. Many actors and actresses did not lead exemplary lives—far from it. Their dissolute lifestyle shocked some churchmen, yet these same people played roles in religious enactments as saints and even the Virgin Mary. Plays of intrigue and passion solely designed to excite human emotions also annoyed some clergy. Taking a dim view of these matters, the church sometimes withheld the sacraments from performers even though it was often the religious organizations in the large towns that owned the theaters and leased them out to managers of the stage companies.

GAMES

Mock battles, fireworks, folk dances, pilgrimages (*romerías*), and hunting (the peasants hunted for food, the nobles for pleasure) were all forms of entertainment. A good deal of activity was generated by mock battles between men dressed as Christians and others dressed as Moors. The reenacting of dramatic battles gave each person in the town or village a part to play, and everyone was kept busy in their spare time making or repairing the costumes and weapons and rehearsing their roles. Most young men preferred the role of the Moor, with his dashing and colorful clothes often creating an imbalance between numbers of Moors and Christians. The former were generally armed with crossbows and the latter with firearms. Christians always won, and the defeated Moors were then led through the streets of the town in chains, while the conquering heroes fired off their arquebuses and waved their swords.

Contests of skill and bravery performed by the nobles in jousting tournaments of the Middle Ages continued into the reign of the Habsburgs but gave way to less dangerous encounters than knocking a heavily armored knight out of the saddle with a stout iron-tipped lance at the head-on speed of two galloping horses. Displays of prowess and horsemanship were demonstrated in cane tilting in which the aristocratic participants, richly attired, formed into opposing groups and rode into an enclosure, where the battle took place, on highly caparisoned horses, displaying wooden or leather shields decorated in the colors of their houses or those of their ladies. To the rattle of drums, the blast of trumpets, and the delight of the crowds, they paraded around the arena. Their colorfully dressed squires then came forward and presented their masters with the cane (bamboo) javelin they would use in the forthcoming combat. All retired then to opposite ends of the field or plaza and formed into squadrons of three or four riders. On the signal of the judge, a squadron broke forth, launching an attack, crossing the arena at full gallop. Once in range, they hurled their javelins at their mounted opponents, who deflected the missiles with their shields. Then it was the turn of the other side to charge forward and release their shafts. The battle continued until all the riders had thrown their javelins. A general but nonlethal charge by all participants concluded the tournament. These resplendent and vibrant spectacles of horsemanship constituted a sporting occasion for the aristocrats and an entertaining afternoon for the plebeians seated on the wooden stands around the enclosure. Often the tournament took place in the Plaza Mayor in Madrid, where the high-ranking nobility could observe it from the balconies of the surrounding apartments. The very competitive ring game in which horsemen took turns charging a small ring at full gallop in an attempt to place their javelin through the hole was also a contest of great skill and showmanship and attracted large crowds.

Games in which a ball was hit back and forth between two opponents with rackets, a primitive form of tennis, and a kind of bowling were common indoor and outdoor activity played by both children and adults, especially at court. Popular among the children were puppetry, hoops, tops, kites, and skipping ropes.

A favorite indoor game of the nobility was chess. Spaniards dominated the chess board in the sixteenth and seventeenth centuries until their supremacy was taken away by the Italians.

A major preoccupation from the king down to the peasant was card games. Felipe III was a passionate player. In Castilla, decks of cards were controlled and sold under license held by the king, and it was illegal to play with a deck of cards not authorized and stamped by the government. To use any other, such as French or Catalan cards, was to defraud the royal treasury and carried a heavy penalty. There were a large variety of different card games, some legal and some not, played in establishments referred to euphemistically as Houses of Conversation, which were located throughout the cities and attended by nobles and wealthy bourgeois. The lower classes also had their own, less ostentatious places to get together and play cards. After clothes, horses, and women, more money was spent on gambling than anything else.

Dice games were prohibited, and it was illegal to manufacture dice or sell them. Penalties included two years' exile for the manufacturer and heavy fines for the players. Many clandestine establishments existed in big cities such as Madrid and Sevilla, however, where professional card sharks fleeced the unsuspecting novice, and dice were rolled in the back rooms. In the gaming houses gambling continued twenty-four hours a day. Food and toilets in such places were provided so that the players might not be inconvenienced. Games of cards and dice were, along with guitar music, supplied by the brothels and attracted all segments of the population from the high-ranking nobleman to the lowliest pickpocket.[15]

NOTES

1. See Defourneaux, 176, for further detail.
2. Swinburne, 267.
3. Kamen, *The Spanish Inquisition*, 118.
4. Ibid.
5. Ibid., 119.
6. Livermore, 56; Starkie, 59.
7. For the development of the *zarzuela*, see Starkie, 132.
8. Chase, 97ff.
9. Starkie, 122.
10. Ibid., 123; Defourneaux, 130.
11. Defourneaux, 131.
12. Ibid., 138.
13. Cervantes, 534.
14. Doblado, 164.
15. For more on gambling, see Defourneaux, 219–220.

15

Military Life

Castillian soldiers had a long tradition of fighting the Muslims in all conditions and terrain and could endure extremes of cold and heat, long marches, and short rations. Further, in a series of battles with French forces in Italy at the end of the fifteenth century and the beginning of the sixteenth, the French suffered heavy defeats by Spanish regiments whose soldiers had a reputation unparalleled in European warfare. Their fame and high esteem remained untarnished until the first decades of the seventeenth century. Although many of those who fought for Spain were not Spanish but German, Irish, English, or Italian, the nucleus of the military force was Castillian and Aragonese who set examples of bravery, fortitude, and arrogance.[1]

The Spanish army was grouped into infantry units called *tercios*, consisting of twelve to fifteen companies of about 250 men each, making the *tercio* about 3,000 or more strong, at least in theory. Often it was not up to full strength. A full muster would compose about 1,000 pike men (foot-soldiers who carried the pike—a long wooden shaft tipped with a pointed steel head and used against cavalry charges), while the remainder consisted of arquebusiers (men who carried the arquebus, a heavy, portable firearm gradually replaced by the musket). The supporting cavalry and artillery units of the Spanish armies were primarily made up of foreign mercenaries. The *tercios* were highly mobile units commanded by captains under whom served lieutenants, sergeants, and the common soldier.[2]

There was no definite length of service, and soldiers were frequently shifted between companies and regiments. Under Felipe II about 9,000 men a year were recruited in Spain and many more in times of crisis. Between 1567 and 1574 nearly 43,000 men left the country to fight in Italy and the Netherlands. Many others were required to maintain control of Portugal.

Besides troops garrisoned in Italy, the army of Flanders absorbed about 80,000 men during the struggle to maintain control in northern Europe between 1567 and 1648. The overall force, including seagoing soldiers on Mediterranean galleys and Atlantic sailing ships along with army units in Italy, North Africa, the Netherlands, and those stationed in Spain, was around 300,000 men in the early seventeenth century. About 12,000 new Spanish recruits a year were then required to meet military needs.[3]

Soldiers received little training except that which came from battle experience, and they could not always rely on regular pay, clothing, or food. Providing manpower for policing the empire represented a significant drain on financial resources. The chronic shortage of money from which the royal treasury suffered often left soldiers without pay for months on end. In 1599 reports from various regions in Spain and garrisons in North Africa allege that troops were starving and in rags. Desertions were heavy; some contingents of soldiers had not been paid in four years.[4]

RECRUITMENT AND MILITARY CAREER

With the exception of convicts and slaves to row the king's galleys, the standing army of Spain was made up of volunteers. A captain having received a special commission from the king was required to form his own unit. In the towns assigned to him he flew his banners and solicited recruits, promising them booty, adventure, and glory. The antithesis to these attributes of martial life was never mentioned: the loss of a limb; blindness; gaping, festering wounds from an enemy pike or arquebus; and if death did not intervene or the king award some small pension, a life of hunger and misery on some city street, begging for a shawl or morsel of food.

It was not always easy for the officer to recruit the required number of men for a campaign and assemble them at a given port where they could be shipped out to the theater of conflict. Some who were sworn in deserted after the first dole-out of pay. Others joined the army to escape justice for an offense and bolted at the first opportunity in a far-off place.

Nevertheless, a military career, once the prerogative of the aristocracy, presented the ordinary man with opportunities. Many of those who enlisted, no matter how humble their backgrounds, expected to increase

Soldier with plume and arquebus.

their fortunes and to stand above the common herd by duty in the king's service. Besides honor and dignity that came from the sword and from prowess in battle, there was always the chance of promotion. Housing was provided even if it was in some poor peasant's cottage, and the soldier was exempt from taxes. At least in theory, a soldier received one and one-half pounds of daily bread, which constituted the primary ration. Contractors supplied the loaves, which at times were worse than no bread at all. Sometimes the bread contained offal, bits of plaster, unmilled flour, and other unsavory ingredients, causing death to some soldiers. The choice too often was eat the bread and be sick or don't eat it and starve.

A soldier's wounds were cared for as best they could be. Gunshot wounds were the worst, since they were likely to cause internal bleeding, blood poisoning, and smashed bones. Besides battle wounds, diseases were treated in the hospitals, the most prolific being venereal infections. The soldier was supposed to be ransomed by the army if taken prisoner, although this did not always happen.

In the Netherlands, when troops were not imposed on the local citizenry, accommodation in barracks was normal. To keep warm in winter the recruits scoured the countryside collecting fuel for their fires and sometimes in desperation burned parts of their barracks.

The Spanish presence in Italy was to protect against local rebellion and against attack by the French or the Turks. For most of the sixteenth century the country was peaceful and the Spanish army spent its time in intermittent warfare against the Barbary pirates. Military service in sunny Italy was popular with soldiers for the assurances of women, wine, and wages and the possibility of booty taken from pirates. The majority of the Spanish troops sent to the Netherlands first sailed to Italy and then marched from there through central Europe to their destination over what became known as the Spanish Road. The 700-mile trek took about seven weeks. The bleak and generally hostile Netherlands, where cities were scattered throughout boggy terrain and prolonged sieges were required to subdue them, was not an attractive place for the Spanish soldier.

For those inclined to the military life, there was ample scope for adventure in a variety of distant and strange lands. Personal dignity and arrogance of one who bore arms for God and king led to extravagant attire. There was never a strict ruling on what was proper to wear in the Spanish infantry, and a soldier dressed himself as best he could afford, exempted from decrees that restricted the amount of money spent on finery and that forbade excessive dress. Morale and élan were raised by his apparel, and it would not be uncommon to see him wearing a long cloak, a doublet, hose and belt in bright colors and embroidered with silver, and a wide-brimmed hat embellished with multicolored plumes. The expense for such finery was often derived from booty acquired in or after a battle. Frequently a soldier was wealthy for a period of time, having looted a palace, shop, or a richly laden vessel, before the money or goods were dissipated on women, clothes, and gambling. Sometimes he returned home with enough loot to live in modest comfort for the rest of his life. When a man attained the rank of captain and was put in charge of a company, including its pay, there was ample room for fraud, especially for pocketing the pay of dead men.

Considerable freedom was allowed soldiers when off duty. Efforts to check gambling with both cards and dice, which often led to quarrels among the troops, proved ineffective. Another cause of friction, women, sometimes did lead to tragic results. While lawful wives of soldiers and officers (and even their children) might accompany the men on campaign, the majority of camp-followers consisted of prostitutes along with peddlers and knaves looking for easy money. Prostitutes were given a semilegal status with their numbers fixed by regulations, generally of eight women to every hundred men. The presence of the women and the passion for gambling most often accounted for the occasional murder among the soldiery.

The havoc, violence, and resentment caused by the military among the civilian populations by living off the land when provisions were short, ruining farms and farmers, or stealing whatever could be carried away from households and merchants' shops constituted a grave problem for

Spanish authorities. The billeting of Spanish soldiers in private residences was a major irritant for the populace.

THE SPANISH FURY

The soldiery, calling itself the Catholic army, was motivated by a complex aggregate of chivalry and barbarism, by idealism and cynicism. While lack of bravery was seldom a concern, insubordination and atrocities were always lurking in the shadows. When pay fell into arrears, soldiers would refuse assignments and remain inactive or make up the money owed to them by pillage. Under such conditions they recognized no authority.

In 1576, after many months without their promised pay as a consequence of the state's bankruptcy the year before, the army in the Netherlands mutinied. On Sunday, 4 November, the rich city of Antwerp was brutally sacked. The assault by the disgruntled Spanish army continued for three days in an orgy of looting, raping, and murder in what has been known ever since as the Spanish Fury. Some 8,000 civilians were killed, and merchants fled the city in vast numbers, leaving a smoking ghost town in their wake. The rich were despoiled of their wealth, and the poor hanged because they had nothing to give.[5] This was not the only city to suffer from renegade soldiers. Between the years 1572 and 1607 there were about forty-five mutinies in the army of Flanders. It has been said with justification that Spain did not lose the Netherlands due to Dutch resistance, nor French and English interference, but through the behavior of its own armies and ultimately, of course, by the lack of money in the Spanish treasury.

MILITARY DECLINE

In the seventeenth century interest in the military waned, and voluntary recruitment dwindled to the point where conscription to fill the ranks, regardless of the hardships this placed on the villages, became necessary. Often, those of draft age disappeared rather than go to war, but their wives or parents might then be imprisoned until the recruits presented themselves. The decline in the number of potential soldiers was in part due to the lack of interest of the nobility who, after the great fiasco of 1588 resulting in the loss of the Armada, were more and more inclined to enjoy the good life as courtiers and not endanger themselves on foreign battlefields. With a payment, they could avoid serving in the military.

As the flow of volunteers shriveled to a dribble, the recruiting officers were obliged to accept anyone who presented himself. As a result, vagabonds, ruffians, and scoundrels whom local authorities wanted to be rid of were taken into the ranks. Quantity prevailed over quality as the recruiting officers tried to fill the quotas. The *tercios* could often manage at best 300 men under arms. As money dried up, malnourished soldiers went about in tattered rags, begging for food. The proud *tercios* sometimes degenerated into a ragtag army of scarecrows.

There was little choice but to allow the companies to live off the land and pillage the homes of the local population. Even in Spain itself the billeting of soldiers on the villages that then had to feed and shelter them often led to disastrous consequences. Excesses committed by the troops in Cataluña who had been sent to repel a French invasion led to an uprising in Barcelona against the king in 1640.

Protected by their privileges (military *fueros*) from prosecution by civil law courts, veterans with little or no pensions, and irregular payments for those who did have them, took to robbing houses, assaulting women, and brawling in the streets. There were reportedly seventy dead and forty wounded people in the hospitals of Madrid during the space of two weeks due to such behavior.[6] Of more concern for the king and government was the decline in the morale, prestige, and spirit of the military. The good reputation of the army gave way to that of the *fanfarrón* (swaggert, boaster, or bully), a figure more adept with the bottle and stories of his conquest of young ladies than in facing the enemy.

In 1635 hostilities with France made it mandatory to maintain troops in Spain. A resounding victory was achieved at Fuenterrabía in the Basque country in 1638 against the French, but Portugal and Cataluña objected to their troops fighting out of their own kingdoms and especially to the depredations committed in their lands by the foreign (Castillian) *tercios*.

With the revolt in Cataluña in 1640 and the war with breakaway Portugal at the same time, the nobility abandoned the army in large numbers, and loyal troops were in short supply. In the towns, recruiting agents began their work and the great lords were ordered to muster regiments on their estates. It was still not enough. Recruiting officers resorted to brutal means to fill the quotas set for them, and in order to collect their pay, they seized the defenseless of the working class and dragged them away in chains to the front. Needless to say, many deserted at the first opportunity.[7]

The battle of Rocroi in northern France on 19 May 1643, entailing the first major defeat, shattered the illusion of Spanish invincibility on the battlefield. In October 1648, by the Peace of Westphalia that ended the Thirty Years' War, Spain was forced to recognize the United Provinces, a part of the Netherlands (Holland) as an independent nation.

When the order came from the crown in 1659 to produce thirteen soldiers in the Andalucian town of Luque or pay a fine of 50 ducats for each one, the municipality decided to raise the levy. The city council determined who was the least beneficial to the welfare of the town or the most expendable and in a dawn raid seized them in their homes and sent them off to the army. Again in 1695 volunteers were in short supply when the officials of the king came calling, this time for sixteen soldiers. The less useful citizens were rounded up and confined in the butcher shop (since the jail was in ruins) and shipped out for military duty.[8]

Summons were sent out to hidalgos with the blunt warning to show up for duty or lose their privileges. Some came; others sent substitutes, which was allowed. The methods partially paid off. Cataluña was re-taken, but Portugal, on the other hand, gained its independence. There had not been enough Castillian troops to keep the unhappy western neighbor subdued, nor did they show any willingness to fight for that cause.

The military was no longer an honorable calling. The Spanish infantry, once so feared, was now a rabble. Old soldiers who had served many years and were wounded numerous times in battle received little compensation or remuneration for their efforts on behalf of king and country. A few ex-soldiers who attained high rank might go on to become the warden of a castle or a commander in a military order or receive some other commission, but the majority returned to their homes under conditions no better than when they left. They swelled the lines of the many looking for a job or a handout at the various charitable institutions or those who sought to obtain a license to run a gambling house or retail wine in the city. Those who had a small pension often did not receive it on a regular basis.

Conscription was made more systematic under the Bourbons when manpower was drastically needed, especially at the beginning of the Spanish War of Succession. The loss of the European possessions at the time made recruitment of mercenaries more difficult. To maintain the military, the *quintas* were introduced in 1702 in which one out of every five young men were conscripted by lottery. Later, lists of unmarried men aged seventeen to thirty-five years of age were drawn up who would serve eight years. Nobles, skilled workers, and professionals were exempted. The new system led to riots and proved unworkable. The older form of recruitment was reinstated in which quotas were assigned to local communities, which were free to decide whether to raise the contingents by conscription or to offer bounties to volunteers. By this time the military was smaller: About half were still foreign mercenaries, and some of the rest were vagrants sentenced by the courts to military duty. Of the Spaniards that served the colors in the Americas, few returned to Spain.

ONE SOLDIER'S FATE

In 1571 Miguel Cervantes, as a soldier, was engaged in the sea battle in the Gulf of Lepanto (Gulf of Corinth) against the Turks. After the victory, the Spanish fleet retired to Sicily for rest and repairs, where Cervantes, wounded by gunshot, recuperated. When fit for service, he was sent to Naples to join another regiment and eventually to Tunis in a campaign to capture the city. The successful outcome freed many Christian captives in the hands of Muslim pirates.

With letters of recommendation for exemplary service and requesting that he be promoted to captain after only six years instead of the customary ten, Cervantes joined a flotilla for Spain. No ship dared sail alone in the pirate-infested waters of the Mediterranean, but the fleet was scattered in a storm and Cervantes's ship was captured and taken to Algiers, where he was locked up in prison to await his fate. The letters he possessed worked against him. Taken as a man of rank, his ransom was set high, well out of reach of his family and more than his value to the army. Cervantes became a slave in the city, an outpost of the Ottoman Empire swarming with Christian captives, pirates, renegades, expatriate Spanish Muslims, and adventurers from all lands and walks of life. His war injury that had resulted in a damaged hand kept him from the galleys. As his captors hoped eventually for a large ransom, five years passed during which time he made several heroic but unsuccessful attempts to escape before money, collected from various sources including his family, arrived. He was released in 1580 and returned to Spain.

The trade and use of slaves was not all one-sided: Christian ships from Spain and elsewhere raided the coasts of North Africa, taking fishing boats or other vessels when the opportunity arose and enslaving the crews, often for a short life in the royal galleys.

THE NAVY

The Spanish navy, like the army, was a heterogeneous composite of men reflecting the diversity of empire. Sailors were poorly paid; most had little prospect of improving their status. Seamen were voluntarily recruited from town and village by the king's representatives, but there were never enough men willing to serve in the expanding fleets and they were forcibly pressed into service. Except in Cataluña where the *fueros* prohibited it, young men were seized in their homes and on the streets, locked up until their numbers were sufficient, and then sent in chains to the ports. In seaport towns themselves, fishermen were a desirable commodity, and the young ones lived in some anxiety of falling prey to the press gangs.

Ships were mostly of two types: oared galleys, used throughout the Mediterranean, and the sailing ships or galleons in the Atlantic Ocean. The military galleys, replete with seagoing infantry, oared by slaves or common criminals assigned to the king's service, fought by coming to grips with the enemy and boarding. Punishment in the galleys was a cheap source of labor, and it was the most feared by prisoners of the Inquisition after the stake itself. To meet rising demand for rowers on royal ships, this sentence became more frequent after the mid-sixteenth century. Homosexuality and bigamy were often punished by a stretch in the galleys, less often punishments for heresy. Five years was generally the maximum sentence of the Inquisition, but secular court sentences were often longer. This saved the inquisitorial tribunals and the state money since it freed the tribunals from maintaining prisoners in cells and the state from hiring rowers. After the uprising in Andalucía in 1568, the galleys became a frequent form of punishment for Morisco prisoners. Four to eight oarsmen, chained on the same bench, pulled a single large oar and rowed under the hot Mediterranean sun all day with poor food and little water. For many, a ten-year stretch in the galleys was tantamount to a death sentence. Those who perished were thrown overboard.

The typical galley had about 150 rowers, and the total crew aboard consisted of about 220 men. The hulls were 120 to 130 feet long and just over 20 feet wide. They carried three to five heavy guns pointed foreword and a number of pivotal light guns. A sixteenth-century development was the galleass, a larger version of the same ship.

The duty of the military galleys was generally to give protection against the Turkish and Berber pirates of the Barbary Coast who, after 1516, made assaults on Spain itself, carrying off Spanish prisoners, and to protect shipping to Italy. The battle of Lepanto was the last of the great galley battles; thereafter the naval importance of this type of ship steadily declined, but it continued in use as a transport vessel for goods and troops in the Mediterranean. Unlike galleys, the galleons with their heavy canon fought their battles at a greater distance. They escorted the merchant vessels plying the trade to the West Indies and, on occasion, the Netherlands. The heavy galleons ruled the waves but were never in sufficient numbers to police the far-flung empire effectively.

There was not much enthusiasm for the sea route to the Netherlands. In 1620 when the French cut the Spanish Road, only a sea route remained available to replenish the northern garrisons. Communications by sea between Spain and the Netherlands was always precarious due to storms and tides in the Bay of Biscay and the North Sea and the constant threat of English corsairs, Dutch freebooters, and Huguenot pirates out of their base at La Rochelle, all of whom lay in wait for Spanish shipping on its way to and from the Low Countries.

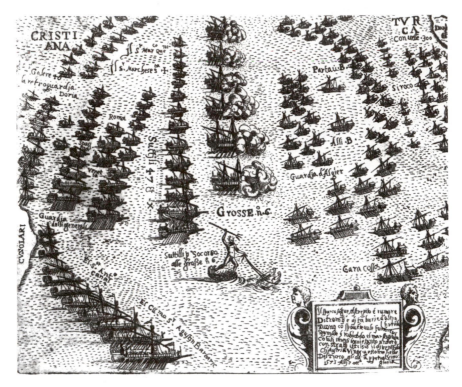

Anonymous. *Battle of Lepanto (1571).* (Madrid: Biblioteca Nacional).

SHIPS TO AMERICA

From the beginning of the sixteenth century, communications between Spain and the Indies, as well as the New World settlements themselves, had to be protected from privateers of other countries and pirates. The Spanish crown was forced to allocate an increasing amount of funds to land fortifications, artillery, and troops and to naval defenses consisting of coastal patrols and transatlantic escort ships for the merchantmen. These measures cost about 25 percent of defense spending in the first half of the sixteenth century.

The second half of the century saw the English, under the command of men like Sir John Hawkins and Sir Francis Drake, raiding the Spanish sea lanes with great audacity. Independent voyages across the ocean gave way to sailings in escorted convoy for better protection and eventually to two large annual sailings. There were never enough experienced men to fill the jobs, especially those requiring expertise such as pilots and navigators. Still, for tens of thousands of Castillians and Aragonese, a place in the ranks was a desirable alternative to a life of toil on a farm

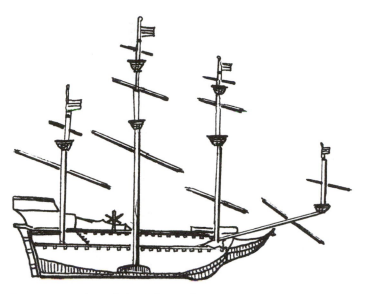

Oceangoing ship of the Atlantic fleet.

with little to show for it except more taxes and the uncertainties of the next meal.

The convoy merchant fleets protected by the royal navy carried to the New World numerous items needed by the colonists. Cargoes consisted of items such as olive oil and wine, nails, tools and iron bars, bales of cloth both coarse and fine, vinegar, olives, almonds, wax, soap, glassware, books, weapons, ceramic tiles, and barrels of mercury from the mines at Almadén in Andalucía used to extract silver from their ores. Sometimes horses, sheep, and goats were transported, requiring supplies of fodder. In the American settlements these items were exchanged for gold and silver, pearls, precious stones, animal pelts, spices, cocoa, sugar, dyes, and exotic wood, all of which were brought back to Sevilla.

Since Spain could not supply all the needs of the colonies but reserved the exclusive rights to all commerce, goods also arrived from other parts of Europe: cloths and linens from northern France, fine brocades from Italy, salted cod and herring from the Baltic towns of the Hanseatic League, and other sundry products for the eager colonists on the other side of the ocean. These were collected and piled high on the wharves of Sevilla and the banks of the river Guadalquivir, awaiting transport down the river and across the Atlantic. Loading the cargo, including victuals for the crews of the ships and cannon balls and powder for the escort warships, gave employment to many stevedores, captains, and crews of the lighters as well as administrative jobs keeping track of all the goods.

When the ships were filled, the inspectors from the *Casa de Contratación* came on board to check the cargo against the bills of lading, and commissioners from the Inquisition arrived to search for illicit books and pamphlets banned by the Holy Office. Heretical literature, it was feared, might reach the colonies smuggled in with other legitimate goods arriving from northern Europe. On the day of departure, most of the city turned out to watch the great ships slowly get under way as their sails billowed large and bright in the breeze. Then came the long wait for the return voyage, with many investors anxious about their ships and cargoes.

With the safe arrival home, festivities began in the city even before the ships were unloaded. The precious metals and stones were consigned to the ships of war and not to the cargo vessels, and the first question asked when they arrived in Sevilla was, "How much?" As anxious as anyone for news of the fleet was the king, who always needed his one-fifth share. Laden with gold, silver, and pearls, ox carts slowly crept forward away from the wharves along the road to the royal chamber in the *Casa de Contratación*. When the storeroom coffers overflowed, as they did on at least one occasion, bars of gold and silver were stacked high in the courtyard outside.

Many men who went to sea did so out of desperation. Nevertheless, the life of a sailor offered opportunities not open to a lackey of some nobleman or to someone working as an unskilled laborer in a hamlet or village. There was always the possibility to make money by engaging in contraband goods smuggled to the Indies and sold for a profit or brought from the Indies home to Spain. On the merchant ships, one might also advance up the ladder to become a pilot, navigator, or a master, in charge of provisions, cargo, and equipment. In time a clever man might even become a captain of a vessel with better pay and more opportunities for enrichment such as the transport of well-paying illegal emigrants.

Some who signed on board had no intention of returning and at the first chance deserted the ship in the New World to seek their fortunes. This short-circuited the slow bureaucratic process and the many necessary and costly bribes to obtain legal papers to emigrate as well as payment for the passage and food for a three-month journey. It could amount to twelve months' pay for an unskilled laborer, few of whom would have been able to save that much money.

CHILD SAILORS

Young boys were often dragooned aboard ship to serve as pages or were sent to sea by families who could not feed them. They entered maritime service between eight and ten years old and did the jobs that no one wanted, scrubbing the ship, clearing up after meals, keeping vigil at night, and maintaining the rituals of religious observances. The passage of the hours was marked by the boys, one of whom turned over the sand clock, a glass through which the sand flowed every half hour. The measurement of time was essential to navigation, as the navigator estimated the speed of the ship and compared it to the time lapsed to determine how far they had traveled. Every turn of the clock was announced by a traditional ditty along the lines of

> One glass done
> One filling
> More sands run
> God willing.

After the seventh turn of the clock, the lad in charge sang out for the next shift to be ready. After four hours or eight turns of the glass, the watch was changed.[9]

The young boys watched over the religious aspects of the ship, reciting the principal prayers of the Christian faith. Their youth and innocence was considered a better vehicle for the transmission of prayers to the Lord than the crude, jaded sailors who often could care less about such matters.

Unlike the army where daily Mass was obligatory, it was not performed on ships for fear that the rolling, pitching vessels might cause damage to or even the loss of the Blessed Sacrament. The boys sang prayers at the foot of the main mast every morning and *Ave Maria* at sunset. There was usually some kind of altar on the ship decorated with candles and images, and services were held on feast days and Sundays. Most sailors carried amulets around their necks of the Virgin Mary or their favorite saint. Again unlike the army with its numerous chaplains, sailors confessed to one another when faced with death in a storm or action. (The great Armada of 1588 with many priests on board was an exception, and the royal galleys had chaplains who looked after the spiritual welfare of the oarsmen who were allowed to hear Mass and confess their sins.)

The pages took orders from all the seamen and from the apprentices, the latter on average about eighteen years old and still learning the trade. Apprentices and pages were subject to abuses both verbal and physical, among which were homosexual advances by some members of the crew in spite of dire penalties. A conviction for homosexual behavior could lead to execution.

LIFE ABOARD SHIP

The officers of the ship and the rich passengers had the best spots to sit and sleep toward the stern of the vessel, whereas the mariners and poorer passengers slept wherever they could find a place in the forward areas. Senior officers might have a bed of sorts, but the sailors slept wherever they could stretch out on the deck. The fact that one-third of them were standing on watch during the night relieved the situation for space somewhat. Not until the eighteenth century did hammocks come into general use on Spanish ships. Sailors marked out their private spot by situating their sea chests there, and fights with drawn daggers were not uncommon over a few inches of space.

In summer the favored positions were on the upper decks, which were also the gun decks, as cannon on Spanish ships were mounted as high as possible to avoid the smoke from the black powder. Passengers fitted trundle beds on deck and partitioned off space for some privacy, although it sometimes interfered with the use of the guns and impeded the work of the sailors.

In the confined space, dozens of people were crammed together for weeks on end. For example, a caravel of sixty-five tons and about 100 feet long, not a large ship, departed in 1507 for the Caribbean with a crew of fifteen, eighty-three passengers, and all their provisions including live animals for food and eighteen mares and twelve yearling calves as cargo.[10]

As oceangoing ships grew larger, so did the crews, cargo, and number of passengers. The cramped and unhealthy conditions were little improved. Besides animals such as sheep and goats carried aboard to be slaughtered for fresh meat, passengers often brought their own fresh supplies in the form of live chickens, partridges and geese, and even pigs. All occupied the deck space, and passengers kept close watch on their birds and other animals, as they were apt to disappear in the night and fill the stomach of a hungry sailor. Live chickens in the galley to feed the sick was part of the general supplies, as the meat of this bird was considered to have great recuperative powers.

With seasick passengers and sick pigs vomiting all over the deck in severely crowded conditions, and the distinct possibility of drowning in a storm, the ships were worse than any prison to which they have been frequently compared. Climbing the rigging on slippery ropes to shorten the sails in driving rain and wind was a feat few sailors relished. Neither passengers nor crew had adequate shelter from the elements in the northern latitudes, and in the tropical heat of the central Atlantic, no fresh water.

There were also a large number of uninvited animals: Legions of mice and rats infested the storage areas, and cockroaches appeared from every crack and cranny. Lice, fleas, and bedbugs were constant companions of the sailors, inhabiting their clothes and blankets and finding new territory among the passengers. Foul-tasting water was for drinking; there was none for bathing or washing clothes.

Besides a table and a few chairs for the officers, the common article of furniture on board was the sea chest of each sailor, usually a wooden box containing clothes and personal effects. These were lashed down on the deck in the open air and also served as a table, chair, or even a bed for their owners. On these, card games were played, with others pulled around to sit on.

Everything on the deck of a ship was public, including what would be private bodily functions in other circumstances. The officers and wealthy passengers had some degree of seclusion inasmuch as they had their own latrines astern, but the sailors stood in line each morning in various states of dress, trousers in hand, waiting their turn on the wooden grating jutting out from the prow directly over the sea.

MEALS

On a ship, at least meals were regular. No one starved; but they were limited to food that did not readily rot or that was preserved in salt, and in practice, victuals were often short due to lack of money or problems in supply. Half rations or poor quality were not unusual.

Ship's biscuit, of which each crew member was given a pound and a half daily, was an unleavened sugarless bread, double cooked to give it longer life. It had to be soaked in water or wine for a few minutes to make it palatable. Water, kept in old barrels, soon developed a bad taste and smell; wine, doled out at two pints a day, was the more popular drink.

Breakfast consisted of the biscuit and wine along with a morsel of salted pork and a few sardines. Lunch, the main meal, was eaten about noon, and dinner, a lighter fare, was consumed before the sun set. Such meals were made up of salted meat or fish, generally cod, cheese, beans, rice, and chickpeas. Salted food naturally brought on greater thirst. In battle or storms when cooking fires could not be lit, cheese was substituted for meat.

Most sailors carried fishing lines in their equipment and sometimes were able to supplement their rations with fresh fish. But lack of food and water was always a danger, especially if the ship was becalmed in windless seas for a length of time. Scurvy, which appeared among the crews after about six weeks' deprivation of fresh fruit and vegetables, was also a dangerous problem.

DRESS AND DIVERSIONS

Most sailors could ill afford fine clothes, and their occupation could generally be identified by their shabby garments. The fashion at the time girded the body in an upright rigid position, head erect, to give the figure dignified elegance. Such attire did not serve to climb the rigging of a ship, and sailors wore loose, unadorned comfortable clothes generally in the color blue. Their entire wardrobe, mainly old and worn, kept in their sea chests, consisted usually of a pair of linen shirts and pants, a couple of jackets, a pair of shoes or sandals, and a sea cape for protection from wind and rain. These items, plus a jug in which to put the wine ration, some fishing tackle, and a knife, always carried on person for work or a fight, were about all a poor sailor possessed.

Singing, telling stories, chatting, and games occupied the spare time of men of the sea. Royal ordinances prohibited games of chance on ships unless, to pass the time, they were played for harmless pieces of fruit or sweets. Cursing and blaspheming were also taboo. The sailors paid no attention to these edicts, and games of dice and cards for money accompanied by profanity and sacrilegious oaths were a common occurrence. Often the officers in charge of discipline on board were the ones who rented out decks of cards for extra cash and usually collected from the winner.

While about four out of five sailors, apprentices, and pages could not sign their own names,[11] for those who could read, books helped pass the time. The favorite stories were of chivalry with their valiant knights, beautiful maidens, and heroic deeds, and religious books such as the lives of saints. Stories of high seas adventures and descriptions of far-off lands were popular, as were those about the grandeur of the Roman Empire. The Reconquest of the Hispanic lands from the Moors and the conquest of the New World were also in demand. These books allowed for discussion of the deeds of Julius Caesar, the Cid, or Hernán Cortés. Reading and possessing books were not without certain risks, however. The Inquisition was always interested in what one read, and the ships, while in port, and even the sailors' sea chests, were often searched for literature that might compromise the teachings of the mother church.

Shipboard heterosexual relationships between sailors and passengers were considered sinful by the church, and if discovered, the culprits could be punished by reprimands, fines, and even abandonment on some forlorn coast (each party in a different place).[12]

THE ROYAL FLEET

On warships, usually galleons, dedicated to the protection of merchant ships, the captain was a military man (unlike the commercial ships). The fleet had two superior officers: the admiral, who was second in command, and a general, who was in overall command. The admiral was charged with allocating justice and was the supreme judge of crimes committed at sea. He had the power to try, torture, and condemn to death anyone suspected of criminal behavior. Generals were responsible for the military preparedness of the galleons and also for the well-being of the sailors.

Every fleet that set sail for New Spain (the Americas) had these two men, often on board their privately owned, heavily armed ships that were leased out to the crown for escort duty. Needless to say, they were in a position to greatly increase their personal wealth through contraband goods stowed away aboard their flagship. The crews of His Majesty's fleet, skilled in the use of cannon and arquebus, like their counterparts on the merchant ships, were often able to supplement their meager pay by buying clothes or other merchandise in Spain and selling them in the West Indies, where there was ample demand.

NOTES

1. Davies, 22–23.
2. Elliott, *Spain and Its World*, 221ff; Elliott, *Imperial Spain*, 134.
3. For costs, see Kamen, *Spain 1469–1714*, 162.
4. Ibid.
5. For aspects of the Spanish Fury, see Kamen, *Spain 1469–1714*, 132; Domínguez Ortiz, 75; Lynch, *Spain 1516–1598*, 405.
6. Defourneaux, 208.
7. Domínguez Ortiz, 39.
8. Casey, 103.
9. Pérez-Mallaína, 76.
10. Ibid., 132.
11. Ibid., 231.
12. Ibid., 165. For illicit sexual behavior aboard ships, see pp. 164–176.

16

Education

A major concern of the king was to select men who would be placed in charge of the education of the heir. The royal tutors had to be loyal to the throne and protect the prince from court factions wishing to control him. They were required to be in agreement on principles and methods in order to create a climate of unity. Strict norms of virtuous behavior were of utmost importance, and the heir had to be kept in touch with the people whom he must be taught to protect and over whom he had to administer justice.

When the prince had grasped the abstract concepts of justice and virtue, other specific subjects could then be taught such as music, dance, poetry, history, mathematics, rhetoric and languages, physical education, and the concepts of the Christian religion. To become a just and prudent ruler was of great importance, overridden only by the necessity to retain the sovereign power of the land. The prince's political education was as important or more so than his humanistic studies, and his training in politics was aided by attending meetings of the various councils. Instilled in young kings-to-be was the notion that they must be the guardians of the Catholic faith, conserve it at all costs, and deplore enemies of the church.[1]

In contrast to the royal family whose education was, at least in theory, the best money could buy, church organizations and private individuals attended to the instruction of young commoners. Charitable endowments helped maintain primary and secondary schools run by the municipality or a patron. In small towns the parish priest or the sacristan often pro-

Classroom scene.

vided rudimentary education in reading, writing, and the catechism. There were, to be sure, numerous young people in the cities and countryside of poor families, or orphans, who never saw the inside of a school. The state took no responsibility for education of youngsters and simply assumed the right of inspection and control. Some charitable endowments were available for the maintenance of primary or secondary schools run by individuals, the church, or the municipality, but many towns and hamlets did not bother at all with the education of children.[2]

For those born into families of means, especially males, the situation was less forbidding. For example, a private instructor might be enlisted to teach the young boys reading and writing and the rudiments of Latin, a language that still enjoyed considerable prestige.

Alternatively, the male offspring of aristocratic or well-off families were sent away from their own homes to the household of some wealthy person, such as the house or palace of a nobleman, a bishop, or even the royal court, where they became pages or foster children. There they were expected to perform domestic service such as waiting on his lordship at table or in his chambers in exchange for instruction under the guidance of a tutor in reading and writing, Latin grammar and classical authors such as Cicero or Caesar, Renaissance humanism, and aspects of basic mathematics. Horsemanship, etiquette, and the art of combat might also be included.

Bishops or in some cases religious orders provided a little elementary and secondary education. Bishops sometimes maintained a number of young nobles in their households and even a few orphans.

Secondary schooling for those who wanted to become priests or go to the university was available. A few academies established by individual entrepreneurs had good credentials, such as the Estudio de Madrid, which provided a humanist education, instruction in poetry, and organized academic competitions. Other schools were operated by charlatans with little more education than the students or by poor rural clerics trying to supplement a meager stipend. The means of instruction was usually a generous use of the cane. Government measures were introduced to impede the proliferation of these institutions since it was thought they deprived the manual trades of conscripts.

From 1560 Jesuit schools began to appear. These were highly disciplined, the students learning through debates and lectures with more emphasis on reward than on punishment. The Jesuits, with a rapidly growing reputation for superior teaching, often succeeded in obtaining exclusive contracts with municipalities, alarming those who saw a monopoly on education in the making. The use of prefects and student fraternities gave aspiring pupils a sense of belonging and distinction.

With the advent of Jesuit schools, sons of the wealthy or nobility also sought a general grounding in history, mathematics, and science. Those students of promise were allowed to enroll in the university and further advance their studies.

For the sons of the nobility, the special Imperial College in Madrid, founded by the Jesuits in 1625, was established to train an elite for high office. Higher education was a powerful tool for perpetuating the social and political dominance of the aristocratic class.

State education of youngsters took on more importance after the expulsion of the Jesuits by Carlos III in 1767: At eight years of age they were taught to read and write; at nine, they were taught mathematics; at ten to twelve, geography and history; and twelve to fourteen, foreign languages. At about age fourteen they could then be sent off to begin university studies in civil law, canon law, theology, medicine, or classics. Many schools did not meet these ideals, however.

At their peak in the 1580s Castillian universities took in about 20,000 students a year, mostly from bourgeois city families and from the hidalgo class. Courses in the humanities gave way to career subjects in law, and the universities produced a homogeneous social group of *letrados* or a corps of trained lawyers who became prelates, councilors, magistrates, statesmen—the bureaucratic elite. In 1555 Latin grammar at Salamanca attracted 35 percent of the students and Greek 1 percent. Hebrew studies had one student and disappeared that year. By 1595 only 9 percent studied Latin, and no one took Greek. In that year some 57 percent preferred canon law and another 16 percent studied civil law. In short, nearly three-fourths of all students took courses that would give them a career in the bureaucracy of state or church. Universities became training grounds for office seekers. They became dominated by professors who were generally *letrados*, not scholars. The graduates developed into dynasties that ruled through key posts over Spain and its empire.[3]

UNIVERSITY LIFE

For noble youth and increasingly more often for boys of the bourgeoisie (but rarely for young men of the peasant class), the university became a way of life where students and professors were isolated from the mundane and lived in an exceptional atmosphere of their own making. The rules that governed their society were unique, and student life was, for some, carefree and exciting, for others, brutal and wretched. University students, even those of upper-class background, were not necessarily well off. Many parents saved and scraped by to send their children to an institution of higher learning, and money was not always forthcoming from home when it was needed.

Founded in 1243 the university at Salamanca, embedded in medieval origins, was the oldest and most prestigious in the country. In the sixteenth century the library contained about 38,000 books and manuscripts. The professor, who had to have a doctorate degree and wear his academic gown, delivered his lectures from a pulpitlike seat towering above the students. Sometimes a student just below this lofty position read from a book while the professor commented on the recitation. Some students took notes for everyone, and no one spoke in the classroom. Questions were relegated to the corridor following each lecture, the latter lasting up to about an hour and a half.

Noble youth were often accompanied to class by their retinue and sometimes sent only their servants to take notes for them. On occasion the servants were the ones who became educated, but having no money to continue a university education on their own, they formed singing groups and took to the streets to entertain passersby, hoping for a small remuneration; or sometimes they enlisted their services to serenade young ladies at their windows on behalf of a wealthy patron. Representing the various faculties of the university (law, medicine, theology), they became known as the *Tuna*, whose practice continues today.

New rivals sprang up to challenge the authority of the University of Salamanca: In the middle of the sixteenth century institutions of higher learning were begun at Zaragoza, Valencia, Toledo, Sevilla, and even in a few smaller towns. There developed, however, only one serious rival

Martín de Cervera. *A University Lecture*. (Universidad de Salamanca).

to Salamanca, which was the University of Alcalá de Henares, about twenty-five miles east of Madrid. It was founded in 1508 by Cardinal Jiménez de Cisneros, archbishop of Toledo and Inquisitor General of Castilla. When Madrid became the capital of the country in the mid-sixteenth century, the university prospered. While at first it was concerned chiefly with theology and classical literature, it soon became a typical product of the New Age. In the space of about half a century the University of Alcalá became the symbol of Renaissance learning, breaking with the traditions of medieval Scholasticism. The little town became a well-known center of scholarship throughout Spain and beyond. Nevertheless, the prestige of Salamanca attracted over three times as many students. The minor universities led a precarious existence and were often the butt of jokes regarding their academic qualities.

The University of Alcalá de Henares was initiated as an authoritarian and centralized institution with much power vested in the rector, who was appointed by the even more powerful archbishop of Toledo. The university of Salamanca, on the other hand, was more democratic in its organization and was to a large extent governed by the students.

In 1492, the Catholic Kings Isabella and Fernando confirmed the immunity of students from ordinary civil law, making them subject only to the jurisdiction of the professor of theology, who at the time was nominated by the pope. His duties included the protection of the rights of students, which exempted them from military service and from all taxes affecting their person and their goods. Responsible for the welfare of the university community and its finances, the rector was elected by a committee made up of half students (selected by their peers) and half professors. For prestige purposes the scion of one of the great families was generally chosen.

Professors were also selected by the students at a public meeting in which the views of various candidates for the academic position were examined. While decrees had been issued by the kings of Spain to curb the practice of bribery through gifts or subornation by threats and entreaties, the often impecunious and hungry student was subject to the inducement of a little silver or a sumptuous meal to vote one way or the other. Not until 1624 did Felipe IV place the appointment of professors at Salamanca, Alcalá, and Valladolid in the hands of the Council of Castilla, where they were chosen strictly on the basis of academic merit.

In the early sixteenth century the influence of Humanism—which emphasized the dignity and worth of the individual with the basic premise that people are rational beings who possess within themselves the capacity for truth and goodness—began belatedly to make itself felt in Spanish universities. The new academic spirit, a reaction to the tenets of Scholasticism, began to take root. Scholastics maintained that there was a fundamental harmony between reason and revelation, and as God was the source of both types of knowledge, they could not be contradictory. Any apparent conflict between revelation and reason must be attributed either to an incorrect use of reason or to an inaccurate interpretation of the words of revelation. As the direct teaching of God, revelation possessed for the Scholastics a higher degree of truth and certitude than did natural reason. In differences between religious faith and philosophic reasoning, faith was thus the supreme arbiter, and the theologian's decision overruled that of the philosopher. Fearing that new ideas might threaten religious orthodoxy, proceedings were taken by the Inquisition against certain professors at the University of Salamanca as warning to those who might seek new approaches and independence of thought.

INTELLECTUALS AND THE INQUISITION

Antônio de Nebrija, born in 1441, was the foremost Spanish humanist of his time. He began his studies at Salamanca but, impatient with his professors, traveled to Italy at age nineteen, where he spent ten years in diligent study. Upon his return to Spain his talents and learning were quickly recognized, and he was given a chair at his old university. His scholarship embraced many fields including law, natural sciences, and philology. He revived and stimulated Latin studies in Spain, and after some years at Salamanca, he was summoned to teach at the University of Alcalá. Nebrija was well known for his *Gramática de la Lengua Castellana* (Grammar of the Spanish Language), the first serious study of a modern European language.

Some of the most caustic intellectual battles of the period were those that took place among university professors. Personal rivalries between religious orders and partisan interests were always present, and many bitter arguments arose between literary scholars like Nebrija and the theologians. In 1504 Inquisitor General Diego de Deza, archbishop of Sevilla, confiscated the papers of Nebrija, who had dared to state the view that as a philologist he was no less capable than a theologian such as Deza of determining the text of holy scriptures. Nebrija, however, enjoyed the support of Cisneros, and the matter went no further. Others were not so fortunate.

Fray Luís de León has been called the most representative man of his age, the supreme expression of the Spanish Renaissance. He was one of the country's first-rank lyric poets and an impressive writer. Son of a lawyer, at age sixteen he attended Salamanca university, after studying at Valladolid and Madrid, and joined the Augustinian Order in 1544. Having earned a degree in sacred theology, at the age of thirty-two he returned to Salamanca as a professor, where he began his lectures with five minutes of communal foot-stamping to warm up the students shivering in the unheated classroom. A brilliant lecturer, he defeated all other opponents for the post in theology—but not without making enemies, chief of whom was León de Castro, who held the chair in Greek studies. He and another unfriendly Dominican colleague denounced Fray Luís to the tribunal of the Inquisition in Valladolid, accusing him of having questioned the accuracy of the Vulgate translation of the Bible, the edition of the Latin Bible that was pronounced authentic by the Council of Trent.

Fray Luís was also accused of preferring the Hebrew version to that of the Vulgate and of translating the Song of Songs into Spanish. He had done this for a nun in Salamanca, but any translation of the Bible into vernacular languages was forbidden by the Inquisition. His orthodoxy was now in question. It did not help his case that his great-grandmother had been a Jew who had converted to Roman Catholicism some sixty years before at an auto de fe. Fray Luís was arrested on 27 March 1572 and confined in the inquisitorial prison at Valladolid about fifty miles northeast of Salamanca, where he remained for nearly five years while his case was examined. He survived the often lethal atmosphere of the cells and was finally pronounced innocent. He returned to the university and is reputed to have begun his first lecture after the long absence with the words "*Dicebamus hesterna die . . .*" (as we were saying yesterday . . .).

Other professors of the university who fell into the clutches of the Inquisition were not so lucky. Several died in prison before their cases were heard. One professor, Martínez de Cantalapiedra, spent even longer in the cold cells of the prison in Valladolid than did Fray Luís. Upon his release he was denied reinstatement at the university. With each new quarrel at the venerable seat of learning resulting from professors examining each others' work for errors and deviations from orthodoxy, the great fear was always that the Inquisition would be brought into the disputes. Rivalry between theologians and grammarians was intense, and professors with Jewish blood in their veins, even if staunch Christians, were always the ones most suspected of straying from Catholic dogma. The Inquisition generally sided with the theologians.

Under the pernicious eye of the Inquisition, the humanist spirit engendered by the Renaissance during the first two-thirds of the sixteenth century gave way to the traditional and entrenched ways of thinking. Every professor was instructed to lecture in the spirit of the teacher in whose name the professional chair of each faculty of the university was founded such as Saint Augustine, Saint Thomas Aquinas and Duns Scotus, the Scottish theologian and Scholastic.

Adherence to what many considered reactionary intellectualism resulted in violent quarrels. In their teachings and in public debates the pundits belonging to the various monastic orders slavishly followed the opinions of their masters, depending on whether or not they were Augustinians, Dominicans, or Jesuits. One such debate between Augustinians and Trinitarians led to punching and kicking each other over the question of whether or not Adam remained incomplete after God removed one of his ribs! The public debates were made more riotous than ever by a chorus of students enthusiastically encouraging their favorite professors.

EXAMINATIONS AND DEGREES

The crowning achievement of the student came when he was awarded the sought-after degree of bachelor, licentiate, or doctor. The bachelor's degree could be earned in the Faculty of Arts where students worked on their Latin and scholastic philosophy. There were no examinations in subjects for the degree, but a requirement was to attend courses for a number of years and take part in ceremonies and public debates. This served to prepare the students for more specialized programs in theology, civil and ecclesiastical law, or medicine.

The licentiate received a license granted by the university to practice a profession; it was an academic degree ranking below that of doctor, and it was conferred at a special ceremony when the candidate presented a thesis and responded to his detractors, not unlike some modern master's degree programs. Feasting and celebrating were at the graduate's expense, as was the high cost of the examination fee. Poor students were often hard-pressed to find the money. However, the degree of licentiate was a good deal less expensive and less ruinous for the student than the doctorate.

The presentation of the doctor's degree invoked rejoicing in which the entire town took part. According to Juan Ruiz de Alarcón,[4] writer and dramatist who attended the University of Salamanca for five years at the end of the sixteenth century, every detail of the degree was recapitulated in the university ritual of the ceremonial along with the description of the menu and service of the banquet soon to be presented, at the doctoral student's expense, to all members of the faculty. This was not all the student or his family was obliged to pay for, however. Honorariums had to be given to the supervising professor, to the beadles, and to the examiners and tips doled out to everyone who helped with the undertaking, including the master of ceremonies, trumpeters, bell ringers and drummers who announced the event, and workmen who, among other things, hung tapestries on the front walls of the university.

For the banquet itself, expenses were staggering. It began with salads that included a variety of fruit, vegetables, preserves, and sugared almonds—whatever was best in the season. Eggs were served next, followed by game birds such as partridge or pigeon and chicken. A well-seasoned dish of chicken hash served with slices of bacon and sausage along with morsels of rabbit and veal came next. The fish course of salmon, dorado, or swordfish followed and had to be the finest and freshest available. Desserts such as eggs *à la royal* were followed by cheese; best-quality olives from Sevilla, anise-flavored candy, sugar-coated fruit, wafers, and finally toothpicks ended the meal.

On the eve of the investiture there was a procession of all the masters and doctors of the university, dressed in black robes trimmed with white lace and covered by a colored cape that denoted the different faculties. Blue capes represented the arts, white the theologians, physicians were in yellow, canonists in green, and jurists in red, all wearing fringed hats and heralded by trumpeters and drummers. Then came the dean, the rector, the beadles, and the professor sponsoring the candidate, who followed mounted on a magnificently caparisoned charger and dressed in velvet or silk with sword and dagger at his side. Bringing up the rear of the long procession in the narrow streets of the city came the students. Reaching the university, a light meal was served at the expense of the candidate. The next day the interrogation of the future doctor by his teachers began in the great hall of the university.

In the chapel of Santa Barbara in the old cathedral, professors sat on benches on three sides, while the doctoral student, who customarily had been there all night thinking about his ordeal, sat with his back to the wall on a kind of throne, his legs thrust forward and his feet firmly pressed against the feet of the statue of the eleventh-century bishop Juan de Lucero, laying in a prone position on the floor in front of him. The professors fired their questions and listened for the answers that the student fervently hoped would be inspired by his physical contact with the statue of the holy bishop.

Upon the successful conclusion, the procession left the university and moved to the cathedral. Here, the new doctor received the insignia of his degree and put on the doctoral cap. Sitting down in a chair, he took an oath and then read the opening words of the Gospel according to Saint John while all present knelt down. When the ceremony finished, the rejoicing began. As was customary, five bulls were put to death in a corrida. Pope Sixtus V, adhering to the condemnation of the bullfight by Pius V, had himself condemned the professors at Salamanca for allowing and attending the cruel and bloody spectacle. The university assembly, however, in a letter to the pope asked that he not enforce a measure that would be detrimental to the peace and order of the university. The pope did not insist.

While failure of the examination before the council of professors was a huge disgrace, the medieval practice of forcing the student to leave the hall by the small back door of the cathedral, where he was apt to encounter an unsympathetic crowd of people and a barrage of ridicule, stones, and rotten fruit, was no longer in vogue.

Besides the high cost of the bullfight and other expenses, the new graduate had to reckon with a series of gifts that were fixed by university tradition and its constitution. Fifty florins to the dean and to the sponsor, 2 gold pieces to each doctor, 100 silver reales to the beadle and to the college notary. It did not end here. A pair of gloves, bags of sugar, and half a dozen chickens were also given to each. Sometimes several students teamed up to have their doctoral degrees conferred on the same day to share and thus lessen the expense. When this occurred, the university staff expected a more bountiful display, thereby lessening the amount of money that would have been saved by the students.

STUDENT LIFE

In spite of the democratic nature of the university in appointments of faculty and common privileges among students, class distinctions reflecting society as a whole continued to exist. The sons of the nobility and the wealthy bourgeois sat on the wooden benches of the lecture room alongside students whose families had made enormous sacrifices to send their boy to try to earn a degree. They might look alike in their short cassock and square cap, the uniform of the university, but their social lives were immensely different.

The son of a grandee arrived at the university with numerous servants and took up residence in a house specially bought or leased for the occasion. One Gaspar de Guzmán y Piamenatal, later conde-duque de Olivares and prime minister to Felipe IV, appeared in Salamanca in 1601 accompanied by eight pages, three valets, four footmen, a chef, grooms, servants, and a tutor. He rode to lectures on a great steed with his household trailing along to then wait for him at the doors of the university until he should reappear after lectures when they escorted him home.

Students generally lived outside the colleges, and university authorities exercised supervision over the houses and landlords in which they found lodging. At Salamanca, regulations set standards and charged the landlords to watch over the morals of the residents and their guests. Doors were closed every evening at half past seven and the residents accounted for every evening and morning. The landlord was urged to make certain the students attended the classes on their syllabus and organized sessions in which they could discuss the lessons of the day. Cards and dice games and amorous adventures were prohibited. Violations could result in the loss of the license issued to the house by the university.

The house master was obliged to provide a pound of meat a day for each student, along with snacks, dessert, and a reasonable quantity of bread and wine. On major feast days supplementary food was expected to be added to the fare. Not all universities had the same regulations, but in all cases the landlords, judging from the satirical comments from the quills of contemporary writers, had a reputation for economizing. It was said, for example, that it was interesting to watch the skinny fingers of the students probing the bottom of the soup bowl in search of an orphaned pea.[5]

The students were, nevertheless, assured of a roof over their heads and something to eat. This was in sharp contrast to the poor pupils for whom existence was an everyday problem. With little money from home, they found part-time jobs as servants for their more affluent colleagues who had their own houses or rented apartments, or found employment as waiters or in the kitchens of taverns.

For the most desperate, when all the books had been pawned—Aristotle with the grocer, Saint Thomas Aquinas with the wine seller—and still no money came from home, there was always recourse to a beggar's certificate (controlled by the state). Both Carlos I and Felipe II had decreed conditions under which poor students might seek some livelihood. They could plead for alms if they could obtain a license from the rector of the university or from the ecclesiastical court of their diocese. They would then have the right to eat at the soup kitchens opened each day by the monks in front of the gates of the monasteries. The only obligation was to wait impatiently for grace to be said. All-consuming student hunger is a recurrent theme in the literature of the times.

EXTRACURRICULAR ACTIVITIES

While the university frowned upon amorous associations involving the students, they nevertheless could not prevent them, and it became accepted practice to visit the parlors of the nunneries, more numerous than the colleges, and converse with the nuns who were often ready to console the student and commiserate with him. On occasion rivalry for the affections of a young sister ended in duels and even murder. Many students wore a coat of mail under their garments and carried a sword or dagger when they went out at night.

Sources of trouble also came from the rivalry between students from the various regions of the country, as they tended to stick together and support one another. Each group would back their own candidate in the election of a new master and showed little hesitancy in mocking those from another region. These encounters sometimes broke out into a brawl until the gentlemen of the watch appeared and put an end to it. Immunity from the rigors of civil law allowed considerable scope for student misbehavior.

A royal commission established in 1645 studied the problems and abuses of student immunity. It found an abundant number of names on the registers of the university of students over the age of twenty who appeared to have no intention of pursuing their studies. Their sole ambition, according to the commission, was to lead a disorderly and immoral life, tending thereby to corrupt the younger students. The recommendations of the commission insisted that all undergraduates attend all their lectures and learn to speak Latin. Those who failed to follow these instructions were to be handed over to the ordinary courts of law and prosecuted as vagabonds.

The livelihood of the university towns depended, of course, on the students. Booksellers, boardinghouses, printshops—most of the trade—would come to a swift halt if the collegiate population vanished. But with a certain immunity from the law for the denizens of academe, the citizens of the town had to tolerate shoplifting, housebreaking, purse-snatching, brawls, and the seduction of their daughters, among other nefarious acts. When something particularly villainous occurred, the townspeople sided with the police, and in spite of the university *fueros*, the culprits were hanged.

By the seventeenth century, in the firm grip of the Inquisition, professors had to swear that they believed in the Immaculate Conception in order to fill a post at the university. But about this time academic life began to wane, and the best universities started down the road to becoming backwaters of intellectual life. Hostility to the new ideas of the

Renaissance, the persistent entrenchment of Scholasticism, the challenge of the new Jesuit schools that attracted the more intellectually dexterous, and the establishment of the Imperial College of Madrid, despite the objection of the universities of Salamanca, Alcalá, and others, all contributed to bring to a close an illustrious period in university life.

FEMALE EDUCATION

The great majority of peasant girls of both country and town received not even a shred of the most rudimentary education, and only a very few learned to read and write. They acquired just what was necessary to perform domestic tasks.

Among aristocratic girls, the emphasis was less on physical labor and more on household management, needlework and social graces, and reading and writing. In the seventeenth century a few progressive thinkers took the position that women should not be restricted in what they might achieve through study and schooling, nor in what subjects they wished to pursue. But such views were propounded in order to make them better housewives. With some education they could teach their children, better contribute to the running of the house, and raise the cultural level of the family. However, these voices, with their albeit temperate views, were cries in the wilderness. Most men and certainly the powerful church rejected even this modest assessment of women's capabilities. Some prelates hinged their opposition to female education on the basis that women were naturally intellectually inferior to men. Women were simply not suited to a study of science or to complicated business negotiations but were capable only of conducting simple transactions performed in the marketplace or relating to domestic affairs.

The education of many young ladies was often neglected because their fathers considered that any kind of intellectual edification would lead to loose behavior. Some parents felt a well-educated daughter would never be able to find a husband. Given the general outlook of the times, this was undoubtedly close to the truth. It was considered sufficient that a woman's needs in the form of education could be obtained from sermons, religious books, and the domestic instruction conveyed by their mothers.

Since education of women was dismissed and deprecated, they often engaged in silly chatter or kept silent to conceal their ignorance. Any female who tried to break the mold, who had a desire to learn, came to be known as a bluestocking (a derogatory term). In order to avoid ridicule, they often had at least to pretend they were interested in the mindless prattle of other women about fashions and makeup. For most women of the middle or upper class, these were about the only subjects they could discuss.

A young girl from a noble or wealthy family learned to read and write from a private tutor, perhaps study a little French, recite a few lines of poetry, embroider, play an instrument such as the harp, sing and dance, and practice her poise and posture and other social graces. She might even master some household chores. But even among the upper classes there were fathers who thought any learning for a daughter was a bad thing.

What some of them did read to pass the hours while confined to their houses were novels of chivalry. This was the most popular genre, and whether of high birth or low, married or single, all seemed to enjoy the situation in which the male was prostrate at the feet of his ideal love, dedicated in body and soul to serve and protect her, to attend to her smallest desire, and ready to die if she rejected him. Such books could not help but dispel the sordid reality of daily life while the tender and enchanting love of the knight for his lady fair occasioned tears in the eyes of the reader.

Nevertheless, there were a few educated women who read Latin, knew the classics, studied philosophy and current literature, and gathered in their homes small cultural groups of other women. For their efforts they were often held in contempt.

María de Zayas y Sotomayor[6] was an early feminist who, in 1637, denounced the tyrannical injustice done to women by encouraging their innocence and ignorance. She asserted that if as children they were given the means to an education with teachers and books instead of lace work and patterns to embroider, women would be able to occupy chairs in a university quite as well as men. It was not brains but simply lack of opportunity that was the root of the matter. A veil was quickly drawn over such outbursts of feminine independence. A woman's role in society was to dedicate herself to the well-being of her husband, family, and church—no more, no less. It was much better for a man to have an uneducated wife than to have married a bluestocking.

Women who demanded a larger stake in education were finally given a glimmer of hope in 1785 when Carlos III decreed that a woman could be awarded the doctorate degree in humanities. María Isidora Quintina Guzmán, from an illustrious family, entered the university of Alcalá to become the first female in the history of Spain to be granted the honor. It would still be some time before girls of a less privileged class could aspire to academic ideals.

EDUCATION OF JEWS AND MUSLIMS

Jewish communities put the highest value on learning. "The world is based on three things: study, divine service and the practice of charity," states a line in a document drawn up by a council of Jewish delegates in the city of Valladolid in 1432.[7] Up to the time of expulsion, Jewish children were educated in the ghettos in which they lived by private tutors or by the rabbi. Education revolved around the Torah, consisting of the five books of Moses, which constituted the basis of Jewish religion and which governed all aspects of Jewish life, and the Talmud, a body of civil and religious law.

Older students would also study the Hebrew language, astronomy, mathematics, medicine and logic passed down through generations, and the outstanding works of the great eleventh-century Córdoba-born Jewish philosopher Maimonides. For poor families who could not afford a tutor for their children, a tax on the slaughtering of animals, on weddings, and on other events was levied in some communities to go to the cost of educating those in need.[8]

In secular studies, the Jewish student relied on private teachers and study of manuscripts that transmitted knowledge in Hebrew, Arabic, Greek, and Latin.

Hebrew, Aramaic, and Arabic were all taught at the University of Salamanca until 1492, after which time Conversos replaced the Jewish professors and took up teaching positions at Salamanca and other universities. The statutes of purity of blood promulgated years earlier were not strictly observed at many institutions of higher learning.[9] Some universities refused to condone it, and various popes were against the statutes. Conversos also studied in foreign universities in Italy and France if they encountered difficulties in Spain.

Muslim children of the families who could afford a tutor studied the Koran, the book containing the divine revelations given to Mohammed concerning the Islamic religious, social, civil, commercial, military, and legal codes. Punishments and rewards are vividly depicted and are exemplified by stories of the kind that also are found in the Jewish and Christian scriptures. Laws, directions, and admonitions to virtue also parallel those of the Jewish writings. Muslim children of poor families, the great majority, were uneducated and illiterate.

NOTES

1. Feros, 15–31.
2. Domínguez Ortiz, 231.
3. Kamen, *Spain 1449–1714*, 153.
4. Quoted in Defourneaux, 168.
5. Ibid., 172.
6. Gaite, 255.
7. Neuman, 2:64, for the first chapter of the document.
8. Ibid., 2:66.
9. Kamen, *The Spanish Inquisition*, 241.

17

Health and Medicine

During the war with the Muslims of Granada, Isabella founded the first military hospital in Europe, consisting of six large tents equipped with bandages, medicine, and beds, which were carried from one besieged town to another. In 1499 the Catholic Kings founded a general hospital in Santiago de Compostela dedicated to housing pilgrims and caring for the infirm and for foundlings. They also established the royal hospital of Granada, which was devoted to treating syphilis, a disease new to Spain in the late fifteenth century. Further, a royal building in Sevilla was converted into a retirement hospital for indigent or incapacitated soldiers who had served the crown.

Medieval hospitals were generally operated by charitable confraternities or guilds, composed of artisans and workers who shared a common class and interest. They were responsible for hospital procedures and upkeep and gave their members medical and spiritual assistance.

In the sixteenth century, the city of Toledo had 143 confraternities, some of which operated hospitals according to their preferences including contagious diseases, internal disorders, and wounds and broken limbs.

During the reign of Felipe II, further royal hospitals and almshouses were founded, in part to keep the church and the guilds from total domination of the medical facilities. The leper houses fell under crown jurisdiction for similar reasons. There was nevertheless some cooperation between church, confraternities, and crown in the field of public health.

In the late sixteenth century, following the dictates of the Council of

Trent for more effective use of charity, the government of Castilla initiated an inquiry into benefaction in general that resulted in some innovative undertakings.[1] A new general hospital for orphans, for pilgrims requiring recuperation, and for the sick was established in 1587 through the pooling of resources of various confraternities. Numerous small medical establishments merged into general hospitals in Madrid, Valladolid, and Sevilla. In the latter, seventy-five small hospitals were reduced to two large centers for the infirm.[2]

The crown provided for workers in its own service, for example, in government mines, who were cared for if they became ill or injured. Beds, medicine, a physician, and a barber-surgeon were provided, but a chronic shortage of staff and supplies always plagued the outlying and remote mining districts. A royal hospital was also created during the construction of the king's palace at El Escorial to attend to the laborers. A resident apothecary prepared the medicines, and a building was provided for the sick and injured; but sermons and prayers took up an equal or greater amount of time in curing the ill. Attention to the soul was considered to be more important than caring for the body.

THE *INCLUSA*[3] AND OTHER HOSPITALS

Charitable hospitals with provisions for foundlings were established in Toledo in 1504, in Valencia in 1537, and in Valladolid three years later. Sevilla followed in 1558 to help the plight of newborn, abandoned children found with alarming frequency in the streets, in the public squares, and at the doors of churches. They often died of exposure or were killed by scavenging dogs. A hospital in Madrid was started by a group of laymen and Franciscan friars, and it began taking in abandoned children in 1572. Its name, *Inclusa*, spread to other such institutions dealing with these children.

The *Inclusa* served as a shelter where the unwanted infant could be brought, baptized, and sent out into the care of a wet nurse. Mortality rates were high, but the soul of the child was thus looked after. The hospital was financed in the traditional way through an alms box as well as by the church that supplied administrators, by the nobility, by the royal family who donated money or goods, and by contributions of well-off merchants and artisans. The staff ranged from people of means to impoverished workers.

In 1615 the *Inclusa* was incorporated as a royal hospital and became entitled to tax money set aside for hospital support. Some volunteers were then aided by paid staff under the jurisdiction of the Council of Castilla. The hospitals functioned to protect the honor of families from the shame that they might incur from the birth of an illegitimate child and presented an alternative to abandoning the newborn on the street or in a ditch or field.

The honor of a family, both high or low on the social scale, was dependent on the sexual behavior of the females. If a child was born out of wedlock, it had no place in society and was deposited with the foundling hospital in order to protect the good name of the mother's family. While it was assumed that most of the children would die either in the hospital or in the care of the wet nurse, it was a consoling thought that at least they would have been baptized.[4]

The women who found jobs as a wet nurse were often from the poorest of the poor, and the pay was dismal. The foundling hospitals never had enough money to pay decent salaries for this essential job. To survive, strategies had to be worked out. A woman might have the midwife drop off her own baby at the *Inclusa*, then go and become a wet nurse for it, drawing the small pay while bringing up her own child. Some drew salaries long after the baby had died. Others, unable to nurse a baby, still took it and tried to feed it by other means such as the usually fatal goat's milk and gruel.

As the economic crisis of the seventeenth century deepened and carried over into the eighteenth, more and more of the abandoned children of the *Inclusa* were not illegitimate but left by their hungry and destitute parents. Women abandoned their infants because they could not afford to feed them or because, in their own wretched malnourished condition, they could not nurse them. Notes sometimes attached to the ragged cloth around the child would state that the parents were honorable people and would one day return for the infant.

In hard economic times, such as when crops failed, the number of children admitted to the *Inclusa* rose by leaps and bounds. In better days the number dwindled down. It was a fact of life that in many areas of the country such as Castilla, farmworkers often could not support a family from the land. They needed a working wife, a good harvest and grain prices, and reasonable pay. When one of these components was lacking, there was little else to do but go off to the larger cities in search of work.

Among babies that were abandoned, the death rate must have been near 100 percent. Among those taken to the *Inclusa* it was nearly as bad (about 75 percent over the seventeenth century). These forlorn foundlings sometimes died from prolonged trips to the hospital in a basket on the shoulder of a porter with no training or interest in his job, sent out by the bishop to collect them.[5] They died by the hundreds in the hospital from influenza, disease, and infections, or neglect, and when taken away, from the poor quality of the milk or the incompetence or indifference of the wet nurse. Emotional distress was no doubt a cause for many problems the infant suffered. Never cuddled, never played with or talked to, it was just handed about from one woman to another or left alone in its seldom-changed rags. Children raised at home had about a fifty-fifty chance of survival to age seven. The death of a baby was not such a serious matter as it would be today, as it was commonly believed that the child was not fully human until it showed clear signs of love, anger, sadness, and happiness. The tiny infant was a creature in which the humors had not yet solidified.

The mortality rate was so high that the *Inclusas*, of which there were now eight in the country, were thought by some to be simply legalized institutions for infanticide so that influential and more fortunate people were spared the public inconvenience of more child beggars.[6]

Not only were the impoverished often unhealthy due to a poor diet, but the surroundings were equally so. An infant sent to the country with a healthy wet nurse or who was adopted had a better chance to survive than one in the city where sewers were nonexistent before 1760 and the houses in the poor neighborhoods were cold and unsanitary.

In some of the worst-affected sections of the city only about 6 percent of the children taken there by wet nurses lived to the age of seven, an age when they would be returned to the hospital for distribution to other places such as orphanages run by nuns or monks and supported by charity or to private homes. Neither poverty nor death discriminated between the sexes. Girls and boys perished in about equal numbers.

As traumatic as it was for these babies, some survived. About one in ten overall returned to the hospital at age seven during the course of the eighteenth century, for which there are records, and a little over 10 percent of these were reclaimed by their natural parents, while about 4 percent were adopted.

The mattress maker supplied fresh straw every year to the hospitals. In the *Inclusa* nursery of Madrid in 1710 were two large mattresses where fourteen to twenty infants were tossed together. Thirty years later there were twice as many infants on the same mattress. Sanitation was primitive at best: Lavender was scattered around the floor every month or so to combat the nauseous odors emanating from sick and dirty children. Ventilation and vinegar were the other countermeasures to the problem.

The kitchen of the *Inclusa* resembled that of a regular home. An assortment of coal tongs, pitchers, wooden spoons, and brass or copper pots hung on the walls along with an iron pan, an oil jar, and other oddments of crockery. It may be conjectured that everyone ate from the same pot. Other items found in the kitchen that were not used to hold water or hang over the fire were made from the strong fibrous esparto grass, which was inexpensive, brought into town from the countryside on the backs of mules and used to make mats, baskets, fans, dusters, bolsters, brooms, dustpans, and dishes. Straw mats covered the tile floors in winter to ward off the chill. One of the benefits of working in the kitchen in winter was the hearth, an open fireplace on a raised brick or stone base, and fire. To keep warm the cook might sleep there, where a large chimney siphoned off the smoke, and water was kept permanently hot in a huge black kettle suspended over the fire by a chain.

Heating facilities in other rooms of the building were meager and dangerous. Heat was supplied by a charcoal-burning brazier, which was usually a brass bowl fitted into a wooden frame. The charcoal itself could be hazardous, and to rid the fuel of soot and dangerous gases, it was often ignited in the open air before being transferred indoors. The fumes, nevertheless, were detrimental to children sleeping closeby. Coal, an expensive item, was delivered to the *Inclusa* and the hospitals once a year by the wagon load.

One of the most famous hospitals of the time was that founded by Juan de Díos in Granada. At first it was situated in a rented house in the poorest district and admitted anyone who asked, no matter what the ailment. **One Case of Hospital Development** The hospital sheltered pilgrims, travelers, beggars, the old, the insane, lepers, syphilitics, the blind or crippled, and prostitutes as well as undesirable vagabonds sent by the city when it wished to clean up the streets. In 1540, the hospital was moved to a vacant nunnery, a building large enough to house the sometimes 200 or so patients.

Juan de Díos felt his duty was to shelter and look after everyone who asked for his aid. Others disagreed and argued that more discriminate measures were necessary in order to help the people who needed it most and not those who took advantage of charity to avoid work. Juan de Díos died in 1550, and his hospital, deeply in debt, was taken over by Archbishop Guerrero, who paid off the creditors and, along with the remaining five followers of Juan de Díos, constructed a new hospital and a Hieronymite monastery on land donated by the city council. These were then placed under the supervision of the Hieronymite superior. A short time later, they established hospitals in Madrid, Montilla, Sevilla, and Jerez de la Frontera, among other places, after which Felipe II gave them an old royal building in Córdoba to convert for their own needs.

The movement attracted some aristocratic patrons who objected to the subservience of the followers to the Hieronymite superior in Granada and sought to make the hospitals more independent. They eventually fell under the jurisdiction of the Hospitalers, who continued their expansion in the seventeenth century, founding more hospitals. Much of the money to support them came from begging for alms by the brothers. They were not adverse to hard work and administered their humble talents to the poor for no remuneration while they cultivated the hospitals' lands for sustenance.

The government's involvement in public health was also increased in 1528 when Carlos I decreed that leper **Leper Houses** houses, usually located outside the walls of the larger towns of Castilla, were to be visited by officials appointed by the Royal Council and their accounts audited twice a year by the local *corregidor*. The *protomédico*, besides acting as an overseer of public health and licensing, was also charged with the responsibility of ensuring that all victims of leprosy were confined to a leper house. It was thought among some physicians that castration was a cure for this most dreaded of diseases. Results must have been very disappointing!

HEALTH HAZARDS

If the hospitals themselves were a danger to public health through the spread of contagious diseases, the existence of cemeteries in crowded, built-up areas was equally a threat.

The middle classes were generally entombed in the local parish church, the poor in the churchyard cemetery. There was restricted room in the cemeteries and a limited time for the dead to remain there. The bodies were placed in shallow graves with a light coating of earth, pending the transfer of the bones elsewhere after the body had decomposed. Regularly the ground would be raked over and the bones removed, usually at night to hide the unpleasant sight. Dogs in search of food were known to disinter the bodies, and heavy rains or melting snow sometimes washed away the soil, carrying off decomposed flesh in rivulets down the streets.

In 1787, reacting to the concerns of public health officials, Carlos III forbade burials in cities except, of course, for the wealthy, who owned private chapels or mausoleums. A large cemetery was constructed outside the walls of Madrid in 1809, but it was little used until mid-century.

As concentrations of people posed problems of hygiene, clean water for drinking and bathing could not be taken for granted at a time when so little was understood about pollution and disease. Rivers and streams were generally safer than water from wells, which were often contaminated by sewage and the runoff from cemeteries. Aqueducts, some built by the Romans such as the one at Segovia, and others by the Muslims, carried water long distances from clean, fresh sources.

A few cities such as Valencia had inherited a sewer system from the Roman era, and from time to time this was flushed out with river water by the municipal authorities. In most places, however, waste sewage was a health problem. In the cities of the plateau, for example, Madrid and Valladolid, where such systems did not exist and urinals and household waste were emptied into the streets, creating a breeding ground for disease, conditions were far from sanitary. Not until the eighteenth century were sewers laid out in Madrid.

LICENSING

Licenses to practice medicine by qualified physicians, and barber-surgeons, and to members of the professions and trades involved in public health such as apothecaries, herbalists, and spice vendors, had been granted to the towns of Castilla and Aragón by their monarchs in the fourteenth century. Local justices issued the permits. Isabella and Fernando had tried to recover this jurisdiction and place it in the hands of the throne by sending out royal officials to oversee the matter, but the towns resisted this intrusion into their privileges, one of their major complaints being the selling of licenses and the taking of bribes by royal officials.

Carlos I issued a decree in 1523 confining the activities and authority of the royal officials, now called *protomédicos*, to a radius of five leagues from the court, leaving the licensing and inspection of local practitioners to municipalities. The measure was confirmed by Felipe II in 1567. A major drawback to this scheme was that practitioners who had been refused permission to practice in the towns traveled to the court to seek the necessary papers from the *protomédico*. If these were granted, it allowed them to set up shop anywhere in Spain. Needless to say, many conflicts ensued between town and crown.

MEDICAL PRACTICES

There was no royal council of public health equivalent to the councils of state, finance, or the Indies to oversee medical affairs, and the number of royal hospitals was small compared to those of religious organizations, confraternities, or even establishments financed and run by individuals. The vast majority of the king's subjects received no medical assistance from the crown, but in some towns the municipality administered public health through the town council, which set aside land for a building, fixed the fees, contracted a doctor, organized the medical provisions, and arranged for free treatment of the poor. Country people were attended by the local clergyman or itinerant healers whose knowledge and abilities were often of a doubtful nature.

There were many fraudulent medical practitioners and concomitant poor care. While the doctor might make a good living with high fees and few overheads, the sham doctor was always just around the corner, and many of the poor were forced to seek his services, which involved a good dose of superstitious ritual. Failed medical students with only a smattering of knowledge frequently passed themselves off as doctors, and others who could prove their qualifications sometimes had only mediocre training, having bought their degrees with gold. Still others had obtained their credentials not by learning facts and participation in clin-

Bleeding the patient.

ical procedures but by means of a talent for elegant Latin rhetoric during their examinations. In 1563, the Cortes, meeting in Madrid to assess the situation, set some standards. Thereafter, the student was required to graduate in arts from an accredited university, then do another four years of study in medicine, to be followed by two years' training with an experienced physician.

The poor depended on the local barber-surgeons for certain medical treatment, however. These craftsmen were more common and widespread than physicians and less expensive. They treated trauma, set broken bones, cauterized bleeding wounds with the use of a red-hot iron, stitched up torn flesh, and bled ill patients. They also cut hair and shaved beards. Many moved around from village to village, tramping the country roads with their bag of instruments ready to bleed a sick cow, mule, or pig if no human patients required their services.

Physicians usually had a deep contempt for apothecaries and chemists and for barber-surgeons (who, they considered, were well beneath them in skill and class since they were once only barbers, pure and simple). These occupations involved manual labor, which was far beneath the dignity of the university-trained doctor. Bleeding and purging were the two most important measures used to cure almost everything, and repeated bleedings were even better, although they often cured the disease by killing the patient. The physician, of course, did not dirty his hands by bleeding the patient himself but left the job to the barber-surgeon.

The cities clamored for better training of the barber-surgeons, as too many people seemed to die under their care. City councils wanted a chair of surgery in the universities, although this was opposed by professors of medicine who, jealous of their own prestige, maintained that the surgeon did not require university training but only four years' preparation working in a city hospital.[7]

In 1593 Felipe II, belatedly responding to calls of the Cortes for chairs of surgery in the universities, wrote to the institutions of Salamanca, Alcalá, and Valladolid, encouraging them to establish courses in this field of medicine.[8] The occupants of the chairs would be given the title of Surgeon Royal, and students who completed the courses would be honored with the degree of *licenciado*. The following year two chairs were filled, and students began their studies. Ten years later, however, the requirements for surgeons were dropped on the grounds that the plague had killed too many of them and the shortage called for less stringent regulations. Unqualified healers filled the gaps, treating kidney stones, ringworm, cataracts, hernias, dislocated joints, and a host of minor ailments. Towns welcomed them, but the medical establishment remained hostile toward them.

Diagnosis, prognosis, and prescription constituted the domain of the surgeon's academically trained superior—the physician. Physicians did not often examine the patient bodily but took note of the symptoms as described by the person, sometimes examining the regurgitated food or urine to determine the remedy. Public confidence in the medical profession was not high in spite of the notion among doctors that they had reached the highest possible standards. Plays, cartoons, and satires of the times depict them as arrogant, greedy, money-grubbing villains whose only interest in the patient was focused on his purse.

A Cortes of 1548 asked the king to order doctors and surgeons who had visited a patient twice not to return a third time unless the patient had undergone confession and could produce a certificate from the village priest to prove it. Too many people were dying unconfessed at the hands of medical practitioners, usually having been bled to death.

The knowledge of theory and practice was still based on Hippocrates, the ancient father of Western medicine, and the Greek physician Galen (who died about A.D. 200). The self-satisfied medical faculties of the universities only aroused themselves to condemn some innovation in thinking by a bright young student that occurred from time to time. Anyone that was alleged to have discovered something new could expect to reap only scorn from complacent professors. Nevertheless, by bribing the hangman, some enterprising students were able to obtain corpses for

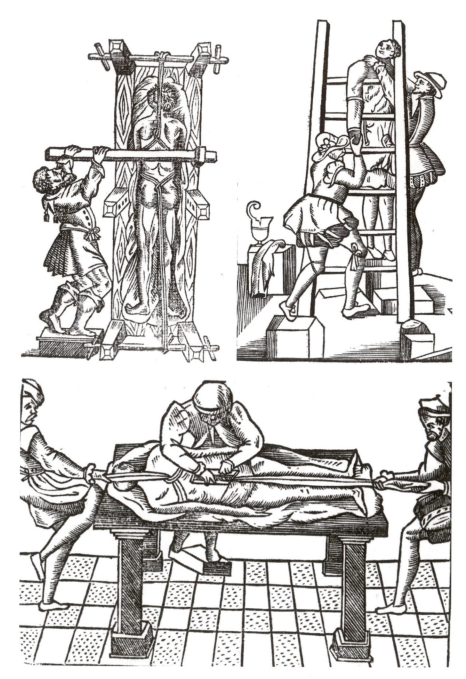

Luiz Mercado. *Instituciones que Su Magestad mando hazer al Doctor Mercado para el aprovechamiento y examen de los algebristas. Madrid, 1599.* (London: The Wellcome Library). Three woodcuts of officially prescribed techniques for treating dislocations. The first shows rigid support and applied compression treating the spinal vertebrae. The second is setting a dislocated shoulder, and the third treating the dislocation of the vertebrae with manual pulling, the patient extended face down on a firm table.

anatomical research and to gain more understanding of bodily functions and disease. Sixteenth-century medicine could have marked the beginning of a new epoch in medical science with the discovery of the pulmonary circulation of blood by the Catalan theologian and physician Miguel Servet working in France. His opposition to the doctrine of the Trinity and infant baptism resulted in his arrest by the papal Inquisition in Lyon, France, from which he escaped only to fall into the clutches of Calvin in Geneva, where he was burned at the stake as a heretic in 1553. Not until the English physician and anatomist William Harvey, who formally presented his findings in 1626 in which he rediscovered the circulation of the blood and the role of the heart in propelling it, were the theories of Galen laid to rest. This was a concept that eventually could not be denied by even the most conservative of the medical establishment.

Medical practitioners also needed a knowledge of astrology and often inquired into the patient's horoscope before prescribing. For example, treatment should not be taken when the moon was in the sign of Saturn, as the humors would congeal; it was considered best to bleed the subject during the periods of the quarter moon since the humors would then have retired to the center of the body; most illnesses began at the time of the new moon when the heat of the sun overpowered the watery moon and left body functions feeble and susceptible; progress toward healing was best made between the new and full moon.

HUMORS

The theory of the four humors, dating back to the ancient Greeks of the fifth century B.C., was still much in vogue in Early Modern Spain. The thesis was that human beings and the food they ate contained the same elements that constituted the universe—that is, air, fire, water, and earth. In human physiology these corresponded to certain humors, which in turn formed the basis of human health and temperament.

Ingredient (element)	Humor	Temperament
air	blood	sanguine—hot, dry
fire	yellow bile	choleric—hot, dry
water	phlegm	phlegmatic—cool, moist
earth	black bile	melancholic—cool, dry

Some people contained an excess of one or the other ingredient that led to ill health, but good physical condition could be achieved by finding the proper balance. All disease fell under the four headings of hot, cool, moist, and dry. For example, a choleric or hot-tempered person would be advised to refrain from hot foods and partake of cool food. With the opposite being the best method to follow, diets could be prescribed accordingly: Fevers originated from hot and dry causes, indicating excessive choler or yellow bile, and thus were treated with cooling medicines such as coriander or fresh roses. Diseases from cold causes, leading to lethargy and fatigue, could be treated with warming medicines including radish, garlic, saltpeter, and myrrh.

HERBAL REMEDIES

Herbal medicines for all kinds of illnesses were administered by nearly everyone with any knowledge of plants. From the lowest healer to the most prominent physician, herbs and spices such as cloves, china-root (for gout), sandalwood, ginger, pepper, and cinnamon, some grown at home, some imported, were used as the basic ingredients. The royal pharmacies were supplied with herbal remedies prepared by apothecaries from plants nurtured in the royal gardens. Felipe II was interested in such plants and their cultivation, sending experts throughout Spain to seek them out. In 1570 he even commissioned his chief physician, Francisco Hernández, to travel to the West Indies and Peru in search of new varieties of beneficial herbs, as the New World was acquiring a reputation for exotic plants with great curative properties. Three years later Hernández reported to the king that he had completed four volumes illustrating and describing over 1,000 new types of vegetation with enormous benefit for medicine.[9]

PLAGUE AND OTHER MALADIES

The common, often fatal diseases of the period were tuberculosis (which was responsible for many deaths), influenza, dropsy or edema, dysentery, smallpox, diphtheria, syphilis, and typhus, which first appeared in Spain late in the sixteenth century. The latter was characterized by delirious fever and small purplish eruptions of the skin with symptoms much like the plague. Epidemics, especially of the bubonic plague, brought entire cities to a standstill as people panicked and left town for the hills or locked themselves away indoors. The heavy loss of life from this feared disease left towns and countryside decimated. In Valencia, for example, 300 people died daily between March and July during the outbreak of 1508. There were many other epidemics there and elsewhere in the country throughout the period. The plague of 1597 to 1602 affected the entire peninsula, causing half a million deaths.

One of the last of the fearful Valencian plagues, which spread along the coast into Andalucía between 1647 and 1652, left a third of the population dead and eventually killed some 50,000 in Sevilla at a rate of about 500 per day. For a time there was uncertainty as to whether the disease was the plague or typhus. It was unknown at the time that both were carried by fleas.

A blockade of the infected regions was often the response to an outbreak of the plague. In May 1649, a government decree prohibited entry to Madrid of all people and merchandise coming from Sevilla and other towns in Andalucía on pain of death. Guards were placed in the passes of the Sierra Morena mountains to seal off Castilla from the south.

A PERSONAL ACCOUNT OF THE PLAGUE

A tanner from Barcelona, Miguel Parets, recounted in his diary the events he witnessed during the great plague that struck the city in January 1651.[10] It was attributed to the anger of the Lord brought on by the sins of the people. The author of the diary suffered from the loss of his wife, a son of thirteen, another of eleven, and a one-year-old girl, all of whom died within a month.

As the plague spread northward from Valencia to Tortosa, the city of Barcelona banned all trade with the latter in the hopes of preventing it from reaching its own population. Barcelona was already under siege, being at war with Castilla when the plague arrived; it was also going through a severe famine due to lack of rain.

It was learned on 8 January 1651 that plague was in the city when in the house of a blind man named Martín de Langa his wife and a young girl relative died suddenly with the telltale sores—boils that looked like red beans with a black tip. The city councilors acted swiftly, isolating the house, cleaning and fumigating it, and sending other members of the household to isolation in the convent of Angels Vells, a large building next to the refuse ditch outside Saint Daniel's Gate.

According to the chronicler, plague had already existed in several other houses but had been hushed up to prevent panic. As it had broken out in poor neighborhoods, the deaths were attributed to unhealthy carrot and cabbage diets of the inflicted brought on by the famine and lack of bread, and not at first to plague.

As the truth became known, people began to flee the city. Guards were posted at the gates, of which only four remained open, and on the walls to prevent people from coming and going, spreading the disease.

As the city descended into chaos, crime became rampant, and those who remained were fearful of leaving their houses at night. Patrols of armed guards tried to maintain order in the dark streets, and culprits caught robbing the deserted houses or mugging citizens were hanged. One of the cases reported by Parets involved a murder on Hatters Street in the house of a hatmaker named Poll, located in front of Saint Mary's Church on the corner of Mirrormakers Street. The villain had been paid to murder Poll by another hatter named Tiana, who had quarreled with Poll, then plotted his death in the chaos of the city, and had now fled. The assassin, a gardener from a poor quarter, was caught, tried, and condemned in short order. His hand was chopped off in front of Poll's house; then he was whipped along Moneychangers Street to the gallows and hanged. Other crimes of theft from stricken houses or robbery in the streets were treated with severe whippings and sometimes the death penalty to set an example to others.

The plague grew steadily worse, and more and more people were sent to Angels Vells, where plague doctors and surgeons tried to treat them (mostly by bloodletting) and monks administered the last rites. In the city there was no end of prayers in the churches and processions as crowds of barefoot penitents, nuns, priests, and monks marched through the streets, carrying crosses and candles and uttering devotions. Later the city councilors tried to prevent mass gatherings of people in order to inhibit further contagion, as it was thought the disease was passed from person to person through the air. Many people watched the progress of the moon for signs that the plague would abate, but when the full moon came and went and cases increased, the sick were moved from the small, overcrowded Angels Vells to a new plague house, the Franciscan monastery of Jesus, from which the monks had fled. The city provided beds of straw and those doctors willing to attend the victims. In April and May of 1651 the number of sick and dead steadily rose and were carried in heaps to the plague house of Jesus. In crowded and unsanitary conditions, about 4,000 people came to be lodged in the monastery.

Many priests had fled or refused to administer the sacraments, so monks often performed the job. When confessing the sick, they carried a torch held between themselves and the victim and kept their distance to avoid the pestilential breath. To flee the city was difficult since villages throughout Cataluña posted guards along the roads and at the entrances to keep people away. Those refugees seeking asylum from the plague in distant places had to sleep in the open en route. When they reached their destinations, their clothes were burned and they had to undergo forty days of quarantine in huts watched over by guards.

To safeguard Barcelona from further contagion, wide and long ditches were dug in the middle of the highways. Those people from outside the city bringing food and other supplies to sell stayed on their side of the ditch, whereas the city dwellers remained on the opposite side. Three long planks spanned the ditch, and a pole attached to a metal axle held up the middle plank and allowed it to turn around like a toy wheel. The farmer placed his chickens, eggs, fruit, or vegetables on the end of the plank and spun it around to the other side of the ditch. If the purchaser on the city side liked what he saw, they agreed on a price. The goods were then removed, and the money placed on the plank was spun around, back to the farmer, who placed the coins in a pot of vinegar brought for the purpose. When they were cleansed, he counted them. Soldiers guarded these exchange stations to make sure no one crossed the ditches. To cross required a pass from the city councilors. To violate these rules meant a penalty of death.

A terrifying sight was of the carts piled high with the dead, moving through the deserted streets of the city, one after the other, as the plague continued into July of 1651. Some of the corpses were dressed, others naked, and some wrapped in sheets, to be taken beyond the city walls and buried in mass graves. Huts had to be constructed in the gardens of the monastery of Jesus, which overflowed with the sick. If the plague didn't kill them, neglect and hunger often did, as food was extremely scarce.

Empty houses whose occupants had died were nailed shut to prevent people from entering, especially thieves who might then contract the disease and carry it elsewhere. Houses of the sick were marked with a white cross to warn people of the danger inside. Some occupants died in their houses for want of someone to come and attend to them. Those that were willing to nurse them charged high prices and in some cases helped them to a speedy demise in order to go off and sign a high-paying contract with another patient or, if alone in the house, to strip it of its valuables and leave. When their mothers perished, nursing babies died in droves due to lack of milk as few wet nurses for any amount of money were willing to take an infant whose mother had died of the plague. Many older children wandered bewildered throughout the streets of the city, having lost their parents to the disease.

Parets escaped the city and, with his surviving four-year-old son, went to live with a brother-in-law, Benet Mans, a peasant in the town of Sarria to the north. They lived in a hut near Mans's house, where they remained twenty-seven days before moving into the house. As was usual in such cases, the brother-in-law brought them food and left it nearby; Parets went out to fetch it while avoiding all close contact with Mans or anyone else.

The plague began to lessen in intensity in July 1651. There were few people left in the city, as some 30,000 had died according to the chronicler, and the intensive fumigation of dwellings and streets started to take effect. People began to return. At night they threw everything out of the windows and doors of the houses into the streets—mattresses, blankets, pillows, sheets, and pallets and anything else that had belonged to those who died. The city sent out carts to collect these items and took them out beyond the walls to be burned.

But the city now faced a new threat—war. Barcelona had rebelled against the crown of Castilla in 1640, protesting high taxes, among other things, and placed itself under the king of France. Now a Castillian army was at the gates to bring it back into the fold. The city surrendered before long, while the plague lingered on among some of the foreign troops who had come from plague-infested areas and had plundered houses in which the disease had been rampant. Again, by November, it began to grow in intensity. A petition to the king of Castilla was sufficient to have the troops removed from Barcelona, and the contagion again subsided and eventually disappeared.

REMEDIES FOR THE PLAGUE

Over time doctors began to learn that bleeding was a useless remedy against the plague. They were also starting to understand that a clean environment was beneficial. As a result, the sick were transferred to isolation hospitals outside the city, and the dead were collected by slaves and buried in lime pits well away from the town walls. In some cases, prompted no doubt by fear, the corpses were dragged from the houses at night by the occupants and left in the streets or on church steps, along with their belongings, without waiting for the municipal cart to collect them. The idea then prevalent that the airborne plague was spread through putrefaction led to some good results. For the first time, city officials sent carts around to collect refuse, and householders were instructed to keep the areas in front of their dwellings clean. Hospital floors were continuously scrubbed, and in some cities such as Sevilla rosemary and thyme, or juniper in Segovia, were burned in bonfires to help purify the air. These actions and the liberal use of vinegar spread around the streets were, of course, unhealthy for the infected carrier-flea and the rats that were host to it but more beneficial for the populace.

Along with wholesome food, another remedy for the dreaded disease was a positive attitude. Church bells were kept silent in Sevilla so as not to spread gloom and doom around the city; instead, the sick and dying heard musicians in the streets as mandated by the city magistrates in order to keep up good spirits and forestall the detrimental condition of melancholy.

While some people attributed typhus and plague to witchcraft and others, even doctors, to astrological phenomena (or more precisely to a malign conjunction of the planets impacting on bodily humors), the church invariably saw all ills as punishment for sin and in some cities organized processions with holy statues, relics of saints, crosses, and wailing flagellants dragging heavy chains through the streets. Prayers to ask for God's mercy were intoned in all the churches, and the faithful solicited their favorite saints for divine deliverance.

Some doctors had great faith in the curative powers of precious stones, which were thought to be useful against poison in the system. Ground-up pearls, rubies, and emeralds were particularly good; nine grams of the latter were considered sufficient to resist all poisons.

Cities and towns maintained their pharmacies well stocked with medicines against the plagues such as bezoar (concretions of mineral salts formed in gastrointestinal organs of human and animals believed by many to possess magical properties and to be a powerful antidote against poisons) and mithridate, an antidote extracted from the dogtooth violet. Another, theriaca, a pulverized concoction of some seventy drugs mixed with honey into a kind of medicinal paste or treacle (a recipe known to the ancient Greeks), was a further potion thought to counteract the poison inherent in the disease.

THE INQUISITION, CONVERSOS, AND MORISCOS

In medieval Spain, doctors were in short supply, and Jewish physicians often took up the slack. There were few aristocratic households in Castilla and Aragón, including the royal family, who did not have a Jewish physician. They could also be found applying their skills in all the larger towns. Muslim doctors were not uncommon in the south and southeast, where they tended to the needs of their own people and even to Christian communities when called upon. After the establishment of the Inquisition, the expulsion of the nonconverted Jews, and the suspicion surrounding New Christians of both Jewish and Muslim origin, medicine entered a dark phase.

Conversos and Moriscos were now barred from practicing medicine, including surgery and pharmacy, in many of the towns. The church was the vanguard of the persecutors. The bishop of Plasencia, Andrés de Noronha, urged Felipe II to enact the strongest measures possible to prevent New Christians from becoming physicians or surgeons, asserting that he had uncovered a conspiracy among Conversos for the destruction of Christians through medical treatment. The information was supposedly contained in some letters that he alleged were given to him by the inquisitional tribunal of Llerena.

It was ironic that when the best physician or surgeon was solicited for special requirements such as a position in the royal household that Converso origins were overlooked. Even the Inquisition employed Converso physicians when it needed specialists. A case in point underscores the hypocrisy. When the inquisitional tribunal of Logroño wanted to consult a physician but could find no one who met the qualifications of *limpieza de sangre*, it asked for permission from the *Suprema* in Madrid to enlist the services of Doctor Béles, a Converso. The response was that he could be consulted if it was done without recognition of his title.

On several occasions Felipe II employed Morisco healers to treat ailing members of the royal family when the court physicians had failed to achieve cures. Morisco practitioners, however, were often persecuted even before their expulsion from the country in 1609. In that year the Cortes of Castilla expressed the fear that allowing Moriscos to practice medicine would put them in a position to kill more Spaniards than the Turks and the English.

An accusation of heresy or apostasy was always a danger to Converso doctors, and a number of Jewish physicians appear in the records of the Inquisition. Arrested by the Holy Office were a number of Morisco practitioners for engaging in magical medicine and soliciting the aid of demons. Magical cures for most illnesses were part of Muslim folklore, and amulets were often worn by the populace to ward off evil spirits. Itinerant Morisco healers and herbalists conjured up demons and mixed herbs for specific cures, and the fakirs, or religious leaders, treated disease by writing Arabic letters on parts of the sufferer's body or inscribed passages from the Koran on paper to be swallowed by the patient. To the Moriscos in Cuenca is attributed the practice of discerning the potential fatal consequences of an illness by the patterns in a spoonful of molten lead poured into a pot of cold water placed on the head of the sick person.

Old Christian fears that the Morisco practitioners were out to kill them, aggravated by the story that one of them caused the death of twenty clergymen at Huerto in Aragón through the ministration of his medicines, maintained tension between the two cultures. Some of the Moriscos accused by the Inquisition did not survive the torture chamber and the confinement in the cold cells.

DENTISTS

Oral hygiene was sorely neglected, as people were not in the habit of cleaning their teeth with any thoroughness. A woolen cloth or a finger wiped over them after eating, or a toothpick to extract debris from between them, generally sufficed. Tooth decay was rampant and often ignored until pain forced the victim to seek the help of a tooth-puller or the surgeon-dentist. The use of a file to remove decayed portions of a tooth was not unknown, and a visit to the surgeon-dentist was an experience not to be taken lightly. There were plenty of charlatans in this profession, too, and again, the poor were at their mercy. Hordes of quacks ranged the countryside, looking for victims, which were not hard to find. Bleeding was once more the primary remedy for toothache, while essence of cloves or spirit of nicotine might temporarily lessen the pain. Cotton soaked in oil of sage or poppy was also recommended for toothache. An actual extraction on a bench in the village square, often with dirty tools, by an itinerant dentist and clumsy assistant with a crowd looking on, was an adventure undergone only in dire circumstances. No doubt, a flask of strong brandy within close reach was desirable. A false tooth or two carved from animal bone might be wired into a gap in the teeth, but few would have bothered to have this done. Complete dentures (the first known set discovered in Switzerland date from the sixteenth century) were probably not in use in Spain.

NOTES

1. Casey, 126.
2. Ibid., 126; Goodman, *Power and Penury*, 210.
3. For detailed information on the *Inclusa*, see Sherwood, *Poverty in Eighteenth Century Spain*.
4. Ibid., 4.
5. Ibid., 129.
6. For social conditions leading to infanticide and public opinion concerning it, see ibid., chapter 8.
7. Goodman, *Power and Penury*, 217.
8. Ibid., 217.
9. Ibid., 233ff.
10. The account of the plague in Barcelona has been taken from Parets.

Appendix A: Rulers of Spain During the Inquisition

HOUSE OF TRASTÁMARA AND ARAGÓN

1474–1504 Isabella of Castilla (Trastámara) and Fernando of Aragón

HOUSE OF HABSBURG

1504–1506 Felipe I (Habsburg) and Joana, daughter of Fernando and Isabella, rule Castilla

1506–1516 Fernando rules Aragón and Castilla (as regent) after death of Felipe I

1516–1556 Carlos I, son of Felipe I and Juana, rules Castilla and Aragón

1519–1558 Carlos I becomes Holy Roman Emperor (Carlos V)

1556–1598 Felipe II

1598–1621 Felipe III

1621–1665 Felipe IV

1665–1700 Carlos II

HOUSE OF BOURBON

1700–1746 Felipe V (grandson of Louis XIV of France and Maria Teresa, daughter of Felipe IV) abdicated in 1724 in favor of his son Louis I but resumed throne in same year

1746–1759 Fernando VI

1759–1788   Carlos III, brother of Fernando VI
1788–1808   Carlos IV abdicated in favor of Fernando VII
1808   Fernando VII deposed

HOUSE OF BONAPARTE

1808–1813   Joseph Bonaparte, brother of Napoleon I, deposed

HOUSE OF BOURBON REINSTITUTED

1814–1833   Fernando VII restored
1833–1868   Isabella II

Appendix B: Sources of Information

Official records preserved in Spanish municipal and state archives are a fruitful source of political, religious, economic, and military conditions of earlier times. The Archives of the Indies in Sevilla, for example, kept detailed documentation on maritime trade and the activities of sailors. Ambassadorial and legates' reports in the archives of Spain and other countries are also important sources. Thousands of surviving files from the tribunals of the Inquisition relating to the people put on trial help illuminate this aspect of the period. An upsurge in interest in the Inquisition began in the 1970s and 1980s with numerous symposia, conferences, and publications. These studies have revised the general knowledge of the Inquisition and its impact on the country. Extremely informative concerning the cultural characteristics of the country are the sketches and scenes found in the literature of the period, for plays, poems, and novels often depict an accurate reflection of society. Innumerable plays such as those by Lope de Vega, Calderón, Tirso de Molina, and the works of Cervantes (for instance, *Don Quijote*) mimic and often mock the conventions of the times. Similarly, the works of satirists and their cartoons in surviving papers and pamphlets express aspects of life during the period.

The *costumbristas* (painters of fashion) give a glimpse of the clothes, whereas wills and inventories that have been preserved in large quantities present an idea of family life. Travel guides, of which there were a number, reported not only itineraries and the best routes to travel but also distances, conditions of roads, bridges, and fords, as well as villages and inns along the routes.

In the sixteenth century, maps designed as far back as the second century by Ptolemy, among others, were still used, but they were far from accurate. Attempts were made to map the peninsula on a more precise scale. Fernando, son of Christopher Columbus, tried such a venture, as did Pedro de Medina in 1548.

The king, Felipe II, also made impressive attempts to map the resources of his realm. In 1645, the Portuguese Rodrigo Méndez Sousa described the regions of Spain, their crops, industry, and population.

In 1546 Juan de Villuga published in Medina del Campo *Repertorio de todos los caminos de España* (An Inventory of All the Roads of Spain), followed in 1576 by a similar endeavor by Alonso de Meneses. Martín Zellerius in 1656 wrote his *Hispaniae et Lusitaniae itinerarium* (Hispanic and Lusitanian Itinerary). These travel guides and others were revised and brought up to date in later years. J. W. Neumair von Ramssla went to Spain in the year 1600 and described the *ventas*, or inns. Thomé Pinheiro da Veiga visited the country during the reign of Felipe III and left his impressions in a number of manuscripts, now in the British Museum, on the court and daily life.

French travelers who visited Early Modern Spain and left accounts are Barthélemy Joly, adviser to the king of France, who made the journey in 1603–1604; Antoine de Brunel, a Protestant from Dauphiné who visited in 1655 and wrote his *Voyage d'Espagne*; and François Bertaut, a chief clerk in the high court of Rouen who visited in 1659 and wrote his *Journal du voyage d'Espagne*. In her work *Relations du voyage d'Espagne*, Madame d'Aulnoy, who visited the country between 1679 and 1681, presented details of upper-class daily life. Father Labat, a French observer who visited Andalucía in 1705, and Jean-François Bourgoing, a diplomat in the French embassy in the 1780s, both left impressions of their sojourn in Spain.

Accounts of the ceremony of the auto de fe of the Inquisition have been reported by eyewitnesses, notably the Fleming Jean Lhermite, who attended one in the company of Felipe II at Toledo in 1591 and witnessed the executions of convicted heretics by burning, which he found distressing; and the French ambassador, the Marquis of Villars, who attended the Madrid auto de fe in 1680 and was puzzled by the contrast between the irreligious everyday life of Spaniards and the religious intensity of the event. Other travelers included Giacomo Casanova, the Venetian adventurer who traveled in Spain in 1767 and commented on the Inquisition, the filth of Madrid, and bullfighting, and Augustus Fischer, a German who in the 1790s set himself up as an authority on Spanish women and gave advice to travelers.

Among visitors from England and America who wrote descriptions of what they encountered in the country were Charles Cornwallis, an English ambassador in the early seventeenth century who complained about poor roads and national politics; James Howell, a Welshman and popular author whose first visit to Spain was in 1617. His *Spanish Commentaries* covered numerous aspects of life including popular superstitions. The outspoken Scotsman William Lithgow was imprisoned by the Inquisition a few years later; Lady Fanshawe, wife of the English ambassador, wrote on Spanish women and food in 1664; in the mid-eighteenth century Edward Clarke spoke of the influence of the church; while seven years later, Joseph Baretti, a distinguished man of letters, spent much time on the roads and among the common people describing many aspects of travel and local customs. He called Madrid a *cloaca maxima* (a great sewer); Richard Twiss, a rich young English tourist, discussed women, food, Córdoba, Gibraltar, and inns in 1773; and John Talbot Tillon, an Irishman, studied the physical geography of Spain and left his impressions of Valencia, Málaga, and Sevilla, among other places. Major William Dalrymple, in 1774, wrote about his views on the Inquisition, travel, sanitation, prostitution, the aristocracy, Galicia, and La Mancha.

In 1775–1776, Henry Swinburne wrote about the Alhambra, idleness, and bullfighting. The latter was also discussed by the Reverend Joseph Townsend a decade later. William Beckford, an English millionaire, delved into aspects of flamenco in the 1780s, while Alexander Jardine, British consul at La Coruña, described such matters as the economy and Spanish individualism. Admiral Horatio Nelson in 1793 described his aversion to the bullfight, a view shared by Lady Elizabeth Holland some years later when she wrote about it, as well as about agriculture, shepherds, and medical care. Robert Southey, a young English poet, gave his impressions of Extremadura in 1795 on his route to Lisbon.

Lord Byron visited Andalucía in 1809 and described in glowing terms Cádiz and its women. George Ticknor, from Boston, traveled to Madrid and Granada nine years later and wrote about banditry, the character of Castillians and Andalucíans, dancing, bullfighting, and the Inquisition. The American Washington Irving in 1829 discussed travel, bandits, and the Alhambra palace in which he lived while writing his book *Tales of the Alhambra*.

Henry Inglis, a Scottish writer, toured Spain in 1830 and left an account of banditry, smuggling, the Spanish character, and several cities including Madrid, Toledo, and Málaga. In that same year Richard Ford, who traveled extensively, wrote about nearly everything including table manners, flamenco, the Inquisition, passport controls, bandits, and medical care. Benjamin Disraeli, the future British prime minister, visited Spain in 1830 and gave his views on subjects as diverse as Spanish fans, food, women, bandits, the Alhambra, and several towns.

In the middle of the nineteenth century George Borrow, peddling bibles, wrote a book of his experiences entitled *The Bible in Spain*. Many of the regions in which he traveled, such as Asturias and Galicia, had changed little, if at all, for centuries, nor had the Gypsies and clergy of whom he wrote.

The vast majority of the peasantry were illiterate and kept no records, and chroniclers of the time who kept some account of events did not generally consider the peasant worth their efforts. Conditions and activities of the peasant class, however, can be gleaned from travelers' accounts and government edicts that attempted to regulate the rural areas, from local records, from censuses, and from lawsuits. Personal diaries such as that written by tanner Miguel Parets of Barcelona, describing the great plague of 1651, are of utmost importance.

Characteristics of the shady realm of society come in the form of adventure stories written at the time; from legal proceedings, royal decrees, and private correspondence; and from accounts of travelers.

Glossary

alcalde. Municipal official primarily serving as a judge with civil and criminal jurisdiction.

alfaquí. Muslim clergy who administered to the Muslim and Morisco population.

alguacil. Municipal constable or sheriff.

aljama. Community in which Muslims or Jews lived separately from their Christian neighbors.

alumbrado. Mystic or illuminist who minimized the role of the church and its ceremonies.

auto de fe. Act of faith; an event in which those who had been tried by the Inquisition had their sentences read out.

ayuntamiento. City or town council.

beadle. Official whose duties included ushering and preserving order.

caballero. Knight or gentleman; someone who fought on horseback.

comisario. Local clergy who aided the Inquisition in administrative matters.

comunero. Member of the communities that participated in the revolt against Carlos V.

Converso. Person converted from Jewish (or Muslim) faith and their descendants.

corregidor. Civil governor in Castillian towns (corrector) who presided over the *regidores*; official of the crown placed at the head of a municipality and president of the municipal council; had judicial, administrative, and financial powers.

Cortes. The parliament of each realm; Corts in Cataluña.

diezmo. One-tenth of production that went to the church.

ducat (or ducado). Castillian unit of coinage = 375 maravedís or 11 reales; originally a gold coin, but by the seventeenth century a unit of account.

edict. Declaration of faith read out in public by the inquisitors or their officers at the beginning of proceedings.

effigy. An image representing an absent victim of the Inquisition and burned at the stake.

escudo. Gold coin worth 10 reales or 340 maravedís; from 1609, equaled 440 maravedís.

Familiar. Lay official of the Inquisition.

fuero. Local law or privilege granted to a town, district, or realm.

grandee. A nobleman of the first rank.

heretic. Dissenter from established church dogma; especially, a baptized member of the Roman Catholic Church who disavows its teaching.

hidalgo. One of the lowest of noble rank, ranging from the wealthy squire to the impoverished gentleman; about half a million men claimed this status.

illuminism. Personal religious enlightenment outside the church, often obtained through meditation and fasting; it might involve direct communication with God or the saints.

judería. See *aljama*.

junta. Board or council.

limpieza de sangre. Pure blood, free of Semitic blood.

maravedí. Copper coin in units of four, eight, and sixteen.

marrano. Abusive word meaning swine applied to Conversos, that is, converted Jews.

Mayor. Major, chief.

mayordomo. Chief steward or majordomo.

mentidero. Place where gossip is exchanged.

Mesta. Sheep owners' association.

millones. Tax introduced in 1590 on wine, olive oil, vinegar, and meat for rebuilding the Armada after the fiasco of 1588.

Moors. In reference to Mauritania in North Africa; Muslims living in Spain.

Morisco. Term applied to Muslims (Moors) after their conversion to Christianity, that is, Spaniards of Moorish descent.

Mudéjares. Muslims living under Christian rule.

pícaro. Vagrant, scoundrel, or petty thief; word first used in 1548.

procurador. City's representative to the Cortes.

quinta. Recruitment call-up by lottery.

real. Silver coin worth 34 maravedís.

reconciled. Those people prosecuted by the Inquisition but received back into the Christian church after punishment.

regidor. Municipal councilman.

relaxed. Those condemned by the Inquisition for heresy and handed over to the civil authorities for burning at the stake.

sanbenito. Penitential garment worn by victims of the Inquisition.

Santa Hermandad. A brotherhood or police force in some Castillian towns and given official status by the crown.

Suprema. Central council of the Inquisition.

tasa. Legal maximum price for grain.

tercio. Characteristic infantry regiment about 3,000 strong.

valido. Royal favorite and chief minister.

Bibliography

Alcalá-Zamora, José N., ed. *La vida cotidiana en la España de Velázquez.* Madrid: Ed. Temas de Hoy, 1989.

Baigent, Michael, and Richard Leigh. *The Inquisition.* London: Penguin, 1999.

Baskin, Judith R., ed. *Jewish Women in Historical Perspective.* Detroit: Wayne State University Press, 1991.

Bennassar, Bartolomé, and Bernard Vincent. *Le temps de l'Espagne XVIe–XVIIe siècles.* Paris: Hachette, 1999.

Bertaut, François. "Journal du voyage d'Espagne (1659)." *Revue Hispanique* 46 (1919): 1–315.

Blayney, Major-General Lord. *Narrative of a Forced Journey through Spain and France as a Prisoner of War, in the years 1810 to 1814.* London: E. Kerry, 1814.

Bober, Phyllis Pray. *Art, Culture and Cuisine. Ancient and Medieval Gastronomy.* Chicago: University of Chicago Press, 1999.

Borrow, George. *The Bible in Spain.* London: Simpkin Marshall, Ltd., n.d.

Boucher, François. *20,000 Years of Fashion. The History of Costume and Personal Adornment.* New York: Harry N. Abrams, 1987.

Boyd, Alexander, ed. *The Journal of William Beckford in Portugal and Spain. 1787–1788.* London: Rupert Hart-Davis, 1954.

Boyd, Malcolm, and Juan José Carreras. *Music in Spain during the Eighteenth Century.* Cambridge: Cambridge University Press, 1998.

Braudel, Fernand. *The Structures of Everyday Life. The Limits of the Possible.* Tran. and rev. Siân Reynolds. Vol. 1. New York: Harper & Row, 1979.

Brunel, Antoine de. "Voyage d'Espagne (1655)." *Revue Hispanique* 30 (1914): 119–137.

Burman, Edward. *The Inquisition. The Hammer of Heresy.* Wellingborough: Aquarian Press, 1984.

Casey, James. *Early Modern Spain. A Social History.* London: Routledge, 1999.

Cervantes Saavedra, Miguel de. *The Adventures of Don Quixote.* Trans. J. M. Cohen. Harmondsworth: Penguin, 1950.

Chase, Gilbert. *The Music of Spain.* New York: W. W. Norton, 1941.

Cooperman, Bernard Dov, ed. *In Iberia and Beyond. Hispanic Jews between Cultures.* Newark: University of Delaware Press, 1998.

Crow, John A. *Spain. The Root and the Flower.* 3rd ed. Berkeley: University of California Press, 1985.

Darby, Graham. *Spain in the Seventeenth Century.* Harlow: Longman, 1994.

Davies, R. Trevor. *The Golden Century of Spain 1501–1621.* London: Macmillan, 1958.

Defourneaux, Marcelin. *Daily Life in the Golden Age.* Trans. Newton Branch. Stanford: Stanford University Press, 1979.

Díaz-Plaja, Fernando. *La vida cotidiana en la España del siglo de Oro.* Madrid: Ed. EDAF, 1994.

Doblado, Don Leucadio. *Letters from Spain.* London: Henry Colburn, 1822.

Domínguez Ortiz, Antonio. *The Golden Age of Spain, 1516–1659.* London: Weidenfeld and Nicolson, 1971.

Edwards, John. *The Spanish Inquisition.* Stroud, Gloucestershire: Tempus, 1999.

Elliott, J. H. *Imperial Spain, 1469–1716.* London: Penguin, 1963.

———. *The Count-Duke of Olivares. The Statesman in an Age of Decline.* New Haven, CT: Yale University Press, 1986.

———. *Spain and Its World 1500–1700.* New Haven, CT: Yale University Press, 1989.

Faur, José. *In the Shadow of History. Jews and Conversos at the Dawn of Modernity.* Albany: State University of New York, 1992.

Feibleman, P. *The Cooking of Spain and Portugal.* Alexandria, VA: Time-Life Books, 1981.

Fernàndez-Armesto, Felipe. *The Spanish Armada. The Experience of War in 1588.* Oxford: Oxford University Press, 1988.

Feros, Antonio. *Kingship and Favoritism in the Spain of Philip III, 1598–1621.* Cambridge: Cambridge University Press, 2000.

Fletcher, Richard. *Moorish Spain.* London: Weidenfeld & Nicholson, 1992.

Gaite, Carmen Martín. *Love Customs in Eighteenth Century Spain.* Trans. Maria G. Tomsich Berkeley: University of California Press, 1991.

García Cárcel, Ricardo. *Viajes de extranjeros por España y Portugal.* Vol. 2, *Siglo XVII.* Madrid: Aguilar, 1959.

———. *La leyenda negra. Historia y opinión.* Madrid: Alianza, 1992.

Garrido Aranda, Antonio, ed. *Cultura alimentaria Andalucía-América.* Mexico: Universidad Nacional Autónoma de México, 1996.

Gerber, Jane S. *The Jews of Spain. A History of the Sephardic Experience.* New York: Free Press, 1992.

Gies, Frances, and Joseph Gies. *Daily Life in Medieval Times.* New York: Black Dog & Leventhal, 1999.

Gilabert, Francisco Marti. *La abolición de la Inquisición en España.* Pamplona: Universidad de Navarra, 1975.

Goodman, David C. *Power and Penury. Government, Technology and Science in Philip II's Spain.* Cambridge: Cambridge University Press, 1988.

———. *Spanish Naval Power, 1589–1665.* Cambridge: Cambridge University Press, 1997.

Griffiths, Arthur. *In Spanish Prisons. Persecution & Punishment 1478–1878.* New York: Dorset Press, 1991.

Haliczer, Stephen H. "The Castilian Urban Patriciate and the Jewish Expulsions of 1480–92." *American Historical Review* 78.1 (February 1973): 35–62.

Hillgarth, J. N. *The Mirror of Spain.* Ann Arbor: University of Michigan Press, 2000.

Hinde, Thomas. *Spain.* London: Newnes, 1963.

Irving, Washington. *Tales of the Alhambra.* (Granada: Sanchez, 1981. First published, 1832.)

Joly, Barthélemy de. "Voyage en Espagne (1603–1604)." *Revue Hispanique* 20 (1909): 460–618.

Kagan, Richard L. *Lucrecia's Dreams. Politics and Prophecy in Sixteenth-Century Spain.* Berkeley: University of California Press, 1990.

Kamen, Henry. *Spain in the Later Seventeenth Century, 1665–1700.* London: Longman, 1980.

———. *Spain 1469–1714. A Society of Conflict.* 2nd ed. London: Longman, 1991.

———. *Philip of Spain.* New Haven, CT: Yale University Press, 1997.

———. *The Spanish Inquisition. An Historical Revision.* London: Weidenfeld & Nicolson, 1998.

Kedourie, Elie, ed. *Spain and the Jews. The Sephardic Experience 1492 and After.* London: Thames and Hudson, 1992.

Kilsby, Jill. *Spain: Rise and Decline 1474–1643.* London: Hodder & Stoughton, 1986.

Lane-Poole, Stanley. *The Moors in Spain.* New York: Putnam's Sons, 1903.

Lea, Henry Charles. "The First Castilian Inquisitor." *American Historical Review* 1.1 (October 1895): 46–50.

———. *The Moriscos of Spain: Their Conversion and Expulsion.* New York: Burt Franklin, 1901.

———. *History of the Inquisition of Spain.* New York: Macmillan, Vols. 1, 2, 1906; Vols. 3, 4, 1907.

Le Beau, Bryan F., and Menachem Mor, eds. *Religion in the Age of Exploration: The Case of Spain and New Spain.* Omaha, NE: Creighton University Press, 1996.

Le Strange, Guy, ed. *Spanish Ballads.* Cambridge: Cambridge University Press, 1949.

Livermore, Ann. *A Short History of Spanish Music.* London: Duckworth, 1972.

Llorente, J. A. *Memoria histórica sobre . . . la Inquisición.* Paris: Presses Universitaires de France, 1977.

Long, Janet, coord. *Conquista y comida.* México: Universidad Nacional Autónoma de México, 1996.

Lynch, John. *Bourbon Spain 1700–1808.* Oxford: Blackwell, 1989.

———. *The Hispanic World in Crisis and Change 1598–1700.* Oxford: Blackwell, 1992.

———. *Spain 1516–1598. From Nation State to World Empire.* Oxford: Blackwell, 1994.

Manley, Deborah, ed. *The Guinness Book of Records 1492. The World Five Hundred Years Ago.* New York: Facts on File, 1992.

Mariéjol, Jean Hippolyte. *The Spain of Ferdinand and Isabella.* Trans. Benjamin Keen. New Brunswick, NJ: Rutgers University Press, 1961.

Martz, Linda. *Poverty and Welfare in Habsburg Spain. The Example of Toledo.* Cambridge: Cambridge University Press, 1983.

Mier, Fray Servando Teresa de. *The Memoirs of Fray Sevando Teresa de Mier.* Trans. Helen Lane. Oxford: Oxford University Press, 1998.

Mitchell, David. *Here in Spain.* Fuengirola, Spain: Lookout, 1988.

Morel-Fatio, Alfred. *L'Espagne au XVIe et au XVIIe siècles.* Madrid: Murillo, 1878.

Netanyahu, B. *The Marranos of Spain from the Late 14th to the Early 16th Century, according to Contemporary Hebrew Sources.* 3rd ed. Ithaca: Cornell University Press, 1999.

Neuman, Abraham A. *The Jews in Spain.* Vols. 1–2. New York: Octagon, 1969.

Nickerson, Hoffman. *The Inquisition. A Political and Military Study of Its Establishment.* Boston: Houghton Mifflin, 1923.

Nuñez, Estuardo. *España vista por viajeros hispanoamericanos.* Madrid: Instituto de Cooperación Iberoamericana, Ediciones Cultural Hispanica, 1985.

Parets, Miguel. *A Journal of the Plague Year. The Diary of the Barcelona Tanner Miguel Parets 1651.* Trans. James S. Amelang. Oxford: Oxford University Press, 1991.

Paris, Erna. *The End of Days. A Story of Tolerance, Tyranny, and the Expulsion of the Jews from Spain.* Toronto: Lester, 1995.

Parker, Geoffrey. *The Army of Flanders and the Spanish Road.* Cambridge: Cambridge University Press, 1972.

Pérez-Mallaína, Pablo. *Spain's Men of the Sea.* Trans. Carla Rahn Phillips. Baltimore: Johns Hopkins University Press, 1998.

Perry, Mary Elizabeth, and Anne J. Cruz, eds. *Cultural Encounters. The Impact of the Inquisition in Spain and the New World.* Berkeley: University of California Press, 1991.

Pfandl, Ludwig. *Cultura y costumbres del pueblo español de los siglos XVI y XVII.* Barcelona: Araluce, 1929.

Read, Jan. *The Moors in Spain.* London: Faber & Faber, 1974.

Reade, Brian. *The Dominance of Spain 1550–1660 (Costume of the Western World).* London: Harrap, 1951.

Root, Deborah. "Speaking Christian: Orthodoxy and Difference in Sixteenth-Century Spain." *Representations* 23 (Summer 1988): 118–134.

Ross, Sir E. Denison, and Eileen Power. *Madame d'Aulnoy. Travels in Spain (1691).* London: Routledge, 1930.

Roth, Cecil. *The Spanish Inquisition.* London: W. W. Norton, 1996.

Rowdon, Maurice. *The Spanish Terror. Spanish Imperialism in the Sixteenth Century.* London: Purnell Book Services, 1974.

Sabatini, Rafael. *Torquemada and the Spanish Inquisition. A History.* London: Stanley Paul, 1937.

Salazar, Adolfo. *La música de España.* Buenos Aires: Espasa-Calpe, 1953.

Shahar, Shulamith. *The Fourth Estate. A History of Women in the Middle Ages.* Cambridge: Cambridge University Press, 1983.

———. *Childhood in the Middle Ages.* London: Routledge, 1990.

Sherwood, Joan. *Poverty in Eighteenth-Century Spain. The Women and Children of the Inclusa.* Toronto: University of Toronto Press, 1988.

Shneidman, J. Lee. *The Rise of the Aragonese-Catalan Empire 1200–1350*. Vols. 1–2. London: University of London Press, 1970.

Singman, Jeffrey L. *Daily Life in Medieval Europe*. Westport, CT: Greenwood Press, 1999.

Smart, Alastair. *The Renaissance and Mannerism in Northern Europe and Spain*. London: Thames and Hudson, 1972.

Southey, Robert. *New Letters of Robert Southey*. Vol. 1, *1792–1810*. Vol. 2, *1811–1838*. Ed. Kenneth Curry. New York: Columbia University Press, 1965.

Starkie, Walter. *Spain. A Musician's Journey through Time and Space*. Geneva: Edisli, Editions Rene Kister, 1958.

Stewart, Gail B. *Life during the Spanish Inquisition*. San Diego: Lucent Books, 1998.

Stradling, R. A. *Europe and the Decline of Spain*. London: George Allen & Unwin, 1981.

Swinburne, Henry. *Travels through Spain in the Years 1775 and 1776*. London: P. Elmsly, 1779.

Tunis, Edwin. *Weapons. A Pictorial History*. Baltimore: Johns Hopkins University Press, 1999.

Turberville, A. S. *The Spanish Inquisition*. New York: Henry Holt, 1932.

Vassberg, David E. *Land and Society in Golden Age Castile*. Cambridge: Cambridge University Press, 1984.

Vicens Vives, Jaime. *Approaches to the History of Spain*. Trans. Joan Connelly Ullman. Berkeley: University of California Press, 1970.

Wood, Melusine. *Historical Dances 12th to 19th Century*. London: Imperial Society of Teachers of Dancing, 1952.

Index

About the Author

JAMES B. ANDERSON is professor emeritus of the University of Calgary, Canada. He has spent many years in Spain and Portugal both as a Fulbright Scholar and as the recipient of Canada Council and SSHRC grants, contributing numerous articles and books to the field of Iberian studies. He is author of eleven books, including *The History of Portugal* (Greenwood, 2000).